FOUNDER OF SANDHURST

MAJ-GEN JOHN LE MARCHANT

ABOUT THE AUTHOR

Paul Le Messurier is a historian and author who focuses on local and military history. His other books include *Surrey's Military Heritage*. Paul is an Associate Fellow of the Royal Historical Society and a member of the Society of Authors.

FOUNDER OF SANDHURST

MAJ-GEN JOHN LE MARCHANT

'A MOST ABLE OFFICER'

PAUL LE MESSURIER

AMBERLEY

For Ana Maria and William

Cover illustrations: Front cover: John Gaspard Le Marchant, artist Henry James Haley. (© Crown Copyright, courtesy of the Sandhurst Collection); *Back cover:* Royal Military College, Sandhurst, artist William De La Motte. (Courtesy of the Yale Centre for British Art under Creative Commons CC0 1.0)

This edition published 2026

Amberley Publishing
The Hill, Stroud
Gloucestershire, GL5 4EP

www.amberley-books.com

ISBN 978 1 3981 3346 4 (paperback)
ISBN 978 1 3981 1490 6 (ebook)

British Library Cataloguing in Publication Data.
A catalogue record for this book is available from the British Library.

2 3 4 5 6 7 8 9 10

Typesetting by SJmagic DESIGN SERVICES, India.
Printed in the UK.

Appointed GPSR EU Representative: Easy Access System Europe Oü, 16879218
Address: Mustamäe tee 50, 10621, Tallinn, Estonia
Contact Details: gpsr.requests@easproject.com, +358 40 500 3575

CONTENTS

The Siege of Dunkirk and Battle of Hondschoote. Le Marchant joined Marshal Freytag's army in establishing a protective screen to cover the Duke of York's siege of Dunkirk. (Map by George Stanford, in Fortescue, *A History of the British Army Vol 4 1917*)

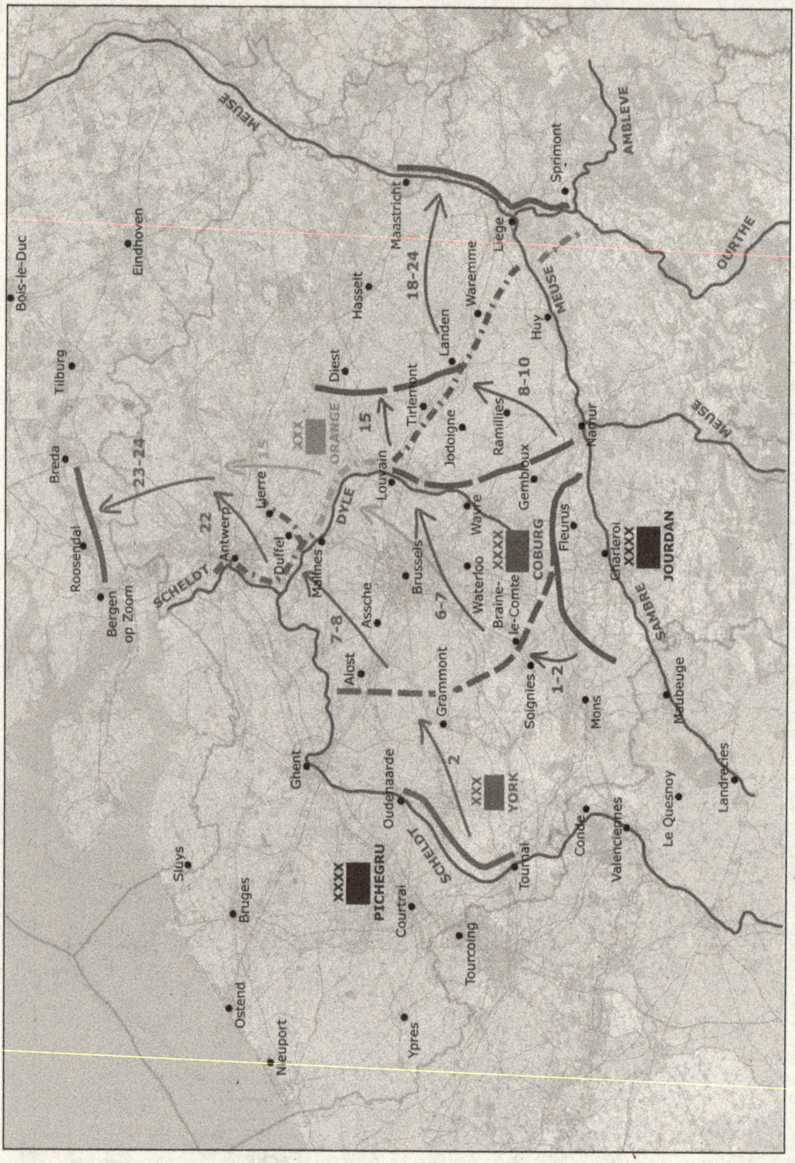

An ignominious retreat for the allies in 1794. Le Marchant acknowledged that 'the game is up, and we are incapable of making a successful war'. In April 1795, British forces were evacuated from Bremen. During the Flanders campaign, Wellington said he 'learnt what one ought not to do, and that is always something'. So did Le Marchant. (OpenStreetMap, Creative Commons 4.0)

The Theatre of War in the Iberian Peninsula 1808–14

In 1812, Le Marchant led successful cavalry charges at Villagarcia, south-east of Badajoz, and at Salamanca.

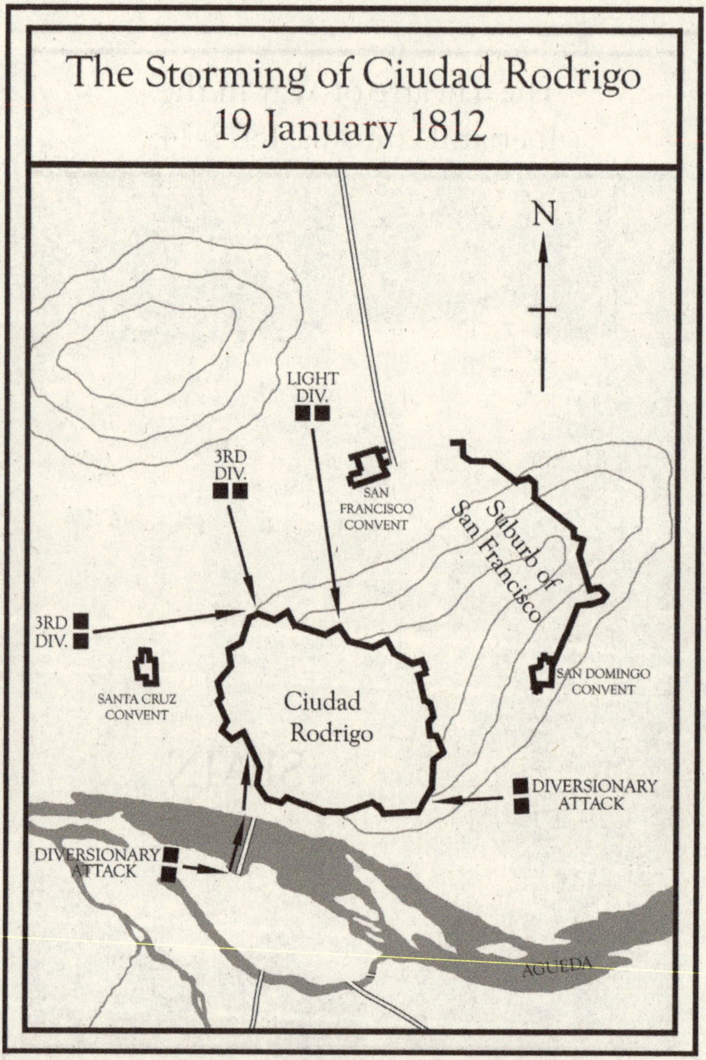

Le Marchant was present at the siege of Ciudad Rodrigo, describing it as 'the most spirited enterprise that has been undertaken this war, & nothing could exceed the good order and judgment with which it was carried'.

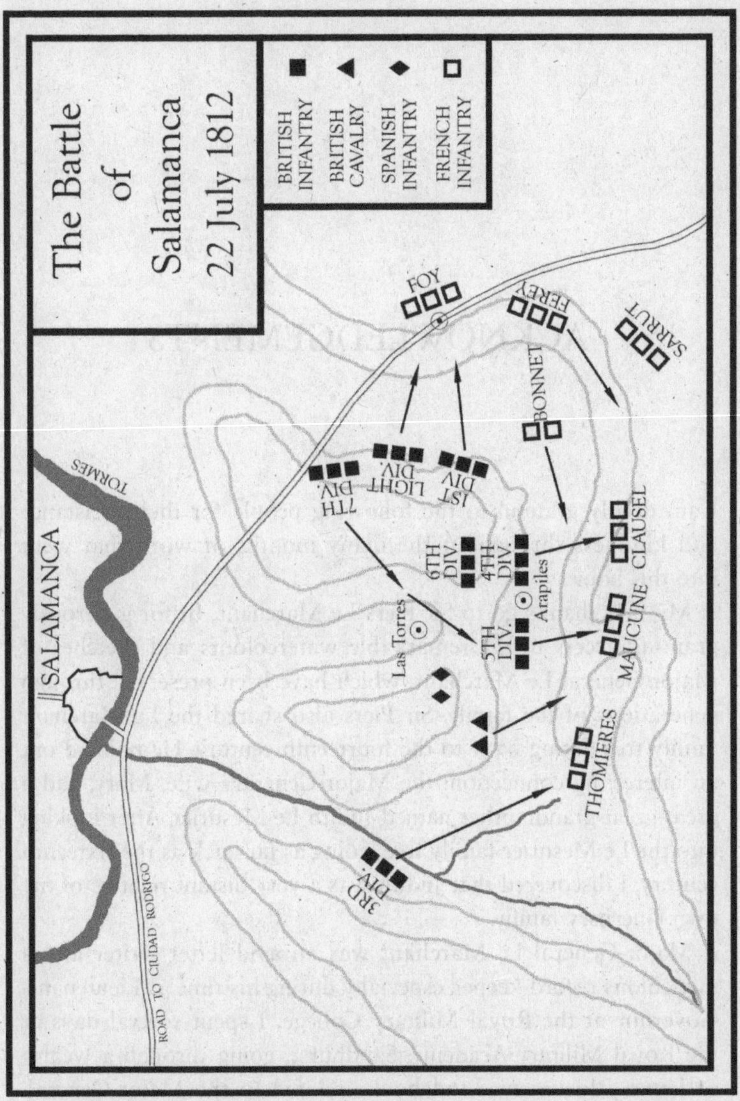

Le Marchant led his cavalry brigade against the French army's left flank: 'The trampling of horses was heard … and the heavy brigade of Le Marchant was seen coming forward in line at a canter.'

ACKNOWLEDGEMENTS

I am deeply grateful to the following people for their assistance and kindness throughout the many months of work that went into this book.

My first thanks go to Sir Piers Le Marchant, Bt for generously granting access to the remarkable watercolours and sketches of Major-General Le Marchant, which have been preserved through generations of the family. Sir Piers also shared the Le Marchant family tree dating back to the fourteenth century. He pointed out an interesting connection: the Major-General's wife, Mary, had a great-great-grandmother named Judith Le Mesurier. After looking into the Le Mesurier family tree, going as far back as the sixteenth century, I discovered that Judith was a very distant relative of my own Guernsey family.

Major-General Le Marchant was an avid letter writer and a meticulous record-keeper, especially during his time as Lieutenant-Governor at the Royal Military College. I spent several days at the Royal Military Academy, Sandhurst, going through a wealth of letters, documents, and books related to the Major-General. My gratitude goes to Dr Anthony Morton, curator of the Sandhurst Collection, for making this research possible.

The letters written by Major-General Le Marchant to his eldest daughter, Katherine, provided a revealing glimpse into the more personal aspects of his life, and my thanks go to the staff at Valence House Archive & Local Studies Centre in Dagenham for providing access to transcriptions of those letters. Some of the letters to Katherine are also held at the Priaulx Library in Guernsey, together with other relevant documents, newspapers and histories of the Le Marchant and Carey families. I extend my thanks to Sue Laker, Chief Librarian, and all the staff at the Priaulx Library, as well as staff at Guernsey Museums & Galleries.

To all those at the British Library, National Archives, National Army Museum, and the Parliamentary Archives in the Houses of Parliament, for providing access to a whole range of documents and books concerning Major-General Le Marchant, the officers under his command, and the Royal Military College.

Where direct quotations have been taken from letters and documents, I have retained, where possible, the same spelling and abbreviations as in the original.

The beautiful city of Salamanca is well worth a visit at any time, and I was able to explore the battlefield with an extremely knowledgeable guide, Raúl Bellido. His tour of the various battlefield locations, including where Le Marchant's cavalry charge might have occurred, was invaluable. Equally impressive was a visit to Ciudad Rodrigo, the location of Wellington's siege in January 1812, where Le Marchant was present. The staff at the information office and the local museum in Ciudad Rodrigo were incredibly helpful.

My gratitude to Shaun Barrington from Amberley Publishing for always being available and for his guidance while writing the book.

There are several others who provided feedback on the manuscript, and those who have continuously shown an interest in my work. Your encouragement kept me going.

Finally, a special thanks to my wife Ana Maria and son William for their patience and unwavering support during the two years and more which I spent researching and writing this book.

FOREWORD

As an Officer Cadet at the Royal Military Academy Sandhurst, I am embarrassed to say that I didn't have the faintest idea who Major-General Le Marchant was, and I suspect that cadets these days are not much the wiser. I was aware that there was a Le Marchant House in the grounds because I was required to run or march past it far too often, and I have become aware in later years that there is a Le Marchant room in the Old College that is beautifully appointed and cared for; but in my day the only time you went to Old College was up the steps when you were commissioned. Over forty years later and living in Guernsey, I'm sorry to say that this proud Guernseyman, John Gaspard Le Marchant, is hardly known here either. He should be, and much better known at Sandhurst as well, for reasons this excellent biography of the founder of the Royal Military Academy, amongst many other achievements, makes clear.

John Le Marchant was indeed 'a most able officer' and a remarkable man, but his success was in no way pre-ordained. As a young man he was prone to be idle, ill-disciplined and headstrong, amongst other things challenging his Commanding Officer to a duel, but he had the strength of character to change his ways and was sufficiently clear-minded to seek to make the most of himself. His first period on operations, as we would now say, was as life-changing for him as it was – and is – for many and the lessons he learned were to change the direction of his professional life. He didn't just identify things that were wrong but set out, often in the face of opposition, to change them. He designed and created a new cavalry sword, wrote tactics manuals when there were none, proposed changes to the structure of the Army and ultimately created a college to train officers; something only offered to Artillery and Engineer officers at that time. When all that was done, he went out to join Wellington as a Brigade Commander, putting into practice with conspicuous success all that he had taught and developed over his professional career.

As this new biography makes clear, he was a complex and determined man, but other traits are very evident. He was very proud of his Guernsey heritage, loved his wife and family deeply, treasured his friends and was loyal to them and the Army. An officer driven by duty to a fault, his was a life of service and he was an exemplar of the modern motto of the Academy he founded – 'Serve to Lead'. This book is a fitting tribute to a man who was ahead of his time, whose impact on his Service and country was immediate and important and whose influence deserves to be properly recognised today. I most heartily recommend it.

Lieutenant General Richard Cripwell CB CBE
Lieutenant-Governor and Commander-in-Chief
of the Bailiwick of Guernsey

Lieutenant General Richard Cripwell was commissioned into the Corp of Royal Engineers in 1982 and commanded 26 Engineer Regiment and the Intelligence, Surveillance and Reconnaissance Task Force in Kosovo. As a Major-General, he was Commander British Forces in Cyprus and served as the British Defence Attaché in Washington before being appointed Deputy Commander of Operation Resolute Support *in Afghanistan in 2017. For his last appointment in the Army he was based in Turkey as Deputy Commander Allied Land Command, the standing headquarters for NATO land forces.*

PROLOGUE

In late May 1793, an imposing young cavalry officer walked down the gangway from the troop ship that had just sailed into Ostend. Tall and muscular, he cut a dashing figure resplendent in his elaborately embroidered scarlet coat. Captain John Gaspard Le Marchant was in command of a squadron of cavalry from the 2nd Dragoon Guards, also known as the Queen's Bays due to the distinctive colour of their horses. He had arrived in Flanders as part of the army under Prince Frederick, the Duke of York, the second and favourite son of King George III, fighting alongside Austria and Prussia in the war against the French First Republic.

On his arrival on the continent, Le Marchant was taken aback at the state of the British army and of the cavalry in particular. Among the several cavalry regiments that had already arrived at Ostend, he noticed a conspicuous absence of order and discipline, that both troops and horses appeared neglected, and that 'the officers, in general, were wholly ignorant of their duty'.[1]

On the night of 29 June, Captain Le Marchant went to inspect his troops prior to an attack on the French camp at Cassel in northern France, planned for early the next day. He found, to his great surprise, his men lying face down in full uniform on the ground next to their horses. When he questioned his men, he was told that they had spent that evening having their hair queued, the common practice by which British soldiers wore their hair in a ponytail or plait, often using a combination of grease and powder. The soldiers, by lying face down, sought to preserve their hair queues intact so as not to repeat the whole process again early the next morning. Army regulations at the time were quite specific about appearance: hair queues were to be no longer than ten inches. The abolition of the practice in 1808 faced considerable resistance from within the army.

Such was Le Marchant's introduction to the unpredictable and misguided discipline of the British Army on active service, with greater emphasis placed on appearance over ability, and presentation over proficiency. As one newly appointed cavalry officer observed, 'We spend a great deal more time on our dress than in learning about our weapons.'[2]

The attack on the French at Cassel in which he participated, his first experience of battle, was a success. Le Marchant was commended for his efforts. Less successful though was the overall campaign, which would see the allied coalition fall apart and the British contingent eventually retreat and evacuate embarrassingly through Bremen in 1795. It was a chastening experience. The French were now in control of the Netherlands. The Duke was only twenty-nine when he had arrived in Flanders, and had no real military experience in the face of a formidable foe. The French were superior in numbers and led by seasoned veterans.

This was a time when the British army would rapidly increase in times of war only to just as quickly disperse during peacetime, as the government set out to reduce the army budget. Officers would be placed on half pay, a type of retirement from active duty, but could be recalled in the event of war. The rank and file would return to civilian life. And this is exactly what happened following the Seven Years' War from 1756 to 1763, a conflict between opposing alliances involving both Britain and France, sometimes referred to as the 'first global or world war'.

When France declared war on Britain in 1793, the British army had a peacetime strength of only 17,000 men at home, excluding those stationed in the colonies, and was ill-prepared to face its adversary. There was a frantic scramble to enlist as many new recruits as possible. The rank and file consisted mostly of volunteers, motivated not necessarily by noble intentions but perhaps seeking to escape from trouble at home, lacking employment or in need of money. It is estimated that around 30,000 were enrolled in the space of six months. There was no time for training and a shortage of guns, uniforms and equipment left soldiers completely unprepared. Officers in the British army would typically come from the landed elite or aristocracy relying on wealth and family connections to purchase commissions. This often led to questionable, or at worst, inept leadership.

In contrast, the French army was made up of conscripts with opportunities for promotion from within the ranks. The soldiers of the revolutionary army were at first poorly trained and ill-disciplined, but their enthusiasm for the rebel cause was unwavering. It was not long before they became organised and effective under the leadership of seasoned, professional officers.

The ill-fated Flanders campaign against revolutionary France left a lasting impression on Le Marchant. Amidst the chaos, he profited from his time, learning much from the other armies within the allied coalition, and above all from the Austrian cavalry. Le Marchant recognised the need for modernisation and reform that would go a long way to preparing the British army for the challenges that lay ahead, in particular the wars that ultimately led to victory against Napoleon Bonaparte in 1815. He saw the need for a new way of thinking, contrary to the long-established practices of the British army. His vision and attention to detail, combined with a drive and determination to overcome all obstacles placed in his way, would result in the eventual establishment of what has now become the world-renowned Royal Military Academy at Sandhurst.

His numerous achievements should normally have earned him widespread acclaim. Or so you might have thought. Yet, after his passing, an article in a national newspaper opened with: 'We would be inclined to suppose, from the perusal of some recent paragraphs in the public prints, that the merits and services of the late Major-General Le Marchant were very little known.'[3]

This is the remarkable story of the life of Major-General John Gaspard Le Marchant on his journey from Guernsey to Gibraltar, through the battlefields of Flanders, by way of High Wycombe and Great Marlow, and finally from Sandhurst to Salamanca.

1
OF ALL THE DUNCES

As a young boy, Le Marchant had shown few signs of the potential that would later shine through during his military career. Sent at an early age to board at King Edward's School in Bath, a highly reputable institution, he showed little enthusiasm for his studies. He was inattentive and impulsive, characteristics that would resurface during his teenage years. From time to time, he would find himself in the occasional scrape. His main distinction at school was when he confronted the school bully in a 'successful fight with a boy of very superior strength, the tyrant and terror of the school, in which only one schoolfellow had the courage to stand by him'.[1]

The schoolfellow in question was his friend William Sidney Smith, who, like Le Marchant, was a headstrong young man. Smith would later rise to the rank of Admiral in Nelson's navy. One of the masters at King Edward's, the Reverend Nathanael Morgan, pronounced Le Marchant and Smith to be 'the greatest dunces in the school'.[2]

John Gaspard Le Marchant was born in the very country that he would later fight against as a cavalry officer. His father was from a well-established family on the island of Guernsey, his mother was French. He was born on the 9 February 1766 at the home of his maternal grandparents near Amiens in northern France, not too far from the Flanders fields where he would first experience battle. The family returned to Guernsey shortly after his birth. Guernsey, the second largest of the Channel Islands, lies approximately thirty miles off the coast of France. It became part of the Duchy of Normandy in the 10th century. William the Conqueror's triumph in 1066 saw him become the King of England while also keeping the title of the Duke of Normandy. When King John lost control of Normandy in 1204, the island remained under the English crown.

The Le Marchant family is believed to have descended from the Normans, having arrived as part of the invasion force and subsequently settling in Guernsey during the reign of King John. Over the years, several of Le Marchant's paternal ancestors held prominent administrative positions on the island. John Gaspard's ancestral line can be traced back to Peter Le Marchant who was the Bailiff, the chief magistrate of the island's Royal Court, in the early fourteenth century. Peter also served as Lieutenant-Governor to Otto de Grandison, Governor of the Channel Islands and representative of the King of England. Several members of the Le Marchant family had subsequently held the office of Bailiff and even more had served as officers of the law in the Royal Court of Guernsey.

John Gaspard's father, John Le Marchant, was one of the first Guernsey men to hold a commission in the army. It was while at Pembroke College, Oxford, that he had seen the 7th Dragoons parade through the city. He was so impressed that he immediately decided to join the army. He left university before he had finished his studies and purchased a commission as a Cornet in the 7th Dragoons under the Marquis of Granby, rising to the rank of Colonel. He fought during the Seven Years' War against France as part of the army of Prince Ferdinand of Brunswick and retired on half pay at the end of hostilities in 1763.

His mother, Marie Catherine Hirzel, was the eldest daughter of Count Heinrich Justus Hirzel de St Gratien, who served as

Marechal-de-Camp in the Swiss Guards in French service. Marie was the niece of Margaret Hirzel, the second wife of John Gaspard's grandfather Thomas Le Marchant. Margaret was the daughter and heiress of Louis Hirzel, Comte D'Olon, a French protestant refugee officer who had fled to England and then become Lieutenant-Governor of Guernsey under his part anglicised name of Lewis or Louis Dollon. John Gaspard received his second Christian name in honour of his mother's distinguished ancestor, Admiral Gaspard De Coligny, a Huguenot leader but also advisor to the French king, Charles IX, in the sixteenth century.

Since there seemed to be little point in leaving Le Marchant at King Edward's, his father decided to remove him from the school and he returned to Guernsey in 1780 at the age of fourteen. Le Marchant later acknowledged that his performance at school was due to his own idleness and placed no blame on King Edward's for his shortcomings. On his return home, he immersed himself in his studies, much to the surprise of his family, making up for lost time. This he did with the help of the family butler, an American who had remained loyal to the British Crown during the American War of Independence. And it was at this time that young Le Marchant started to express a keen interest in following in his father's footsteps into the army.

There were very few ways for young John Gaspard to enter the British army as an officer apart from buying a commission, a practice dating back to the Middle Ages. Some attempts at regulation of the purchase system had been introduced and an official price list established. The cost of a commission varied based on the officer's rank. Following a review of prices in 1766, the lowest officer rank in the infantry, an Ensign, would cost £400, while a Lieutenant-Colonel, the highest rank available for purchase, cost £3,500. In the cavalry, the costs were even higher, ranging from £1,600 for a Cornet, equivalent to an Ensign, to £5,200 for a Lieutenant-Colonel. A commission in the cavalry would require additional funds with officers expected to cover the expense of their uniform, saddles and equipment, which could set an officer back a further £500.

Although efforts were made to control prices, a black market in the purchase of commissions persisted. In 1783, another review revealed that the regulations had been broken on many occasions and higher prices paid, much to the detriment of more experienced and deserving officers. It was not unknown for children under the age of sixteen to purchase a commission and those with substantial fortunes could quickly rise through the ranks. One young cavalry officer reflected on the intricacies of the purchase system in a letter to his father.

> There is some juggling going forward with regard to the Troops in our Regt which I did not understand. We have already one Troop unsold which Shakespear does not purchase because he is promised a Company. Burn promised to purchase it but then cried off on account of the extravagant Price asked for it, or, I rather imagine, because he knows his Brother-in-law will sell his as soon as ordered on Service. After Burn I am the next claimant, but not having served Three Years it would be useless making any application.
>
> Should you purchase me a Troop in the Summer, I shall be a Captain before many others have obtained their Lieutenancies who entered the Army at the same Time, and thus be on a level with others of Seven Years standing, so great has been the Promotion.[3]

In a way, the purchase system was a reflection of wider society at the time where a select and privileged group of landed gentry, estate owners and aristocrats retained a hold on political authority. Those in power exercised their patronage in all walks of life; in court, politics, church and the armed forces. Seats in the House of Commons were sold to the highest bidder. In 1802, a constituency is rumoured to have been purchased for £60,000. The constituency of Gatton in Surrey was sold in 1829 for £170,000. The vote was restricted to landowners and open to bribery. So, it is not surprising that paying for commissions was the standard practice in the army.

Edward Cardwell, Secretary of State for War from 1868 to 1874, would much later make his own feelings about the purchase system very clear in the House of Commons. He considered that there was 'nothing so perplexing and embarrassing to have to deal with; and it constantly reminds me of the saying of a character on the stage with which we are all familiar, "it is one of those things that no fellow can understand"'.[4] It was not until 1871 that the purchase system was abolished as part of the Cardwell army reforms, after which the promotion of officers was based on merit rather than money and influence. Regardless of the disadvantages and complexities of the purchase system, there was little alternative for a young man to pursue a career in the army as an officer. And so Le Marchant's father bought a commission for John Gaspard as an Ensign in the Wiltshire militia in 1782 when he was just sixteen years old.

Young Le Marchant had an inauspicious start to life in the army, much like his time at school. It was not long before his quick temper had landed him in trouble. He took offence at an innocuous remark from his commanding officer, prompting him to challenge the Colonel to a duel. During that time, duels were still commonplace among the aristocracy, upper classes and army officers. Swords had in the main been replaced by pistols, and the primary objective was not necessarily to kill or injure the opponent, but merely to restore honour. In May 1789, Charles Lennox challenged Prince Frederick, the Duke of York, to a duel over some misunderstanding. Lennox was a Lieutenant-Colonel in the Duke's regiment, the Coldstream Guards. They met on Wimbledon Common. Lennox fired first, grazing the Duke, who chose not to return fire. The matter ended there. In 1798, George Tierney, a leading Whig politician, challenged the Prime Minister, William Pitt the Younger, to a duel after Pitt had accused him of being unpatriotic. The duel took place on Putney Heath. Neither of the protagonists was injured.

Fortunately for Le Marchant, the Colonel, displaying wisdom and experience, defused the situation. Le Marchant was reprimanded and a duel was prevented. Even then, he hadn't learned his lesson. He later challenged another gentleman to a duel over a minor provocation, once again convinced that he had been wronged. This time the authorities intervened, and the duel was avoided.

In March 1783, at the age of seventeen, Le Marchant obtained a commission as an Ensign with the 2nd Battalion of the 1st (Royal) Regiment of Foot. He joined his new regiment in Dublin. Although his family was very well known in Guernsey, he had few influential connections elsewhere. His foreign name and relatively modest wealth would normally have made it difficult to progress in the army. The choice of regiment often relied on family ties, and for those with limited financial means, patronage was the next best alternative. While in Dublin, Le Marchant began to socialise in high society and became acquainted with influential individuals. Among those was George Grenville, the Lord-Lieutenant of Ireland and 1st Marquess of Buckingham.

In 1784, Le Marchant's regiment was posted to Gibraltar. It was at this point that his military career very nearly came to an embarrassing end. The night before he was due to leave Ireland, he was invited to join a senior officer in a game of cards in a Dublin club. Le Marchant, with little experience of gambling, soon found himself at a disadvantage and it was not long before he had lost £200. He was too ashamed to tell his father about what had happened. He would have to sell his commission and leave the army to pay off the debt. Le Marchant's career was saved when the Regimental Paymaster offered to lend him the money, to be deducted from his army salary, on the condition that Le Marchant promised that he would never take to gambling again. He set off with his regiment to Gibraltar.

Upon their arrival, they found that the enclave, a territory of less than three square miles, was in a sorry state. Britain had taken control of Gibraltar in 1704, given its strategic importance at the entrance to the Mediterranean. So, it was hardly surprising that

Spain and France made several attempts to take it away from the British. The climax was the siege of Gibraltar by the Spanish and French from 1779 to 1783, during which the British garrison of over 5,000 troops was close to starvation and several hundred succumbed to disease. Yet, the British held out. Now that the siege had been over for more than a year, and the town had been rebuilt, several regiments had been recalled and those arriving as replacements found little with which to occupy themselves.

Since most of his pay was taken up to offset his loan to the Regimental Paymaster, Le Marchant was unable to participate in any of the social activities on Gibraltar or to pay his share in the officers' mess. As a result, his fellow officers considered him to be antisocial and rather aloof. They had no idea of the real reason behind his behaviour, and he was too proud to enlighten them.

With ample time on his hands, Le Marchant took to drawing and painting his surroundings, capturing the landscapes of Gibraltar and the North African shore opposite, then known as the Barbary coast. Although he was not to know it at the time, these paintings would later prove to be invaluable in advancing his career.

While in Gibraltar, Le Marchant contracted yellow fever and was sent home to recuperate. During his stay in Guernsey, he formed a relationship with a young lady, Mary, the eldest of fourteen children. Mary's father, Jean Carey, happened to be a neighbour of the Le Marchant family in St Peter Port. Le Marchant, at the age of twenty, and Mary, one year his junior, were both under the legal age for marriage without consent from their parents. In those days, men, especially army officers, married later in life, sometimes in their thirties. Certainly, marriages at such a young age were quite unusual. So, it was predictable that Mr Carey disapproved of the relationship, and as soon as Le Marchant's own father found out, he sent Le Marchant, now recovered from his illness, back to Gibraltar.

On his return to Gibraltar, Le Marchant discovered that the attitude of his fellow officers towards him had completely changed. During his absence, the Regimental Paymaster had arrived and the reason behind Le Marchant's prudent, somewhat reclusive, behaviour had become common knowledge. The officers now treated him with kindness and respect. Here was a man of integrity who had honoured his debt.

After four years with his regiment, Le Marchant was growing impatient. He was still an Ensign, the lowest infantry officer rank, and the prospect of a promotion within his current regiment was limited. With his debt repaid and a yearning to advance his career, he convinced his father to purchase a Cornetcy in the 6th (Inniskilling) Dragoons in May 1787, marking the start of what would prove to be an illustrious career in the cavalry. Frustratingly for Le Marchant, a mix-up in paperwork meant that there was a delay of several months before he could actually transfer to his new regiment.

At last, he returned to England to join the Inniskillings. There he found a degree of hostility between the officers and their new commanding officer, Lieutenant-Colonel Francis Elliot, the 2nd Lord Heathfield. Le Marchant wisely chose not to get involved in these internal disputes, behaviour that endeared him to his commanding officer. In June 1789, he received his just reward when Lord Heathfield selected him to command a guard of honour to escort George III.

The King struggled with mental illness throughout his life and the government was close to establishing a Prince Regency on several occasions. In this particular instance, His Majesty had started to show signs of recovery and it was felt that he would benefit from a stay on the south coast at Gloucester House in Weymouth, a residence that belonged to his younger brother. George III was a popular monarch and the crowds gathered to see the King on his way down south. His arrival at Weymouth found the town in festive mood. The streets and shops were decorated with banners proclaiming 'God save the King'. Even the bathing machines stationed on the beach displayed similar expressions of good will. The King and Queen entertained themselves by taking daily swims in the sea, strolling along the esplanade as they greeted the throngs of well-wishers, and taking afternoon tea in the assembly rooms. On 8 September, the Royal couple gave a ball in Weymouth to celebrate their wedding anniversary.

It was on this tour of duty in Weymouth that Le Marchant, as head of the King's guard of honour, caught the attention of His Majesty. The King was surprised to see an impeccably dressed young Cornet, aged just twenty-three and the lowest rank of cavalry officer, in command of his escort.

While in Weymouth, Le Marchant also came to the notice of Sir George Yonge, the Secretary at War, who, appreciating Le Marchant's talent for painting, took the young man under his wing. Yonge was so impressed by Le Marchant's sketches and watercolours, particularly those of Gibraltar, that he brought them to the attention of the King. A few months later, a vacancy came up for a Lieutenant in the 2nd Dragoon Guards (Queen's Bays) cavalry regiment, a highly sought-after position for which there was fierce competition. Sir George Yonge put Le Marchant's name forward and the King approved the appointment in November 1789.

Yonge also arranged leave of absence from the army for Le Marchant to travel around Europe. Such a tour was typically the privilege of the wealthy, intended to enhance their education and experience as well as to improve their language skills. Le Marchant spent six months in Strasbourg, but the threat of war with Russia meant he was recalled. He returned to his regiment at Truro in Cornwall.

On 29 October 1789, Le Marchant married his young sweetheart Mary in Guernsey, now with the blessing of both sets of parents. Their first son, Carey, was born in 1791, a previous child having died in infancy. In the same year as the arrival of their newborn son, Le Marchant was appointed Captain of a troop by purchase in the 2nd Dragoon Guards, just over two years after joining the regiment. Le Marchant had become well known amongst politicians and in court circles at a time when patronage was all important. His career was now on the rise. No longer might he be considered a dunce.

2

A DISASTROUS CAMPAIGN

The onset of the French Revolution in 1789 caused significant concern across Europe, and Britain was no exception. The government became increasingly cautious about potential repercussions, particularly as discontent was rising in both Britain and Ireland. The relations between the French revolutionaries and neighbouring countries continued to deteriorate until France declared war on Austria in the spring of 1792. Initially, George III wanted to remain neutral. However, as the Prussians had aligned with Austria with the intention of invading France, Britain found it increasingly difficult to stay out of the conflict.

Later that year, the French army under the command of General Charles Dumouriez invaded the Austrian Netherlands and defeated the Austrians at the Battle of Jemappes. The execution of Louis XVI on 21 January 1793 marked a turning point. George III ordered Parliament to start preparing both the army and navy, 'for maintaining the security and rights of his own dominions, for supporting his allies, and for opposing views of aggrandizement and ambition on the part of France, which would be at all times dangerous to the general interests of Europe'.[1] In response to escalating tension, France declared war on England and the United Provinces of the Netherlands on 1 February.

The Duke of York arrived in Holland with a small British army contingent to join forces with the Austrians under Prince Frederick of Coburg-Saalfeld. The hurried efforts to bolster the size of the British army meant that inexperienced officers and untrained men took to the field. The Adjutant-General of the Forces apologised in a letter to the Duke, acknowledging the poor state of the infantry:

> I am afraid that you will not reap the advantage that you might have expected from the brigade of the Line just sent over to you, as so considerable a part of it is composed of nothing but undisciplined and raw recruits; and how they are to be disposed of until they can be taught their business I am at a loss to imagine.[2]

Given the shortcomings in both the quality and quantity of infantry, eleven regiments of cavalry, including Le Marchant's 2nd Dragoon Guards (Queen's Bays), were mobilised for a tour of duty on the continent. Shortly before leaving, Le Marchant was appointed Brigade Major. The Queen's Bays left Norwich Barracks, and on 25 May Le Marchant boarded a troop ship at Blackwall, arriving at Ostend four days later.

Mary returned with their two-year-old son, Carey, to her father's home at La Bigoterie in Guernsey, concerned about her husband's first venture on active service. Le Marchant wrote to Mary in early June:

> Do not alarm yourself, my dear soul, but rely on that Providence which has hitherto smiled on us, which brought us first together and who, without just offence, will not part us afterwards. The forms of religion I do not respect, but the principle I revere, and as devoutly as any man I seek the protections of the Supreme. Look to His Mercies and from them expect everything you wish.[3]

Le Marchant spent the first few days in the saddle reviewing the advanced guard stationed around Ostend. When he found a vulnerable or unmanned outpost, it would be promptly addressed. On one occasion he noted:

> The detachment of Light Dragoons posted in the front of our line, about six miles from the town, met a detachment of Dutch troops on their march from Furnes to Ypres, took them for French, and were so dreadfully frightened that they galloped away like madmen. They rode their horses so hard, that several died the same evening, and others were seriously injured.[4]

Lieutenant-Colonel George Augustus Herbert, Earl of Pembroke, assumed command of the Queen's Bays, and the regiment joined the main allied army surrounding the French-held town of Valenciennes. The nature of the military operations around Valenciennes restricted the cavalry's involvement, and Le Marchant found there were limited opportunities for action during the siege.

In late June, Le Marchant and his squadron received orders to join a group of Austrian cavalry and Prussian infantry under the command of the Austrian General, Prince of Hohenzollern. Their mission was to launch an attack on the main French camp just outside Cassel, fifteen miles south of Dunkirk. The Prince of Hohenzollern's army marched out from their base at Cysoing, with Le Marchant joining them as they headed towards Cassel. It was on the night before the attack that Le Marchant discovered his men lying face-down to preserve their hair queues. On 30 June, the allies set off before sunrise, Le Marchant's squadron the only British presence in the force.

Early that morning, the French advance guard was taken by surprise, causing them to beat a retreat to their camp. The Prussian infantry failed to pursue the fleeing enemy troops, allowing them to regroup in a nearby cornfield. From there, the French unleashed a volley of musket fire. Seizing the initiative, the Austrian and British cavalry charged, with Le Marchant leading his squadron on the right, driving the French infantry back until they scattered. In spite of this initial success, the allies were unable to take the enemy camp and returned to Cysoing. The Prince of Hohenzollern wrote immediately after the attack:

> I beg the officer commanding the British cavalry in the absence of Lord Herbert, to express my thanks, in my name, to Captain Le Marchant, and to all his brigade, for the precision with which he executed my instructions at the engagement at Cassel this morning, and to assure all the corps, that I esteem myself both happy and honoured to have had him to command troops that showed as much spirit as intrepidity.[5]

The Prince also mentioned Le Marchant's contribution in a report to the Duke of York. This was Le Marchant's first experience of combat and it left him with a lasting impression, both of the realities of war and the noticeable gap in training and discipline between the British army and their allies. He wrote to his wife Mary from the camp at Cysoing:

> I am just returned from a scene that, on cool reflection, makes my soul shrink within me, but it is one of the horrors of war. What gave me most pain was to see that the Austrians gave no quarter. Poor devils on their knees, merely begging for mercy, were cut down. My own people, thank God! were as merciful as possible, and, I think, destroyed none in the pursuit, except such as would not give themselves up. Dives's [his junior captain] party had taken five men alive, but leaving them for an instant in pursuit of others, some Austrians came up and butchered them. I made a complaint to Hohenzollern, who supposed his men might have seen some of their comrades receive similar treatment from the enemy during the engagement. He seemed to be very sorry for it.
>
> My people behaved remarkably well in the face of the enemy, that is, for young troops. They have an implicit confidence in me, so that I hope in time we shall be esteemed by our friends the Austrians, who are, at present, as superior to us as we are to the train-bands [part-time militia] in the city.[6]

This particular incident found its way into the English newspapers, portraying the episode as an act of barbarity. One newspaper strongly condemned the behaviour of the Austrian soldiers, declaring that seizing prisoners from a British detachment and ruthlessly slaughtering them without mercy was a national insult. The newspaper concluded that the Austrians responsible for these actions should be punished.

In the early autumn of 1793, the British government instructed the Duke of York to take Dunkirk, considering it invaluable as a British base. The Duke led a combined force of slightly over 35,000 allied infantry and cavalry to begin the siege. Of these, Field Marshal Wilhelm von Freytag took 14,500 Hanoverian troops and ten squadrons of British cavalry southeast to establish a protective screen to cover the siege.

It was as part of this second force that Le Marchant found himself camped on the banks of the river Yser near Wylder in France between the enemy-occupied towns of Cassel and Bergues. An ultimatum was given to the French commander at Bergues. According to Le Marchant, 'We summoned the garrison to surrender, but I conclude the answer was not a pleasant one, as it never was made known.'[7]

The area in which they were camped was a labyrinth of small rivers, streams and ditches, not ideal for cavalry manoeuvres. Le Marchant's men worked hard to clear the land of hedges and trees to make it more navigable. On 26 August, Le Marchant passed through the village of Esquelbecq, a short distance from their camp at Wylder. Like many of the villages nearby, it was deserted except for a few stragglers who were too old or ill to leave.

> I found all the doors and windows of the houses left open, and all the implements used in the different branches of trade, laying just as if the different artisans had gone to dinner and were about to return in an hour. All the household furniture lay just as if the houses were inhabited, and by going into those houses, one can see what the inhabitants were employed at in each from the place and

situation you find the utensils and implements of work. The sight is one of the most melancholy to be seen, and the only consolation is that the inhabitants have absented themselves from a consciousness of having done their utmost to oppose us. It is incredible how strongly attached the lower order of people show themselves to revolutionary principles.[8]

On 5 September, a detachment of cavalry set out from the camp to engage with the advancing enemy. The French were forced to retreat from their advanced positions back towards Cassel, but not before the allies had captured eighty prisoners. The allies suffered casualties with a captain, three junior officers and 140 soldiers wounded.

The following day, between seven and eight o'clock in the morning, Le Marchant was writing a letter when he heard the sound of musket fire. The advanced outposts of their camp had been overrun before he had time to mount his horse. Recognising the immediate threat and concerned about their ability to defend their position, Le Marchant promptly instructed his servants to remove his baggage to the rear: 'Lord Herbert laughed at my prudence, and bet me five guineas that his own baggage would be safe to-morrow.'[9]

In less than an hour, the allied line came under attack from enemy forces stationed at Cassel and Bergues. The French kept up the attack for seven hours, 'an unintermitted, wonderfully hot, and intense fire'.[10] Le Marchant, positioned on the right flank of the allied army, faced a fierce onslaught that afternoon, the cavalry having to dismount and fight on foot. The allies managed to check the French attack, forcing them to pull back. By six o'clock that evening, the ferocious hand-to-hand combat had subsided. The left of the allied line was less fortunate, and that night retreated to the town of Rexpoede, leaving many wounded behind. Marshal Freytag's allied corps had been split in two.

During the night, Le Marchant was given the task of maintaining communications between the right and left sections of Marshal Freytag's army, riding back and forth between the two. During a thunderstorm, he lost sight of the troops and in complete darkness struggled to find them as he negotiated the muddy country tracks. Anxious not to fall into enemy hands, he came across a few baggage wagons so heavily laden with soldiers' families and possessions that they could barely move. He pressed on until he stumbled across a group of Hanoverian infantry who, like him, were lost and unable to offer any assistance. 'All this happened within a few hours, in the dead of night, when, at times, I could not see my horse's head.'[11]

Eventually, two officers from the Austrian light cavalry raced towards Le Marchant. They had just come from the outskirts of Rexpoede and wanted to return there. But Le Marchant felt that by staying on the main road they risked capture by the French. He suggested that they should proceed across country to Hondschoote. The two Austrian officers agreed, and they reached the town at two o'clock in the morning where they were joined by the rest of the cavalry shortly after.

It transpired that the French had seized the town of Rexpoede, during which both Prince Adolphus Frederick, the seventh son of George III and future Duke of Cambridge, and Marshal Freytag were captured. The Prince managed to escape and Marshal Freytag was rescued some hours later when the town was retaken by the allies. The rest of the allied troops arrived at Hondschoote during the course of the day.

It was now that Le Marchant learned that the allied losses had been severe. In one regiment, only eight had survived out of thirty-six officers. An Austrian company lost forty-nine men out of eighty. The fate that had befallen a Hanoverian regiment was even worse. Only two officers and fifty-two men were left out of 600, the remainder having been killed or taken prisoner. The remaining allied forces gathered and established a camp only to be attacked again. This time, neither side gained a decisive advantage as the allies held their ground.

On the morning of 8 September, the attacks continued and by early afternoon the allies had retreated to the banks of the river Yser. It was at this point that Le Marchant joined forces with General William Harcourt, commander of the 1st brigade of cavalry. Once again, they readied themselves for further enemy attacks. It was then they realised that 'almost all our baggage, ammunition, &c. had fallen into the enemy's hands. Poor Lord Herbert is among the sufferers. My prudence has saved me.'[12] The French attacked the following day, compelling Marshal Freytag's division to retreat again, leaving the Duke of York's army exposed. The Duke abandoned the siege of Dunkirk and withdrew east.

The success of General Jean Houchard in defeating Freytag's force, a victory which prompted the Duke to abandon the siege of Dunkirk, earned him nothing less than the guillotine. Accused of cowardice for not pursuing and crushing the retreating allied forces, General Houchard was executed in Paris in November 1793.

Le Marchant's cavalry marched to Furnes to join up with the Duke of York's retreat from Dunkirk. On the 12 September, General Harcourt and Le Marchant proceeded to Dixmude where he was finally able to rest.

> At Dixmude I slept undressed between sheets for the first time these two months, would you believe it? I did not sleep sound. Perhaps I did not enjoy myself the less in musing on my novel situation. In fact, during these same two months I have not even taken off my clothes or boots, except to change them. Often fatigued to death, so much so as to fall asleep on my horse. A little bit of dry bread that has been lying in the bottom of my great coat, was as carefully divided between the General and his Staff, as would have been the richest dainty between epicures at home. It would appear unaccountable to you, how persons accompanied by the number of servants and horses that we all are, can be in want of the comforts, much less of the necessaries, of life. The fact

> is this: attacks are generally made by the enemy at moments least expected, when we hurry on our horses, and think of nothing but our immediate responsibility as officers; we take our posts, and the army changes its position half a dozen times before our servants can find us out again. All they can do, is to stick to some column, and trust to chance for a rencontre.[13]

Le Marchant went to Cysoing at the end of September. Not long after their arrival, they found themselves under renewed attack by the French, forcing them to withdraw to Tournai. The fighting over the summer months had been so intense that neither side wished to engage in any further bloodshed as the season drew to an end. Le Marchant put the respite to good effect, writing to Mary from Tournai:

> No one can have profited by this suspension of hostilities more than myself. I have been busily engaged in making drawings of all articles in the military equipages of our Allies that differ from ours, such as saddles, accoutrements, arms, &c. I have also paid particular observation to the mode of training the Austrian cavalry to the use of the sabre, in which their superiority over us is incredible.[14]

At the beginning of 1794, Le Marchant's father, who had been suffering from ill health, took a downward turn and Le Marchant was granted a few days leave by General Harcourt to return to Bath. He arrived in time only to meet the funeral procession. He took care of family affairs and before long had returned to Ghent, the headquarters of the allied army, in February.

In Ghent, he was billeted with Baron de Levendeghem, whom Le Marchant described as one of the wealthiest nobles in the city, yet also one of the greatest misers. The Baron extended every hospitality to Le Marchant, inviting him to numerous social events. Le Marchant, however, suspected that these invitations were motivated by the Baron's desire to convert him to Catholicism. The Baron readily admitted that 'the affection his wife and himself bore towards me, made them wretched at the idea of my inevitable perdition in the next world'.[15]

From Ghent, Le Marchant proceeded to Courtrai where a large allied force had gathered, and then on to Valenciennes.

On 15 April, Le Marchant was invited to a dinner attended by several senior army figures, including Prince Frederick of Coburg-Saalfeld, the overall allied commander, and the notorious General Karl Mack, a successful Austrian officer at the time. The allied command had put great faith in General Mack's ability, entrusting him with the planning of various operations during the Flanders campaign. Despite being forty years old, General Mack had the appearance of one much older. His general health was poor, and he had suffered a head injury during a previous campaign, from which he had never fully recovered. Le Marchant observed of Mack's injuries: 'In consequence he wears a black caul on his head which is sewn round the bottom behind with stiff black hair, which gives him an extraordinary appearance, he lays on his bed during the whole day, and with pencil writes all his instructions to the army, and when any action takes place, he is lifted from his bed to his horse.'[16]

It was not until later that General Mack's career went into decline. In 1805, he surrendered his Austrian army, albeit against far superior numbers, to Napoleon at the Battle of Ulm. Mack was court-martialled and imprisoned for two years.

On 16 April, Le Marchant was part of the whole combined army consisting of Austrians, British, Dutch, Hanoverians and Hessians. A total of 187,000 men took up positions north of the town of Le Cateau, where they were inspected by the Duke of York. The allies initiated an all-out attack on the French posts at daybreak the following morning, with Le Marchant in the column led by the Duke. The fighting was fierce, Le Marchant describing a particular encounter in a letter to Mary: 'Very little quarter was given, as one regiment at the beginning of the action of the 26th threw down their arms to our Blues who, giving them grace, passed on to charge another body of cavalry, when the villains took up arms and fired at the Blues who had their backs to them. The dogs were punished everyone with death.'[17]

Le Marchant left the area of Le Cateau, heading north towards Flanders, arriving at Tournai at the end of May: 'I had been fourteen hours constantly in horseback, so that I was too fatigued to be capable of any further exertions. I am always sleepy and stiff, proceeding, doubtless, from cold and exercise united. But I eat and drink well, and have good nights, so that if we have the fortune to be allowed a few days' rest, I shall be myself again.'[18]

Le Marchant soon realised that the allies could not overcome the French. No matter how many reinforcements they might receive, the French could call on more. Le Marchant concluded with a degree of resignation, 'I am therefore confident the game is up, and we are incapable of making a successful war.'[19]

In September 1794, General Harcourt recommended Le Marchant for promotion to the rank of major by purchase in the 16th (The Queen's) Regiment of Light Dragoons. Seizing the opportunity, Le Marchant left the Low Countries and headed back to England to join his new regiment. It proved to be a fortunate escape, since the French army was gaining momentum at the same time as the allied coalition was beginning to unravel. By December 1794, the situation had deteriorated to such a point that the Duke of York was recalled to England. General Harcourt assumed command of the British army as it continued to retreat north through the Netherlands in the bitter winter conditions.

> Far as the eye could reach over the whitened plain were scattered gun-limbers, waggons full of baggage, stores, or sick men, sutlers' carts and private carriages. Beside them lay the horses, dead; around them scores and hundreds of soldiers, dead; here a straggler who had staggered on to the bivouac and dropped to sleep in the arms of the frost; there a group of British and Germans round an empty rum-cask; here forty English Guardsmen huddled together about a plundered waggon; there a pack-horse with a woman lying

alongside it, and a baby, swaddled in rags, peeping out of the pack, with its mother's milk turned to ice upon its lips, – one and all stark, frozen, dead.[20]

In April 1795, the British army reached Bremen from where they were evacuated to England. The Flanders campaign proved to be a disaster. It has been said, most probably incorrectly, that the disdainful nursery rhyme, *The Grand Old Duke of York*, was a reflection on Prince Frederick's failure as commander of the British forces against the French during the campaign. It was perhaps unfair to lay the blame entirely on the shoulders of the young, inexperienced Duke. The dysfunction and conflicting objectives among the main allies made matters more complicated. But there is little doubt that the dreadful condition of the British army played its part in the defeat during the Flanders campaign. The purchase system, where individuals could buy commissions and promotions, was partly responsible.

There was a standing joke within the army at the time. An English soldier taken prisoner by the French tells them that they very nearly captured his commander. A French soldier replies, 'Ah! we know better than that. He does us more good at the head of your army.'[21]

Major-General James Craig, Adjutant-General to the Duke of York, wrote a letter to General Sir Hew Dalrymple, the military secretary to the Commander-in-Chief of the army, following the Battle of Cassel in 1793.

> That we have plundered the whole country is unquestionable; that we are the most undisciplined, the most ignorant, the worst provided army that ever took the field is equally certain; but we are not to blame for it. There is not a young man in the Army that cares one farthing whether his commander-in-chief approves his conduct or not. His promotion depends not on their smiles and frowns. His friends can give him a thousand pounds with which to go to the auction rooms in Charles Street and in a fortnight

> he becomes a captain. Out of the fifteen regiments of cavalry and twenty-six of infantry which we have here, twenty-one are commanded literally by boys or idiots. We do not know how to post a piquet or instruct a sentinel in his duty; and as to moving, God forbid that we should attempt it within three miles of an enemy.[22]

The renowned military historian Sir John Fortescue wrote in *A History of the British Army*:

> ...the commanders of the new battalions, who had been juggled into seniority by the Government and army-brokers, were not fit to command a company, much less a brigade. Some of them were boys of twenty-one who knew nothing of their simplest duties. Though they went cheerfully into action, they looked upon the whole campaign as an elaborate picnic.[23]

And Arthur Wellesley, later to become the Duke of Wellington, who had obtained command of a battalion by purchase at the age of twenty-four, once remarked that in the Flanders campaign, he 'learnt what one ought not to do, and that is always something'.[24]

Likewise, Le Marchant learned a great deal from the shortcomings of the British army during the campaign and from serving alongside what he considered to be superior allied armies. It did not take long for the lessons learned in Flanders to inspire Le Marchant to propose his own innovative reforms for the army.

3

LIVE BY THE SWORD

On his return from Flanders, Le Marchant joined his wife and family in Guernsey. As his ship passed the smaller islands of Herm and Sark, on the approach into St Peter Port harbour, it was challenged by a King's cutter and ordered to stop. The response from Le Marchant's ship was too slow. The King's cutter opened fire, a bullet grazing Le Marchant's head.

He then rejoined the 16th Light Dragoons at Weymouth where his regiment was in attendance on George III, taking his wife and family with him. Seven years had passed since he was last in the King's company, and much to his surprise His Majesty still remembered him.

While stationed on the south coast, Le Marchant turned his attention to the lessons he had learned during the Flanders campaign and the issues he had observed regarding the use of the sword. He heard from army surgeons that many wounds among the British cavalry were self-inflicted, though not deliberately. One officer known to Le Marchant had sustained a serious wound to the foot from his own sword. Horses often suffered injuries around the face and neck from the swords wielded by their own riders. An Austrian officer is said to have joked that a

British soldier in action with sword in hand resembled someone chopping wood.

The training of officers and men was the responsibility of the regimental commanding officer, assuming that he had any interest in training at all. In many cases, regimental instruction extended only to drill on the parade ground, but there was very little understanding of military tactics. A cavalry officer noted:

> In England I never saw nor heard of cavalry taught to charge, disperse and form, which, if I only taught a regiment one thing, I think it should be that. To attempt giving men or officers any idea in England of outpost duty was considered absurd, and when they came abroad, they had all this to learn. The fact was, there was no one to teach them.[1]

And this applied equally to swordsmanship, with each regiment adopting a different approach. Le Marchant began to write down his ideas, drawing on his observations from the Flanders campaign and conversations with some of the best swordsmen in the Austrian cavalry. He devised a system of sword fighting, covering both attack and defence, and developed this into a structured set of instructions.

He enlisted assistance from a few fellow officers, and together they ran through the various sword movements while he fine-tuned the exercises. Beginning with a couple of troopers from his cavalry regiment, he gradually extended the training to a larger group.

He subsequently sought to involve other regiments in the training but faced resistance. Some commanding officers were reluctant to embrace new ideas, while others were just plain lazy. Lieutenant-Colonel Herbert, Earl of Pembroke, wrote to Le Marchant in December 1795, 'I shall be very glad to see what you have to recommend on the subject of the sword exercise, because I am always glad to learn. I am sorry Major is not likely to listen to your proposals of training his people.'[2]

General Charles Stanhope, 3rd Earl of Harrington, was equally approving of Le Marchant's efforts. He sent two of his men down to Weymouth, where the 16th Light Dragoons were stationed, to benefit from Le Marchant's sword instruction. So satisfied was he with the training of his men that he enlisted others to follow on.

> Immediately on the receipt of your last letter I wrote to the officer who commands the 1st Dragoon Guards in London desiring Him to send off 6 Horses, according to your direction to Dorchester & availing myself of your obliging permission at the same time requested Him to order the 3 men, who go with those Horses, to remain with them there, in order to profit by the instruction which you are so good as to allow the former squad to receive under your eye.
>
> I am glad to find by your letter that our men are taking pains. I hope they will continue to behave themselves to your satisfaction, & must once more beg that, if any of them are idle or troublesome or conduct themselves in any way contrary to your wishes, you will have the goodness to order such men instantly to their Regiments & take the trouble to acquaint me with their conduct.[3]

Le Marchant, encouraged by the positive feedback, presented his instruction manual to the Duke of York, who had been appointed Commander-In-Chief of the army in 1795, together with his plans to train the British cavalry. The Duke, having taken advice from a committee of general officers, ordered the instructions to be included in the permanent regulations of the cavalry. Le Marchant's exercises were finalised in *Rules and Regulations for the Sword Exercise of the Cavalry*, published on 1 December 1796 by His Majesty's command.

Le Marchant had now successfully delivered a standard method of training designed to enable men, particularly the inexperienced, to be brought up to a minimum level of swordsmanship. The instructions comprised ninety pages of commands, drills, illustrations and various exercises for both individual soldiers and the regiment as a whole, on foot and on horseback. Le Marchant understood that the exercises that he proposed were not going to be easy, especially for new recruits.

> From want of habit in the exercise of the wrist in the common occupations of life, the weight of the sword will at first be found extremely irksome. The action of the arm bears no comparison with that quickness of which the wrist is susceptible; for the motions of the arm are so wide and circuitous, that they are easily counteracted; from which, in a clear point of view, the strictest perseverance will be found necessary, in order to attain perfection in the first lessons; which are merely confined to acquiring a suppleness in the wrist and shoulder; as without this indispensable requisite, no person can become a good swordsman.[4]

The training manual featured a novel method for developing a combination of sword and horsemanship skills called 'Running at the Ring'. A post was erected, adjustable in height, at the top of which hung a ring of five inches diameter for beginners, gradually reducing in size as the training progressed. The horseman would charge from a distance of around fifty yards, starting in a trot and increasing to near on full speed, and attempt to pass the tip of his blade through the ring. Should he be successful, the ring would detach from the post and slide down the blade as far as the handle.

At the end of 1796, Le Marchant could be found at Newmarket in the east of England teaching his new sword exercises and drill to representatives from several cavalry regiments and yeomanry from surrounding counties. The officers were then directed to return to their regiments to train their own men. The importance attached to Le Marchant's mission was emphasised when it was announced that the Duke of York, and possibly George III, and several high-ranking army officers would attend a review at the end of the training session. George, Prince of Wales and heir to the throne, was sufficiently impressed by the sword exercise that he asked Le Marchant to provide him with one-to-one instruction.

From Newmarket, Le Marchant took his sword drill tour north. General Sir William Fawcett, Adjutant-General to the Forces, issued an order to the commanding officers of several regiments stationed in Scotland and the North of England:

> Two Non Commissioned Officers and eight Privates, under the Command of the Adjutant, or Riding Master of the Regiment, to march agreeably to the Route which accompanies this Letter, to Newcastle upon Tyne, where they will place themselves under the Command of Major Le Marchant of the 16th Light Dragoons, and follow such directions as they shall receive from that Officer, both in regard to themselves & their Horses.
>
> The object of this Detachment is that the Non Commissioned Officers who compose it, should be instructed in the Sword Exercise. You will therefore be careful in selecting such as are intelligent, and none of them should be under eighteen, or above thirty years of age.[5]

In March 1797, a similar directive was issued to cavalry regiments in the south and southwest, instructing them to send men to Bradford-upon-Avon in west Wiltshire for training, once again under the guidance of Le Marchant. Once the tour of England had been completed, preparations were made for Le Marchant to travel to Ireland to train the troops stationed there.

In 1797, Britain was in crisis. The French Revolutionary Wars had imposed a significant financial burden on the country. The French had attempted to land in Ireland with 15,000 men in December 1796, only for their ships to be scattered by a storm. The following February, a small force of 1,400 French soldiers landed near Fishguard in Wales. The invasion soon collapsed and the soldiers surrendered.

Although the attempted invasion had proved unsuccessful, it caused panic amongst the public. Many feared a financial meltdown and attempted to convert their banknotes to gold. There had already been a run on banks in Newcastle upon Tyne,

Sunderland, and Durham. The risk of financial unrest spreading to other regions, and specifically London, led to the government passing the Bank Restriction Act of 1797, designed to safeguard the Bank of England's gold reserves. In the midst of this financial turmoil, Le Marchant wrote from Newcastle to his wife in Guernsey in March 1797.

> Some of the principal banks in this part of the country have stopped payment, and all credit has sunk along with them. Not a guinea is to be seen anywhere, nothing but paper. It is expected that Mr. Pitt will go out, yet what will that produce? If peace, it must be such as will eventually ruin the country, and by a perseverance in the war, what is to be hoped for? You can have no idea of the dejection of the public mind and I cannot help so far participating in it, as to regret that we did not make some small investment last year in the American funds. It would have been a resource for our children.[6]

Before Le Marchant could leave for Ireland, he received instructions from General Sir William Fawcett, Adjutant-General, that he should find a replacement to carry on with the sword drill training. The perilous state of the country and the threat of invasion by Napoleon necessitated that he remain in England.

He nominated his brother-in-law, Cornet Peter Carey, to go to Ireland in his place. Peter had already been involved in assisting Le Marchant with sword training and had also contributed illustrations of various sword movements for Le Marchant's instruction manual, for Le Marchant felt that illustrations were crucial to get his message across. Peter set off for Ireland to continue the training in Le Marchant's absence.

Le Marchant's training manual was reprinted in April 1797 and a directive was issued that every cavalry officer should purchase a copy. Several thousand copies were sold with the proceeds going towards the service. The training methods became an integral part of the regular exercise and practice of the cavalry as well as being introduced to infantry regiments.

The sword drill in itself was not enough for Le Marchant. After dedicating so much time to practising and teaching his sword exercises, he recognised the limitations of the existing weapons.

Even though there had been a new standard sword design in 1788, Le Marchant observed during the Flanders campaign that very few cavalry regiments used the same type of sword. The planned standardisation had not been fully rolled out. The most commonly used swords were heavy with a long straight blade and cumbersome to handle. They would often turn in the hand on striking with little effect. Some had been known to break during combat. Le Marchant came up with a new design.

Le Marchant's preference was for a lighter, curved sword along the lines of the scimitar used by the horsemen of Eastern Europe, the Middle East and North Africa. In his view, the longer straight swords commonly used by the British cavalry were designed for a bygone era, 'at a Time that cavalry attacked at a Walk, when no Impulse was given by the Charge'.[7]

Le Marchant simplified the handle, altered the shape and proportions of the blade, shortened the sword and redistributed the weight to produce a well-balanced weapon that needed less strength to wield. The blade featured a more pronounced curve than previous versions and was wider at the tip than at the hilt.

He visited steel manufacturers in the Midlands and Sheffield, seeking advice from established sword cutlers. In particular, he worked closely with Henry Osborn, combining Le Marchant's experience of fighting on horseback with the expertise of one of the most distinguished sword makers of the time. Osborn operated from a factory in Bordesley, Birmingham, and a shop in Pall Mall, London, and would later be appointed sword cutler to the King in 1802.

Le Marchant submitted his final design to the Duke of York in *A plan for constructing and mounting in a different manner the Swords of the Cavalry*. The Duke arranged for the sword to be trialled by the Royal Horse Guards (The Blues). The response was extremely positive; the regiment adopted Le Marchant's sword.

It is said that Le Marchant wanted both light and heavy cavalry to use the same sword design. The light cavalry rode smaller, quick horses and carried light weapons ideal for scouting, skirmishing, and outpost duties, operating ahead of the main army. The heavy brigade rode stronger, more powerful horses for charging at speed and destroying enemy formations. They were often kept in reserve for that crucial moment during a battle, acting as a shock tactic following on from an initial infantry attack. In practice, these roles became interchangeable. During the Peninsular War, heavy brigades were at times used for picket and outpost duties, as well as escorting infantry on marches. While light brigades would find themselves charging at enemy infantry and cavalry during the heat of battle.

Le Marchant's design was approved for the light cavalry, and a sword based on an older Austrian design, featuring a long straight blade of 36 inches, was adopted by the heavy cavalry. The specifications for both new sword designs were formalised in a Royal Warrant issued in June 1796. The Board of Ordnance acknowledged Le Marchant's innovative sword design by presenting him with an exquisitely engraved sabre, an inscription etched on the blade commemorating the occasion.

At the same time, General Charles Stanhope had also been trialling different sword designs. The men he had sent to Le Marchant for training carried the results of these experiments. They were similar to those used by the Austrian cavalry, but with a hilt made of brass which made for a rather heavy sword. Le Marchant responded with some comments, to which Stanhope replied.

> I am much obliged to you for the very accurate calculation you sent me on the proportional weight of the different Parts of the Sabre, which appears extremely useful; at some future time I shall take it as a favour if you will let me know the name & address of the former armourer of your Regiment whom you mention to have been employed in verifying those experiments; as the ignorance & obstinacy of the sword cutlers in general makes such a man an acquisition.[8]

In April 1797, the Duke of York issued an order mandating that both the light and heavy cavalry replace their old swords with the new patterns. Regimental commanders were able to exchange swords or sabres as long as the blades, scabbards, and hilts were in fairly good condition. In return, they would receive an equal number of new swords or sabres at no extra cost. There would be a charge, however, to replace those swords or sabres that were no longer serviceable.

Le Marchant had not only developed and introduced a standardised sword training program, but also designed a new sword pattern for light cavalry, with the admirable support of the Duke of York. Le Marchant worked long hours, often from six in the morning until twelve at night. His reputation had been enhanced and his tireless efforts were recognised when he was promoted without purchase to Lieutenant-Colonel in April 1797. While such a rapid promotion on merit may have been admired by some fellow officers, it also had the potential to cause jealousy among others.

Le Marchant was initially assigned to Hompesch's Hussars, a light cavalry regiment in British pay that had fought with the allies during the Flanders campaign. Two months later he was transferred to the 29th Light Dragoons. During an audience with George III, the King told Le Marchant, 'I dare say many persons will claim the merit of your promotion. Now I wish you to know that whatever merit there is in it rests entirely between you and me, for no one else is concerned in it.'[9]

His new regiment had been posted to the West Indies, while Le Marchant remained in London at the request of His Majesty and the Duke of York. Le Marchant set about defining further improvements for the British army. He developed *A plan for preventing peculation in the foraging of cavalry* which received approval from the Duke. This plan addressed the issue of fraud, where the captain of a troop or the quartermaster would misappropriate funds intended for the feeding of horses. On joining the 6th (Inniskilling) Dragoons back in 1787,

Le Marchant was alarmed to find that the horses were in such poor condition. He discovered that they were only adequately fed and watered immediately before a review or inspection of the regiment. He also authored *The Duty of Officers of Cavalry on the Outpost* which was based on his observations of the Austrian and Prussian cavalry in Flanders.

Le Marchant became a regular visitor at court. Instead of being sent out to join his regiment, the 29th Light Dragoons, in the Caribbean, he was transferred to the 7th (Queen's Own) Regiment of Light Dragoons in the autumn of 1797. His Majesty was reluctant for Le Marchant to be exposed to the unfavourable climate and the yellow fever pandemic prevalent in the area. It is estimated that around fifty thousand British soldiers and sailors died from disease in the West Indies, sometimes referred to as the fever islands, during the 1790s.

Le Marchant's new regiment, the 7th (Queen's Own), had a long history. Originally raised in the late 17th century, it was regarded as one of the top cavalry regiments in the British army but had recently gone into decline. The regiment was under the command of Lord Henry William Paget, but during his absence, Le Marchant, as the next most senior officer, assumed temporary leadership. Recognising that the regiment suffered from a lack of discipline, Le Marchant initiated a series of changes. He wrote a set of instructions covering all aspects of regimental duty and held classes for officers on two or sometimes three days a week. He also introduced riding practice and drills. It is hardly surprising, then, that his efforts met with resistance from some officers and troops who had grown accustomed to a more relaxed atmosphere. Perhaps he tried to effect change too quickly with a vigour that some found disagreeable. But the improvements were noticeable.

On Lord Paget's return, the troops gathered on parade cheered enthusiastically, anticipating that Le Marchant's strict regime was at an end. They were mistaken. Lord Paget checked his horse, then reprimanded them. He considered that the cheering was an act of insubordination and a personal insult to himself. He praised Le Marchant's work, emphasising the need for strict discipline in the ranks.

Lord Paget was an experienced and successful officer. By the age of twenty-five, he had already assumed command of an infantry regiment. He made a point of living like a soldier, with their rations, for a week: hardly a great hardship but still unusual for an officer at the time. He fought during the Flanders campaign and in 1795 had risen from a Lieutenant to a Lieutenant-Colonel in the space of a few months.

At first, Le Marchant was somewhat dismissive of Lord Paget. In a letter to his wife, Mary, he expressed his initial impressions of his commander: 'Lord Paget's is such an overgrown fortune that it will be unpleasant to live in the same place with a person whose military rank is only my equal; but by the profusion observed by him in every instance in his mode of life, I shall always be considered a very secondary point of view, money being the great engine of popularity.'[10]

Almost a year later, the regiment had moved from Canterbury to Guildford, by which time Le Marchant's attitude towards Lord Paget had changed. Le Marchant noted that some of the officers were still a 'bad set', yet he was now 'very well with them all, but it is by being intimate with none but Colonel Barne and Lord Paget. We three agree very well together, and in time hope to weed the Regiment of the black sheep.'[11]

This they achieved by encouraging those officers they did not want to move on to other regiments, either through purchase or exchange. The practice of officers exchanging regiments for payment was not officially sanctioned, as it might lead officers to seek transfers instead of addressing issues in their current regiment. And then, when regiments were ordered overseas, some officers would pay less affluent acquaintances to exchange commissions so as to remain on home soil.

During their time together in the 7th Light Dragoons, Le Marchant and Lord Paget developed a lasting relationship and as Le Marchant's career progressed, he would on occasions seek out Lord Paget for advice. Over time, the regiment began to improve thanks to Le Marchant's lessons and his commitment to discipline. He was not afraid to set an example by taking decisive action against those who transgressed.

> I take a favourable opportunity of making a striking example of a mutineer who is to be tried by a General court martial for striking an officer, and two others were severely punished for striking non-commissioned officers. I saw the Duke on the subject, who most completely accords with me in the proper steps to bring independent spirits to just reasoning and sense of subordination.[12]

General Sir David Dundas, the regimental Colonel, was sufficiently impressed with the discipline and conduct of the troops during an inspection that he encouraged Le Marchant to write down his code of instructions for general use. This was published as *An Elucidation of Several Parts of His Majesty's Regulations for the Formation and Movements of Cavalry* by order of the Duke of York, as Commander-in-Chief.

In spite of his notable achievements, Le Marchant was still not satisfied and set his sights on the more ambitious objective of elevating the overall standard and knowledge of army officers. His persistence and determination, ably demonstrated in the way he had overcome resistance during the introduction of the new sword drill, would stand him in good stead for his next, much grander and challenging attempt at reform.

4
THE FRENCH GENERAL

Britain stood out as one of the few leading countries in Europe that did not have a national military school or college. In 1751, Louis XV approved the building of an *École Militaire* in Paris, although it would be some years before it was officially opened. Its primary objective was to take in five hundred young men from less privileged backgrounds, based on the military service records of their fathers. The curriculum included mathematics, physics, mechanics, and fortification. There were also several preparatory military schools in France. A young Napoleon Bonaparte attended a preparatory academy on a scholarship at Brienne Le Chateau from 1779 to 1784, before passing the entrance exam for the *École Militaire*.

A cadet academy had been in existence in St Petersburg since 1732, teaching military and general subjects to children of soldiers killed or injured during war. The curriculum included mathematics, history, geography, artillery, fortification, fencing, horse riding and languages. In Prussia, Frederick the Great established a military academy in Berlin in 1765 following the Seven Years' War, where young aristocrats could be trained for military and civil service.

The only comparable military college in Britain was the Royal Academy at Woolwich for artillery cadets. It was founded in 1741 under a Royal Warrant by George II. The academy was subsequently divided into a lower school for boys aged twelve to fifteen, and the main school for those between fifteen and nineteen. While mathematics was naturally of great importance to an officer in the Royal Artillery, the course of study also included the classics, fencing and French.

There were some small, private military schools in Britain. Lewis Lochée, originally from the Austrian Netherlands, opened such an institution in Chelsea in the 1770s, until it closed its doors in 1790. Sir Stapleton Cotton, who would later become Le Marchant's commanding officer, wanted to attend a military school abroad but instead was sent to a private military academy in Bayswater, run by a Major Reynolds of the Shropshire militia, 'where he learned little more than the best method of cleaning firelocks and accoutrements'.[1] Apart from artillery and engineers, those wishing to advance their military education were obliged to attend military schools on the continent. Several young men who later achieved success as officers in the British army had followed this route. This did not reflect well on the government or the country.

At the age of seventeen, Arthur Wellesley attended the Royal Academy of Equitation at Angers in France, where he studied mathematics, grammar, fortification and fencing. He became an accomplished horseman and improved his French. He was not the only young man from Britain to be found on the continent. General William Beresford, who later took command of the Portuguese army during the Peninsular War, was sent to a military school at Strasbourg, as was General Rowland Hill, another Peninsular War veteran.

In Britain, responsibility for training army officers rested with regimental commanders and so varied in quantity and quality. Even though some of the better commanders had already instituted training within their regiments, these efforts were delivered in an ad-hoc manner. There was no standardised officer training across the army.

Sir Henry Bunbury, a distinguished army officer and historian, later wrote about the state of the British forces in 1793 when they entered the fray during the French Revolutionary Wars:

> Our army was lax in its discipline, entirely without system, and very weak in numbers. Each Colonel of a regiment managed it according to his own notions, or neglected it altogether. There was no uniformity of drill or movement; professional pride was rare; professional knowledge still more so. Never was a kingdom less prepared for a stern and arduous conflict; and this fact may be fairly taken as a proof that Mr Pitt had entertained no design of engaging in a war with France.[2]

Previous efforts to introduce a consistent form of officer education in England had met with limited success. Some years earlier, Charles Lennox, 3rd Duke of Richmond, at the time the Master-General of the Ordnance and a member of William Pitt's government, had proposed the creation of a national military college. Several of his colleagues agreed with him. But when the idea was examined in more detail, he encountered too much opposition. The objections in parliament revolved around costs, while there were those in senior positions in the army who simply preferred the status quo. It was an implied criticism that the current method of training officers in the army was ineffective. And some feared that the army would become too powerful. The idea was abandoned.

In 1795, an experienced French army general had arrived in Britain offering his services to the British army. The turmoil during the French Revolution, particularly the arrest of Louis XVI in August 1792 followed by the abolition of the monarchy, prompted the emigration of many French officers. These officers sought to enter the service of the allies, either on active service or providing information of a military nature. Some were motivated by their opposition to the revolution, while others needed a source of income following their departure from France.

François Jarry de Vrigny de la Villette was born in France in 1733. After studying military engineering, he entered into the military service of Prussia in 1763 as a Captain, later rising to the rank of Colonel. He served on the personal staff of Frederick the Great, one of twelve officers whom Frederick instructed in the duties of the Quartermaster-General's department. General Jarry fought during the Seven Years' War on the side of the Anglo-Prussian coalition against France, after which he was appointed director of the military academy in Berlin from 1775 until 1786.

After returning to Bordeaux, General Jarry resumed his military service by joining the French army. He was promoted to Field Marshal, assuming command of an infantry division. In early June 1792, Jarry was part of the French army that crossed the border into the Austrian Netherlands and took possession of Courtrai. The Austrians launched several unsuccessful attacks against the French but managed to establish a position near the city suburbs. On 29 June 1792, Jarry gave orders to set fire to the houses located between the city and the Austrian forces, after which the French withdrew back to Lille. Jarry's actions faced condemnation from both the revolutionary assembly and the press.

When the King and Queen of France were imprisoned in August, General Jarry, along with several other high-ranking officers, fled the country. On his arrival in Luxembourg, he was imprisoned alongside his fellow émigré officers. He was released shortly afterwards and, faced with financial difficulties, he sought to make use of his military skills and experience, taking advantage of his connections in Berlin to offer his services to the Austrian army.

It was through the Austrians that General Jarry eventually came to the notice of the British. He was introduced to Colonel Charles Craufurd, an aide-de-camp to the Duke of York during the Flanders Campaign. It was Craufurd who felt that Jarry's skills and experience could be of some benefit to the allied armies. In May 1793, Craufurd wrote to William Eden, 1st Baron Auckland, British ambassador to the United Provinces of the Netherlands, 'If M. de Jarry comes to the Hague, he may probably be able to give your Lordship some useful information with regard to Dunkirk and Lille.'[3]

Craufurd and Jarry met in June 1793, and one month later the Foreign Secretary, William Wyndham Grenville, agreed to take Jarry into the service of the Foreign Office. Jarry received £20 a month for six months, along with £100 for expenses to cover the costs of acquiring intelligence in France. He was asked to prepare several reports and plans for ongoing and future operations, including his thoughts on the overall campaign in Flanders and on military operations around Dunkirk. He did not hold back from criticising the allies' actions during the campaign, while his hostility to the French revolutionaries ran deep.

General Jarry's contribution allowed him to consolidate his reputation as a military expert. And when he came over to England following the return of the Duke of York's defeated army in 1795, he continued to work for the British government, producing reports on various military matters. His proposal to accompany an army officer to inspect English ports and suggest ideas on how best to defend them was accepted by Pitt. The following year, Jarry wrote a report on the potential threat of a French invasion of England. At the same time, he had been engaged in providing private military tuition to Lord William Bentinck, son of the 3rd Duke of Portland. Jarry also offered to provide military instruction to army officers on a semi-official basis.

In April 1798, Lord Auckland wrote to Henry Dundas, Secretary of State for War, proposing that General Jarry be taken on to instruct a select group of the most promising officers on military theory and practice. The approach suggested by Jarry was based on the methods he had employed at the military college in Berlin. The professionalism of the Prussian army was regarded as a model that the British army should strive to emulate.

Lord Auckland circumscribed this as an experiment for a limited time of eight months, to commence the following March.

He further suggested that Jarry would benefit from working alongside an experienced and talented British officer. The cost of such an initiative was set at no more than £1,000 per year, of which £500 would go to Jarry, £300 to a Colonel or Major on half pay as an assistant, and £200 for other expenses.

On 12 December 1798, the army headquarters at Horse Guards issued the following order:

> His Majesty having been graciously pleased to accept the Offer made by General Jarry (who was for many years at the Head of the Ecole Militaire, at Berlin) to take on himself the Superintendence of a similar establishment in this Country, the Commander in Chief has been pleased to direct, that the following Particulars relative to the proposed plan should be communicated to all Colonels and Commander Officers of Regiments, to the end, that they may recommend for his Royal Highness's Approbation, such Officers as are desirous to profiting by General Jarry's Instructions, and who are ready strictly to comply with the Rules and Regulations which will hereafter be framed by His Royal Highness's Direction for their Conduct while they are under General Jarry's Superintendence.
>
> General Jarry will on the 10th March be established at High Wycombe, in the County of Bucks, and be ready to receive such Pupils as have obtained His Royal Highness's approbation, and Leave of Absence from their Regiments for that Purpose. The Number will be limited to Thirty, each of whom, on his Admission, must pay into the hands of Messrs. Cox and Greenwood, Treasurers for the Establishment, the Sum of Twenty Pounds, independent of which he must be prepared to provide himself with such Books and Instruments as General Jarry may think it necessary; & as much of the instruction will be given actually in the Field, it is very desirable that each Officer should be provided with a Horse, for which forage will be allowed. General Jarry speaks very little English, therefore his Lectures will be given in the French Language.[4]

5
THE OUTLINE OF A PLAN

At the same time as General Jarry was offering his services to the British government, Le Marchant had made a start on a *Plan for Establishing Regimental Schools for Officers throughout the Service*, based on his experience with the 7th Light Dragoons. After careful consideration, Le Marchant realised that his initial proposal was too limited in scope and rejected the idea. It needed a more standardised approach across all regiments.

By the autumn of 1798, Le Marchant had come to the conclusion that a national military institution on a far grander scale than previously envisaged was necessary. By December, his ideas were taking shape, and he spent much time putting his thoughts down on paper and refining his vision. His optimism shone through in a letter to his wife, Mary:

> My plan goes on agreeably to my most sanguine wishes, and I have no doubt it will succeed, though there is much more to arrange than I expected. My mind furnishes me, as I go on, with so many new ideas, that I see the impossibility of its embracing a complete system at once. It can alone be led on progressively. Lord Paget will relieve me in about three weeks, by which time my work will be in

> sufficient forwardness to be shown to the Duke. I need not tell you that I am indefatigable, and I am sure I ought to be so, for my plan is so extensive that it is a most laborious undertaking. At the same time it will be as good a test of my talent for my profession as I can wish for.[1]

Le Marchant was just thirty-three years old when he presented his plans to Prince Frederick, the Duke of York, Commander-in-Chief of the army. The Duke responded with a mix of caution and encouragement. While acknowledging the merit of Le Marchant's ideas, the Duke warned him that persuading the government and the army to adopt such a significant improvement in officer training would be a tough task:

> I have no wish to discourage you, yet I can hardly recommend you to sacrifice your time and talents to a project which seems so very unlikely to succeed. Nothing can be done as long as people think on the subject as they do now, and I despair of your removing their prejudices, for prejudices they are, unless you can absolutely demonstrate them to be groundless. This cannot be done in a moment, and it will require stronger arguments than those you have laid before me. If you will revise your plan, and accompany it with all the details necessary for satisfying the public, it shall have my warm support.[2]

Le Marchant got to work refining and developing his plans in such detail so as to counter any arguments that might be raised against his proposal. Three months after his initial meeting with the Duke of York, Le Marchant returned with a comprehensive plan, including financial estimates, income and expenditure. He drew on the wealth of experience available to him, seeking advice from the Duke, his private secretary, the Adjutant-General and the Quartermaster-General. Le Marchant put together a summary of his vision titled *Outline of a Plan for a Regular Course of Military Education* and circulated it to as many as he could.

His proposal recommended establishing a Royal Military College led by experienced officers, under the control of the Commander-in-Chief of the army. The primary objective would be to provide a basic military education for junior officers, and a more structured training program for those aiming for higher positions. The college would be organised into three departments.

The First Department was designed for officers with regimental experience, preparing them for staff roles in the army. Graduates from this department would most likely become aide-de-camps, or take on other key positions on the general staff of the army. The initial intake for this department would be thirty officers, very much in keeping with the temporary establishment planned under General Jarry.

Drawing on the lessons learned from the allied armies during the Flanders campaign, Le Marchant recognised the value in sending young officers abroad. He suggested that the most promising officers should spend two years in European countries to enhance their military knowledge and prepare them for future command. Le Marchant proposed that the officers maintain journals of their observations while abroad, these journals to be held in the college library for future reference.

The Second Department was for those without previous military training. Students in this department would undergo a six-month probationary period. After passing their final exams, they would be commissioned as junior officers. Before joining the department, each cadet had to obtain approval from their regimental commanding officer that they were in line for a vacant commission. The Second Department would also include a 'Legion' of cadets, the sons of soldiers, aged between thirteen and sixteen. The curriculum would cover basic subjects like reading, writing and arithmetic. The course of studies would last three years, with seventy cadets admitted each year. The objective was to prepare these boys for roles as non-commissioned officers.

The Third Department, also known as the junior course, focused on providing a military education to young men aged between fourteen and sixteen, preparing them for a career as officers in the army. Students would gain a solid foundation in military matters prior to reaching the age where they could hold an army commission. The number of students in this department would be two hundred, including fifty sons of officers who had died while on duty, fifty cadets from the East India Company, and one hundred 'sons of Gentlemen'.[3]

The scale of Le Marchant's military college was hugely ambitious, with a total of 560 students across the three departments, and a staff of ninety-seven. The staff included a Governor, Lieutenant-Governor, Commandants, Field officers, Chaplain, Treasurer, Surgeon, twenty-three Professors and Masters, and forty-six servants.

Le Marchant paid special attention to the finances of the college, recognising that the cost of such an institution would be a significant issue. He estimated that the annual income of the college would be £31,121, with expenditure amounting to £25,323, leaving a surplus of £5,790. He concluded, rather optimistically, that the college would accumulate a surplus of £141,550 after thirty years.

He was so engrossed with his ideas and plans for the military college that his wife and family took second place in his priorities. Le Marchant's vision was now close to becoming an obsession. Mary, who had been living in Guernsey for the past two years, was unhappy at their prolonged separation. He revealed his determination to persist with his ambitious project in a letter to Mary, despite the challenges it posed to his personal life and relationships.

> Since my last letter, I have distributed about thirty copies of my proposed plan, and I am happy to say, that no objections are made to it as a system, whilst the amendments that have been proposed, will enable me to render it more perfect, should government determine upon founding a system of general instruction for the army. Everyone in and out of office, allows the necessity of the

measure, and as far as it is possible to judge, I have more reason than ever to count on its success. But time must be allowed for opinion to circulate and people in power to make up their minds. The Duke told that he approved of my prospectus, and should take it immediately to the King, and I find the leading generals canvassing it with an interest that is very encouraging to me. I cannot, however, say when anything will be known, though I trust my next letter will report further and material progress.

I feel most sensibly the length of our separation, and you cannot regret more deeply than I do the necessity of its continuance. My chief wish, my most anxious desire, has always been to make you happy, and this has proved most fortunate for both of us, as I fear that without the ties which bind me to you and our children, I might have been content to live like too many around me, indifferent to the present and regardless of the future. I have worked hard to bring myself forward in the line of my profession. I have attracted public notice, and I trust good opinion. I have got into that connexion, which is the first in the country, and bids fair to establish whatever I may have the ability to bring forward for the public good. But the progress of an individual who depends on his talents, and not his birth and interest, must necessarily be slow and attended by innumerable difficulties. I am of this description, and considering the circumstances under which I started, we must admit, that I have had more success than I had reason to expect, and after the perseverance with which I have pursued my object, when it may be said to be within my grasp, I am sure you will join with me in submitting to the arrangements which the exigences of the moment require.

The present period of public affairs is big with great events, and it is at such a moment alone, that an opening is given to men of enterprize, and therefore, not to be sacrificed to domestic considerations. Peace is the period for indulgence, war for professional exertions. One year more must determine the good or evil of the present political struggle, and since we have done so much as to sacrifice two years of happiness to my pursuits, I think

> it would be folly for me now to desist and give up all thoughts of the distinction that I have laboured so long to attain. Some men, and those of high rank, leave their homes and comforts to seek their fortunes in the East, others hazard all in the West, surely the same reasons that justify these privations, ought to exonerate me from the imputation of any want of judgment, whilst I pursue the more safe career of home service. I ask you but to wait a little longer, and I think see, upon reflection, that I do not ask too much.[4]

Le Marchant contacted several of his friends and acquaintances, seeking their opinions. He received many letters of support and encouragement, including one from the Duke of Richmond, who had previously proposed a similar institution. The Duke praised Le Marchant's ideas and wished him success.

Colonel Charles Craufurd, who had been instrumental in bringing General Jarry over to England, replied to Le Marchant:

> My anxiety for the success of this Establishment is equal to my conviction of its infinite utility and importance. The advantages of it to the Military Service of this Empire are incalculable. As we stand at present, when an army goes upon service, we are so destitute of Officers qualified to form the Quartermaster-General's department and an efficient Corps of Aides de Camp, and our Officers in general have so little knowledge of the most essential parts of their Profession, that we are obliged to have recourse to Foreigners for assistance, or our operations are constantly liable to failure in their execution. The getting Officers from the Allies that you may be acting with for the most confidential situations in your Army is subject to very serious Political Objections, as well as highly disgraceful, and injurious to the Service from the jealousies and dissensions which it naturally excites. It is to a certain degree resigning yourself into the hands of your Allies, and it brings much too near to you their Cabals and intrigues, the mischievous consequences of which we have sufficiently experienced. But if your Army is conducted in all its branches by your own Officers, you

> have it entirely in your own hands, and of course are not subject to the inconvenience just stated.
>
> The success of the French in the present War is a striking proof of what the superior Talents and Science of Officers may effect. Their Armies, tho' labouring under great disadvantages, in many essential Points of interior Discipline and arrangement have generally been victorious from the superior excellence of their Officers. (They have certainly often been defeated, but I am here speaking of their general success in the War). The vulgar idea of their having been often conducted by men of no knowledge or experience in the profession is perfectly erroneous.
>
> I have examined with attention your printed outline of a plan for the Military College, and I think it is in general well arranged. But in order to make it of the utmost possible immediate utility it ought to be upon a more extensive scale. The Departments ought not to be limited in number, and every step should be taken that can induce Officers already in the Service to resort to this seminary for instruction.[5]

Colonel Craufurd disagreed, however, with Le Marchant's financial calculations. He thought that the proposed expenditure was insufficient and that the professors' salaries were too low to attract suitably qualified candidates. He also questioned the likelihood of the college having a surplus.

In May 1799, Le Marchant and Jarry opened the temporary military college in The Antelope Inn on the High Street in High Wycombe. Le Marchant assumed the role of Commandant, with Jarry serving as the Director of Instruction. The premises, already in use by the local militia, were considered far from ideal by Le Marchant. 'It is an old place, not at all calculated for the purpose, but it will do to begin with this year.'[6] These premises would continue to be in use for another fourteen years.

High Wycombe, with a population of just over 2,300, thrived from being on the main route connecting London and Oxford. The daily coach services between these two cities made regular stops at the numerous hotels and inns along the bustling High Street, with the Red Lion hotel, right next to the college, one of the more prominent hostelries. The town's excellent transport connections contributed to its prosperity as it became a centre for lacemaking and paper mills. The abundance of beech trees in the surrounding area resulted in the growth of a flourishing chair-making industry, with many of the goods taken down to the markets in London. The presence of the college contributed to the vibrancy, prosperity and cultural life of the town. On one occasion, the officers hosted an evening at the New Theatre on St Mary Street, featuring a comedy performance.

Although this semi-official military college for army officers represented only a small part of Le Marchant's wider plan, it was an important first step, in effect a proof of concept. The initial intake of thirty officers consisted of a Lieutenant-Colonel and several with the rank of Major. Le Marchant rented a house in Church Street, while General Jarry moved into Wellesbourne House on the corner of Priory Road and Castle Street.

General Jarry's lessons went into a vast amount of detail, which he documented in several manuals written in his mother tongue. His comprehensive *Treatise on the Marches and Movements of Armies*, of some ninety pages, focused on the intricacies of marches leading up to battle, and included a section on marching in retreat. Jarry's method involved precise calculations of the speed of men marching in columns, taking into account factors such as the condition of the roads and the nature of the countryside. Jarry estimated that, 'in roads considered as bad, infantry can march at the rate of 3000 paces per hour; in middling roads, 3900; in an even good road they can advance as much as 4800 steps an hour, which is at the rate of about 80 steps per minute.'[7]

Jarry's *Treatise* went on to estimate the length of a horse's step as 2 feet 9 inches. On exceptionally good roads, which during a campaign might be few and far between, cavalry could maintain an average of 5,400 steps, equal to almost three miles per hour.

And this was just the start. Given that armies often marched in separate columns, sometimes taking different routes, it was essential that the various units of the army – whether infantry, cavalry or artillery – would arrive in the correct order of battle precisely on time. Officers on the staff or from the Quartermaster-General's department would need to calculate the route for each particular column, factoring in natural obstacles such as forests, marshes, rivers and mountains. They would also have to take into consideration the position and distance of the enemy. Over such matters would a battle be won or lost. The importance of meticulous planning became evident during the Peninsular War against Napoleon. Throughout this campaign, armies spent most of their time marching, countermarching and navigating the difficult terrain of Portugal and Spain across mountains, valleys, rivers and plains.

When it came to cavalry, Jarry argued that a competent commander should always send scouts ahead to identify obstacles before ordering a cavalry charge or forward movement. And in retreat, the cavalry would play a vital role as the rear guard, slowing down the enemy to allow the infantry to withdraw safely.

Jarry's tuition would have presented a considerable challenge for some of the officers attending the new establishment. The lectures were delivered in French, and the students had limited knowledge of the subjects being taught beyond their standard regimental duties. Nevertheless, both Le Marchant and Jarry persevered, and the entire undertaking was regarded as a success.

The temporary college in High Wycombe had opened with only Le Marchant and Jarry present. Le Marchant now set about recruiting additional professors and masters. One of the first was Isaac Dalby, a mathematics professor. He was a self-taught man from a humble background, whose previous experience included a similar role at a naval college in Chelsea. Despite his rather eccentric and unsophisticated demeanour, Dalby quickly became a favourite among both students and staff at the college.

John William Cole of the 21st Fusiliers, an ex-cadet from the Junior Department, fondly recalled Dalby's distinctive teaching methods:

> There were some awful moments, when, with chalk in hand, he designed a complicated problem on the blackboard, and muttered with a gruff tone, 'Let me see what you can make of that!' If you succeeded without boggling, he patted you on the head with a gracious, 'You may go.' As he entered the grounds on those momentous occasions, many would gather round him with obsequious bows and inquiries after his health, but as he saw through the overstrained courting, he replied half jocularly, 'Ah! I suppose you are coming up presently. Take care I don't spin you like tops.'[8]

Dalby was also appointed as an examiner in history, even though he knew little about the subject. Cole continues, 'He usually began with a common-place question in chronology, such as for instance, 'When was the battle of Hastings fought?' which, as a matter of course you were unable to answer; and as you hesitated, he helped you out by saying, 'Never mind a hundred years or so, give me a good round guess.'[9]

Dalby would remain at the college for twenty-one years, retiring in 1820 at the age of seventy-six. He published *A Course of Mathematics Designed for the Use of the Officers and Cadets of the Royal Military College* in two volumes covering a wide range of mathematical subjects, including arithmetic, geometry, trigonometry, surveying, algebra and mechanics.

Le Marchant's second son, Denis, who readily admitted that he was not the most diligent student, received private tuition from the mathematics professor, noting that 'Dalby, though one of the most eminent mathematicians of the day, had a ruggedness and uncommunicativeness which quite disqualified him as a teacher of a youth like me. He was, however, very kind to me and I picked up much curious information from him respecting the eminent men among whom he had lived.'[10]

Dalby would later be joined by three other distinguished mathematicians: Thomas Leybourn, James Ivory and William Wallace. The latter would go on to become professor of mathematics at Edinburgh University. This collective expertise transformed the college into an important centre of mathematical research, with Leybourn, Ivory and Wallace publishing several papers that made significant contributions to the advancement of mathematics in Britain. All four professors would teach at Sandhurst following the relocation of the Royal Military College.

Le Marchant was exacting in his approach to recruiting professors, driven by a determination to uphold the high standards of the college. In a letter to his wife, he explained the importance of choosing professors who possessed the right quality and qualifications. 'Lord Moira has been with me several times to recommend one of his protégées, but I shall not think of him if I can find any one better qualified for the situation: whatever patronage I may hold, shall be for the benefit of men of ability. There is no room in the College for even a single drone.'[11]

He was on the verge of recruiting professors in fortification and military drawing when he received orders to join the 2nd Regiment Dragoon Guards (Queen's Bays) in July 1799. While disappointed at having to relinquish command of the college at that very moment, he regarded this move as beneficial, writing to Mary, 'I am determined to rise to the head of my profession, nothing but death shall stop me.'[12]

He was asked to select an officer who could take over at High Wycombe during his absence. He named his friend, James Brock, as his replacement. Brock was a fellow islander from a prominent Guernsey family, who had recently become a major in the 16th Light Dragoons. Colonel Henry Calvert, Adjutant-General to the Forces, wrote to Le Marchant soon after he had left to join his regiment:

> I could have much wished, for the benefit of our young establishment at High Wycombe, that your services had not been

> required in the field this year, and indeed, for the benefit of the service at large, I wish you could have been spared till the plan you have suggested and arranged, for a complete System of Military Education, (so essentially necessary, and, unfortunately, so long neglected in this country) had been in such a state of forwardness as to have enabled those, who have the honour and reputation of the service much at heart, to have looked forward to its establishment and completion with confidence.[13]

Le Marchant, now with his regiment, prepared to join an Anglo-Russian expedition led by the Duke of York to the north of Holland. The primary objective was to defeat the combined French and Dutch Batavian forces and regain control of the area from France. The Helder campaign proved to be short-lived. The Duke, having been pushed back by the French, concluded an armistice in October and the British army withdrew from Holland. The Russian troops, unable to return home through the Baltic because of ice, yet prohibited from landing on English soil, ended up in the Channel Islands until the following spring.

Le Marchant returned to High Wycombe without having left England. He found that nothing had advanced during the two months that he had been away. No additional professors had been recruited, and his plans were still under consideration by ministers, who were preoccupied with other important matters. Napoleon Bonaparte had led a *coup d'état* in France and declared himself First Consul. And the country was suffering financially with little prospect of adding further to the budget of the army.

6

THE SEAL OF APPROVAL

By October 1799, the college at High Wycombe had thirty-four students in attendance, while Le Marchant was waiting for a response from ministers regarding his broader plan. He did, however, manage to gain the support of two influential men, William Huskisson and John Charles Villiers. Both were close to the Prime Minister, William Pitt the Younger, and they provided Le Marchant with much needed advice on how to negotiate the corridors of power.

At the age of thirteen, Huskisson had been sent to Paris to live with his uncle, where he witnessed the early days of the French Revolution and the storming of the Bastille. In 1790, he became private secretary to George Leveson-Gower, the 1st Duke of Sutherland, who was the British Ambassador to France.

Both returned to England in 1792, when diplomatic relations between the two countries broke down. It was the Earl who introduced Huskisson into political circles. His administrative skills and knowledge of French made for a rapid ascent and in 1795, at the age of twenty-four, he was appointed Under-Secretary to Henry Dundas, Secretary of State for War. The following year he was elected as a Member of Parliament. He would prove to be a valuable ally and supporter of Le Marchant's plans to establish the college.

Huskisson wrote to Le Marchant from Downing Street on 2 November 1799:

> I am glad to see you adhere to this subject with your usual perseverance, as I am convinced it will prove most beneficial to the public. The ministers are so completely satisfied that it will, that whatever delays you may experience with them, from the pressure of other national concerns, you may rest assured of their ultimately giving it every necessary support and protection, either from their own authority, or by application to Parliament, as may appear most proper.[1]

Tragically, William Huskisson would become better known for the circumstances surrounding his death, rather than his achievements as an administrator and politician. In 1830, he fell onto the railway track in front of Robert Stephenson's *Rocket* steam locomotive, at the opening of the Liverpool and Manchester Railway.

Le Marchant continued to seek support for his plan, approaching men of influence during his stay in London. On 7 December 1799, he wrote to Lord Auckland, a close associate of William Pitt.

> Knowing that your Lordship sees the very great necessity there is for military instruction in this country, I take the liberty earnestly to solicit your influence with ministers in support of a plan for founding a military college, and which is at present under consideration.
>
> The rapid progress made by other nations in the art of war is so evident, that the object of this institution becomes a question of great national importance, and which certainly cannot be legislated at a more favourable moment than the present.

> Although the establishment at Wycombe has been attended with the success that was reasonable to expect, yet it is not the exertion of a few individuals, acting under private patronage, that can ever essentially forward the interests of the service.
>
> Innovation, to be well received by the public, requires to be confirmed by an act of the legislature, in order to do away with the prejudices of custom. If the improvement of the service is not considered a measure of sufficient importance, to be acknowledged and brought forward by the Government, it is not to be expected that science will be held in higher estimation by the army itself, therefore, to attempt an establishment on any other than a national foundation, it cannot be permanent; and these considerations will deter men of science engaging on it as professors; whilst officers of rank may be led to consider any employment at a private institution as incompatible with their situations in life.[2]

At the end of the year, his plan reached the Prime Minister, and Huskisson provided Le Marchant with an update indicating a favourable response. Pitt had read Le Marchant's papers and was supportive of the idea, but he wanted input from military experts before moving forward.

In early 1800, two military advisers, General Sir David Dundas, Quartermaster-General, and Colonel Henry Calvert, Adjutant-General to the Forces, submitted a report to Prince Frederick, the Duke of York, regarding Le Marchant's plan. The report provided a summary of the proposal, outlining the plan to create three departments within the college.

The two advisers agreed with Le Marchant's calculations that the income raised from those attending the college would cover all expenses, including the salaries of professors and masters. The surplus that Le Marchant reckoned would accrue would cover any unforeseen costs as well as providing pensions for retired staff. There would be no financial burden placed on the government, except for the cost of new buildings and accommodation.

The report proposed that the new college be situated in a county with countryside suitable for military training and manoeuvres. It emphasised the need to steer clear of London or any other large city, so as not to provide a distraction for students.

In his plan, Le Marchant had stressed that the availability of accommodation would be critical, a concern echoed by General Dundas and Colonel Calvert. The report also recommended the appointment of two key roles; a Governor and a Lieutenant-Governor, who would also serve as the Superintendent General, both to reside on site.

The report concluded with a resounding endorsement of the effort and detail that had gone into Le Marchant's plan:

> On reviewing the whole of the subject and the papers relating thereto we beg leave strongly to express our sentiments of the very great importance of the former, and our opinion that the latter are so well arranged, and so entirely methodized, that it now requires nothing but His Majesty's Sanction and Royal Approbation, to carry into immediate execution a measure long earnestly wished for & most essentially conducive to the Public Welfare.[3]

The Duke of York forwarded the report to Henry Dundas, the Secretary of State for War, accompanied by the following covering letter:

> Horse Guards April 3rd 1800
> Sir,
> In compliance with the suggestion contained in Your Letter of the 10th February, I lost no time in directing the Quarter Master General and the Adjutant General to consider minutely the Plan which had been prepared by Lieut. Colonel Le Marchant for the establishment of a Military College in this Kingdom and to report to me their opinions upon the same.
>
> I now transmit for Your Information the Report which they have made to me, which is so full & which appears to me in every

respect so correct that I do not think it necessary to add any further observations upon the Importance and Utility of an Institution, which if adopted in its proposed extent, promises to be productive of so much Benefit to His Majesty's Service.

I am Sir
Yours
Frederick[4]

Le Marchant was becoming increasingly restless. It had been just over a year since he and General Jarry had opened their temporary college at High Wycombe. Surely there was sufficient support for the college to advance to the next stage of formalising and expanding the institution along the lines of Le Marchant's proposal.

He wrote to Colonel Calvert that it was time to set out the rules and regulations in a Royal Charter, covering all aspects of the college's operation. He believed that without this, there was no point in moving forward with his plan. Le Marchant was determined to avoid the practices that had long prevailed in the army – staff appointments based on patronage and examinations awarded by favour – from being applied to the college. After all, Le Marchant argued, the Royal Military Academy at Woolwich had been established with clear responsibilities and regulations through both a charter and an Act of Parliament. Le Marchant's lengthy letter to Colonel Calvert made its way through the hands of Huskisson to the desk of Henry Dundas.

Whether Le Marchant's efforts to exert pressure on the government had any impact or not, Henry Dundas replied to the Duke on 14 August. Dundas revealed that William Pitt was ready to go to Parliament to get approval for Le Marchant's plan. Pitt intended to seek a reasonable sum of money to build the necessary facilities required for the proposed college. Pitt also recommended that the Duke appoint a committee of senior officers to review and discuss how to implement Le Marchant's proposal. The committee's mission would be to agree on the estimates and details for building the college and finalise the rules and regulations for its management. Prince Frederick, the Duke of York, in his capacity as Commander-in-Chief of the army, was appointed as president of the committee. The remaining members included a number of eminent, high-ranking officers chosen by His Majesty.

General Sir William Fawcett was in his seventies and had recently retired as Adjutant-General to the Forces due to his failing eyesight. He was appointed to the committee for his extensive experience and knowledge of military strategy and tactics. Fluent in both French and German, in 1754 he had translated the *Regulations for the Prussian Infantry* and soon after, *Regulations for the Prussian Cavalry*. He was a frequent visitor to Europe, partly as an observer of military manoeuvres, but also to negotiate with Britain's allies.

General Sir David Dundas, Quartermaster-General, had attended the Royal Military Academy at Woolwich, and was therefore well aware of the advantages of officer training. Like General Fawcett, he had spent time studying the Prussian army under Frederick the Great and was an advocate of army reform. In 1788, he had published the *Principles of Military Movements* and then *Instructions and Regulations for the Formations and Movements of the Cavalry* in 1796. General Dundas would later become Commander-in-Chief of the army from 1809 to 1811 replacing Prince Frederick, the Duke of York.

The other members of the committee included the Earl of Harrington, General Lord Cathcart and General William Harcourt. The latter had been Le Marchant's commanding officer during the Flanders campaign. The committee was completed by Major-General Oliver Delancey, Barrack-Master General to the Forces, Major-General John Pitt, 2nd Earl of Chatham and brother of Prime Minister William Pitt the Younger, and Colonel Calvert.

It is worth noting, and a testament to Le Marchant's standing, that despite holding the position of Lieutenant-Colonel in the Queen's Dragoon Guards, he was invited to join the committee, even though his rank was considerably lower than that of the majority of the other committee members.

The committee convened at Horse Guards and reported to Henry Dundas on 2 December 1800, recommending that the Royal Military College should be established in the name of His Majesty through a Royal Warrant, based on the proposal 'which has been with great labor and ability prepared by Lieutenant Colonel Le Marchant'.[5]

The committee included a budget of £146,877 for the purchase of land and the construction of buildings. The cost would be spread over four years, since it was anticipated that this would be how long it might take to complete the construction work.

The Duke of York, on behalf of the committee, wrote to Henry Dundas. Le Marchant's efforts had been finally recognised at the highest level:

Horse Guards
2nd December 1800
Sir
I am directed by the Committee assembled in pursuance of His Majesty's Commands, for the consideration of Matters relative to the proposed Establishment of a Military College, to accompany my Publick Letter on that subject, with a few observations, which the Committee deem it expedient to submit to you and Mr Pitt's Consideration.

It appears in the first instance, a Point of Justice towards General Jarry, and equally conducive to the benefit of the Establishment (in which they must necessarily be immediately and actively employed) that he as well as the Officer, on whom His Majesty maybe pleased to confer the Appointment of Lieut. Governor and Superintendent General, and likewise the Secretary of the Supreme Board, should enter into the Salaries proposed for them, from the Period, when His Majesty's Approbation of the Warrant is obtained, and that General Jarry and the Superintendent

General, should be authorized immediately to search for such able Professors and Masters, as the future Establishment of the College will require, who shall, as soon as approved by His Majesty, enter on the Pay annexed to their several situations.

The Committee are induced to make the second Proposal, from a Conviction of the length of time it will require to find Persons sufficiently qualified, and under the persuasion, that the Supreme Board will exercise this Power with due discretion, and will not authorize any Expence, which the Circumstances of the case do not fully justify.

The Committee have further desired me to express in very strong terms, the sense they entertain of the Ability, and uninterrupted assiduity which Lt. Colonel Le Marchant has displayed, in preparing and arranging the very intricate and Voluminous Details, necessary to bring this important Object to the State, in which it is now presented to His Majesty's Ministers, and from a Consideration of the unavoidable Expenses, to which he has been exposed during the long Period he has been engaged in this undertaking, they recommend, that he shall receive, not less as a Token of approbation, than as a just Remuneration for the same, the sum of Five Hundred Pounds.

Yours

Frederick[6]

The only part of Le Marchant's plan that the committee did not approve was the 'Legion', which was designed to educate the sons of soldiers to become non-commissioned officers. Concerns were raised about the adverse impact on the army if officers were promoted from within the ranks. General Sir David Dundas remarked that at the start of the French Revolution, many soldiers had deserted rather than be led by their former comrades. Although the idea of the 'Legion' was rejected by the committee, the Duke of York pursued a similar idea independently.

In 1803, the Duke opened the Royal Military Asylum in White Lion Street, Pimlico, aimed at providing an education for the sons and orphans of British servicemen who had lost their lives in action, very much along the lines of Le Marchant's 'Legion'. Perhaps this was the Duke's way of acknowledging the validity of Le Marchant's original idea, while avoiding the objections of the committee of high-ranking army officers. In 1892, the Royal Military Asylum was renamed the Duke of York's Royal Military School. The school moved to Dover in 1909 and is now a co-educational boarding school.

7

THE ROYAL MILITARY COLLEGE

The Duke of York drafted a Royal Warrant for His Majesty, the introduction of which outlined the need for such an institution.

> It having been represented to us by our Dearly Beloved Son Frederick Duke of York, Captain General and Commander in Chief of our Armies, that very essential advantages would arise to our Service from the establishment of a College for the General purpose of military education and instruction, and having observed the benefit derived to our Artillery Service from the establishment of the Royal Military Academy at Woolwich, as well as to the Armies of the European Powers where similar institutions have been formed, We were induced to direct that a Military College for the instruction of the Officers of our Army, tho' on a temporary and limited scale, should be formed at High Wycombe and having remarked with much satisfaction the good tendency already apparent of this measure, and being fully satisfied of the expediency of extending the same to our service in general.
>
> It is our Royal Will and Pleasure, that a military establishment under the title of The Royal Military College shall be formed according to the following Rules, Order, and Regulations.[1]

Unfortunately, the warrant became stranded in the machinery of government. The delay was partly due to a relapse in the King's health at the beginning of 1801, which lasted for several months. Nevertheless, Le Marchant proceeded to recruit four new professors, one for field fortification, two for military drawing, and one for German language.

Le Marchant's cause received a welcome boost when three officers who had attended the college at High Wycombe had an opportunity to demonstrate their value on active service. Majors Thomas Birch, John Pine Coffin and Burgh Leighton were appointed to the Quartermaster-General's staff under Lieutenant-Colonel Robert Anstruther, as members of Lieutenant-General Sir Ralph Abercromby's expedition to drive the French from Egypt. The reports back from the Middle East praised the contribution, conduct and accomplishments of the three young officers from the Senior Department. Le Marchant appeared elated and no doubt proud as he congratulated Major Thomas Birch on 9 May 1801:

> Accept my most hearty congratulations on the very handsome manner Colonel Anstruther speaks of you and the Wycombites. In his last despatches he says, "the officers sent me from Jarry's are of infinite use, and the details of the several actions fought by this army are accompanied by plans in drawing, executed by Major Birch and the officers from Wycombe, in a style of perfection that does them great credit." I saw this encomium upon you and my friends at the Secretary of State's.
>
> Continue your exertions, and they will place you high in the most honourable rank of your profession.
>
> The Establishment is improving in science daily. I have some very intelligent officers here at present, and Government is so sensible of the advantages to the country which the Establishment is producing, that we receive the greatest possible encouragement. The moment an officer is qualified for the Staff, he is immediately appointed, and any who have reasonable claims to promotion are

attended to. In short, we are in high feather, and the credit which the world is willing to allow us exceeds my warmest expectations.

In regard to my progress in rendering the College a national institution, I have been equally fortunate. This week it is to be brought before Parliament, and the Secretary at War assures me there is no likelihood of opposition. Indeed your conduct, joined to those of the Establishment with you, have materially contributed to fix the opinion of the public as to its utility to the service. The poor King's illness, and the unexpected change of Ministry, threw me back for the moment. But I set to work with such expedition, and found the minds of the new Government so well disposed towards my plan, that I experienced no difficulty.

The classes, progress of studies, &c. are all better arranged than when you were here, yet notwithstanding, the Establishment is more difficult to conduct. Fine gentlemen cabal together and discourage the industrious, which must be the case until I have a book of statutes confirmed by order of his Majesty, and this I expect shortly.

You see that your interest is pushing at home, whilst you are labouring to lay the foundation of success abroad. Recollect all I have told you on the head of exertions. It is only by doing what others do not, that you are to build your hopes of preferment.[2]

The skills they had acquired at the college were put to good use. Birch replied from his camp on the Nile:

You give me great pleasure by telling me that Colonel Anstruther has spoken of us with satisfaction & indeed I can conclude today that in no one instance has he found us wanting in inclination & exertion and that I hope we are in some measure deserving of it. Leighton has exerted himself as much as possible always ready & willing to be of service. Coffin found us just before we reached Cairo in high health & spirits. He has made himself of infinite service & shews the confidence that good instruction gives. He was actively & usefully employed immediately.

> In our march from Cairo one or other has always gone forward to reconnoitre for the march of the army the next day, another has assisted in taking in the ground for the encampment, another making remarks on sketching the nature of the Country, course of the Nile to correct the sketches we made on the march to Cairo. I lament much we have not had three more with us as there would have been full employment for them without deviating from our particular line of duty & in this country too it is the more requisite as the duty is fatiguing & requires relief.[3]

In June, Charles Yorke, Secretary at War, stood up in the House of Commons and launched into a spirited address in support of the Royal Military College. He explained that the institution at High Wycombe had already produced nine general officers, including those who had demonstrated their ability in Egypt to such good effect. He contended that in the navy, every officer went through a course of instruction before he could attain even the lowest rank as a commissioned officer.

Opponents of the plan, like Major-General George Walpole, argued against the necessity of a military college. Walpole pointed to the success of the Duke of Marlborough at a time when no formal military education existed. Some voiced concerns about the potential cost and the burden it would place on the public purse. There were others who considered such a military institution as unconstitutional, fearing it could pave the way for a military regime. One Member of Parliament observed that he had

> … sat long enough in that House to witness many strange things. To him standing armies and barracks appeared a gross attack on the Constitution. He wished to see the return of good old times, as with the return of the true constitutional spirit, we might hope to see the return of true English liberty, which, he was sorry to say, was now nearly lost.[4]

At the end of the debate, Charles Yorke proposed a motion for the sum of £30,000 to be granted to His Majesty for the purchase of land and for the construction of buildings for the Royal Military College. The resolution was passed.

Finally, a few weeks after Le Marchant's letter to Birch, the warrant received Royal Assent. On 24 June 1801, the temporary institution at High Wycombe officially became the Royal Military College. The warrant established a Supreme Board of Governors with responsibility for the direction and management of the college. The board's duties included preparing rules and regulations for the running of the college, a task that eventually fell to Le Marchant, and submitting them to His Majesty for approval. The board was also entrusted with recommending officers and staff for appointment to the college, along with determining their salaries and allowances.

The Supreme Board met for the first time at Horse Guards, the headquarters of the army, on 1 July. It was attended by the Duke of York as Commander-in-Chief of the army, Charles Yorke as Secretary at War, General William Harcourt, General Sir David Dundas, General Lord Cathcart and Colonel Calvert. It was at this meeting that the decision was made to appoint Le Marchant as the Lieutenant-Governor of the college and General Jarry as Commandant. The salary for Le Marchant was set at £730 per annum, Jarry was awarded £790 while Isaac Dalby, professor of mathematics, received £250. The pay for other masters and instructors ranged from £100 to £200 a year.

On 13 July, the King wrote to Charles Yorke, formally approving the recommendations regarding Le Marchant and General Jarry. Le Marchant's appointment as Lieutenant-Governor appeared in the London Gazette soon after. He was to report to General William Harcourt, who had been chosen as Governor of the college. Harcourt had been part of the committee appointed by the Prime Minister, William Pitt, to oversee the implementation of Le Marchant's plan. He had joined the army at sixteen and his family wealth and connections meant he had risen quickly through the ranks. He became a Lieutenant-Colonel at the age of twenty-one. His father had served as governor to George III and played a key role in negotiating the marriage between the newly crowned King and Princess Charlotte of Mecklenburg-Strelitz.

Given Harcourt's family connections, it was to be expected that he held prominent positions in royal circles, first as equerry to Queen Charlotte, and later as a groom to the bedchamber, attending to His Majesty. Harcourt's favourable standing with the royal family most likely contributed to his appointment as Governor of the college, a highly coveted position. Harcourt was approaching the age of sixty when he was appointed. He was not in the best of health, having previously suffered a minor stroke. Although it was expected that the Governor would reside near the college, Harcourt claimed that he could not find a suitable house close by and remained at the family residence at St Leonard's Hill near Windsor. He also owned property at Clifton in Bristol, and he would spend time in London and Brighton. His position as Governor of the Royal Military College was largely symbolic. The overall day-to-day management of the institution fell to Le Marchant.

Le Marchant had previously served under Harcourt during the Flanders campaign. It was the General who had recommended that Le Marchant be promoted to major in the 16th Light Dragoons. As Harcourt's brigade major in Flanders, Le Marchant often found himself in the General's company, and at the time Le Marchant held him in high regard. But the relationship would turn sour.

General Harcourt's wife, Mary, was known as someone who liked to involve herself in court politics and could be rather hostile towards those who did not show her, in her opinion, sufficient deference. And Le Marchant, known for his straightforward nature, was not overly concerned with social niceties. John Sanders, the architect to the Barrack Department of the War Office, would later tell his friend Joseph Farington that

Le Marchant, 'had in Lady Harcourt, wife of Genl. Lord Harcourt an enemy, she having a strong prejudice against him'.[5]

In November, Le Marchant began working on estimates and proposals for the Junior Department. It had already been decided that the Junior Department was too large to be located at High Wycombe. Harcourt, Le Marchant and Delancey, the Barrack-Master General, set about looking for suitable premises nearby, and chose Great Marlow. After visiting several properties in the town, they settled on one they considered to be suitable.

At the same time as Le Marchant was making preparations for the opening of the Junior Department, he was finalising the rules and regulations for the Senior Department, which had been omitted from the original warrant back in June. Le Marchant's regulations were included in a second Royal Warrant on 9 December 1801.

The warrant prescribed the entry requirements. Prospective candidates had to be at least nineteen years old and have served a minimum of two years with their regiment. They were expected to be well-versed in military manoeuvres, proficient in arithmetic, and possess an understanding of the French language. Each application had to be submitted through the regiment's commanding officer, acting as a guarantor that the candidate met the entry requirements. The warrant also detailed the duties of officers, provided an outline of the curriculum and specified allowances for forage, coal and even candles for the staff.

In addition to running the new college, Le Marchant, never one to waste time, put his mind to other matters. In 1801 he submitted *A Plan for Recruiting the Army* to the Duke of York. He also provided Charles Yorke, Secretary at War, with *A Plan for the General Enrolment, and Effectual Discipline of the Population of the Country capable of bearing Arms,* part of which was eventually included in an Act of Parliament in 1803. Le Marchant next studied different military systems across several countries and compiled his findings in a document entitled *An Outline for the Formation of a General Staff to the Army.* A report of over two hundred and eighty pages, it focussed on the duties of staff officers and the Quartermaster-General's department.

Le Marchant's dedication and attention to detail knew no bounds. The topics discussed at one meeting of the Supreme Board might seem surprising given the presence of such dignitaries as the Duke of York and Charles Yorke.

> Lieutenant Colonel Le Marchant, Lieutenant Governor & Superintendent General presented to the Board, a drawing of a Bedstead proposed to be provided for the use of Students of the Junior Department at Marlow, and some alterations therein being suggested, the same were approved of, and the requisite number directed to be provided by the Barrack Department, together with such Bedding as may be approved of by the Lieutenant Colonel Le Marchant.[6]

The Junior Department finally came into existence with a Royal Warrant issued on 4 March 1802. The three departments in Le Marchant's original plan had now been combined into two – the Senior Department at High Wycombe and the Junior Department at Marlow. The Royal Warrant outlined the purpose of the new department:

> The Junior Department of the Royal Military College is appropriated to the Instruction of those, who from early Life are intended for the Military Profession, and who, by this means may be grounded in Science, previously to their attaining the Age that enable them, consistently with Our Regulations, to hold Commissions in the Army.
>
> This Department of the College is also intended to afford a Provision for the Orphan Sons of those meritorious Officers who have fallen, or been disabled, in the Service of their Country, as well as for the Sons of those Officers, who, from pecuniary difficulties, might not otherwise be able to give them an adequate education.

The Cadets shall, for the present, be received into the Junior Department, upon three different Establishments, according to the following Specification, viz.

Thirty, the Orphan Sons of Officers who have died, or been maimed, in Our Service, and who have left such Orphans in pecuniary distress:

These shall receive their Education, Board, and Clothing, free from Expence.

Twenty, the Sons of Officers actually in Our Service:

These shall pay Forty Pounds per Annum each, for which Sum they shall receive their Education, Board, and Clothing.

Thirty, the Sons of Noblemen and Gentlemen; and, Twenty, the Cadets of the East-India Service. These shall pay Ninety Guineas per Annum each, for which Sum they shall receive their Education, Board, and Clothing.

Linen is not included under the Head of Clothing.[7]

Le Marchant set specific admission criteria for the Junior Department, admitting only those between the ages of thirteen and fifteen. Successful candidates would need to demonstrate a solid understanding of grammar, arithmetic and have decent handwriting.

The warrant was also very specific when it came to the cadets' clothing. On arrival, they would be provided with a uniform, 'somewhat after the style of a French Railway porter'.[8] The uniform for cadets consisted of a blue great coat, a scarlet infantry jacket adorned with blue cuffs and collar looped with silver, and a scarlet waistcoat without sleeves. It also included two pairs of blue pantaloons, a felt cap, two pairs of short black gaiters, and two or more pairs of shoes. Cadets were given a list of personal items they needed to bring; seven shirts, seven pairs of short stockings, seven handkerchiefs, five towels, three night caps, two black cravats and four pairs of drawers. Le Marchant was committed to equality for all cadets, recognising that they could come from diverse backgrounds, from orphans to boys from wealthy families. He introduced a rule restricting each cadet to a maximum of one guinea as pocket money, regardless of their family background. Any cadet found with more would be disciplined.

A Commandant, reporting directly to Le Marchant, would be appointed to oversee the studies and discipline of the Junior Department. The Royal Warrant also established a Collegiate Board, scheduled to meet every month, consisting of the Governor, Lieutenant-Governor and the Commandants from both the Senior and Junior Departments. The board had responsibility for supervising all aspects of the college, from the recruitment of professors to financial management and purchasing of supplies.

The Junior Department opened on 17 May at Remnantz, in West Street, Great Marlow. Remnantz, a substantial, brown brick house in extensive grounds of around ten acres, provided ample space for a parade ground and exercise area. Originally built in the early 1700s, it had been renamed after its current owner, Stephen Remnant, an iron-founder from Woolwich who supplied guns and ammunition to the British and overseas governments. Remnant agreed to let the property to the War Office for £120 a year for a period of three years. Le Marchant determined how the various rooms in the building were to be used. Given the dilapidated condition of the house, the work required to refurbish the interior and exterior of the premises cost in the region of £400.

At the time of the Junior Department's opening, the picturesque town of Marlow, nestling on the banks of the river Thames, had become a fashionable resort. The arrival of junior cadets, although initially modest in number, would have a substantial impact on the town as the numbers increased, although not always in a positive manner.

A year later, Marlow Place, a five-storey house in Station Road originally built for the future George II, was leased to accommodate up to 100 cadets from the Junior Department. Other premises at Cromwell House, High Street, and Albion House, West Street, were also leased by the department.

A cadet described one aspect of the regime at Marlow that was probably of some importance to him. They would wake up 'every morning at half past 4 o'clock. At 6 a piece of dry bread is given to each of them. At half past 9 they breakfast on dry bread and each a pint of milk. At 2 they dine, on Roast mutton 4 days a week, and on beef 3 days. At 8 they sup on bread & cheese, and at 9 go to bed.'[9] In between, the cadets were subjected to parades and inspections, prayers and study followed by fencing, riding, swimming and sword drill.

Lieutenant-Colonel James Butler of the Royal Artillery was appointed as Superintendent of the Junior Department. General Harcourt promoted Butler to Commandant the following year. Le Marchant, still based in High Wycombe, would make the short journey to Marlow at least twice a week to inspect the department.

Lieutenant-Colonel Butler had never seen active service. He was older than Le Marchant and resented the younger man's authority. Butler successfully ingratiated himself with Harcourt and, more importantly, with Harcourt's wife, Mary. He would attempt to bypass Le Marchant's authority whenever possible by going directly to the General, who willingly complied. Add to this Le Marchant's occasional volatile temperament, and the stage was set for an inevitable clash of personalities.

The early days of the college appeared to be progressing well. A first inspection of both the Senior and Junior Departments by the Earl of Harrington and General Lord Cathcart in July resulted in a very favourable and flattering report, which was presented to the Supreme Board:

> The Studies carried on with great zeal on the part of the Students, and great skill and attention on the part of those employed in their instruction that the progress of the Senior Department is every day more visible, and that it seems likely to produce a number of useful and scientific Officers to the Service.
>
> That the Junior Department (tho' so lately brought together) seems animated with no less Emulation and Industry. The cadets

> are Clothed and already assume a Military appearance. They appear in general to be, for their Age, forward in Arithmetic; and many of them have some knowledge of the French Language. We examined very minutely into the economy of this Department, and can testify that it is well and satisfactorily conducted. The Food good, and well cooked, and the House beyond measure neatly and comfortably kept and arranged.[10]

By the close of 1802, both the Senior Department in High Wycombe and the Junior Department in Marlow were fully operational, with Le Marchant in charge of both. It was an extremely ambitious undertaking, and it is hardly surprising that there were teething problems. The annual report published in December highlighted issues in the Senior Department arising from the age and relative inexperience of some of the officers recently arrived at the college, preventing them from benefiting fully from the instruction provided. The Duke of York, unhappy with the results, directed Le Marchant to review the entry requirements for candidates.

Le Marchant was serious and strict, but fair. He earned the respect of the students through a blend of friendly encouragement and an authoritative presence. On one occasion, a cadet from the Junior Department had taken a book into the main guard room to lessen the monotony of guard duty. Le Marchant suddenly appeared from around the corner of the guard room. The cadet's heart raced as a deep voice suddenly barked out, 'A sentry reading on his post?'[11] Le Marchant reprimanded the cadet and then continued on his way. The student later recalled how relieved he was not to have suffered further punishment.

Le Marchant remained vigilant when it came to the finances of the college. He paid special attention to the accounts, insisting on quarterly reviews and taking immediate action when he found irregularities. He also made sure that all communications were put in writing, which he thought was 'the best check on bad men, and the best security to good'.[12] All discussions about official matters were systematically documented the following day. While it may have been time-consuming, this practice ultimately proved to be a wise decision that would later save his reputation and career.

In February, he retired on half pay from his post as Lieutenant-Colonel of the 2nd Regiment of Queen's Dragoon Guards, and now dedicated himself fully to the role of Lieutenant-Governor, responsible for the management of the Royal Military College. Under another Royal Warrant of 17 April 1803, the number of cadets in the Junior Department was increased to a maximum of 400, although it would take several years before that figure was reached.

The increase in the number of cadets meant that the search for additional professors and masters continued. The net was cast far and wide. Monsieur De Beaumont, formerly an engineer in the King of Sardinia's service, now living in Switzerland, had been highly recommended for the role of professor of fortification. He was appointed without going through the usual process of advertising the post and conducting interviews. A professor from Magdelene College, Oxford, joined the Junior Department to teach classics and history.

The house at Marlow was soon found to be too small, and a second house rented adjacent to Remnantz for £200 per year. Other locations for the college were considered at Winchester and Chatham, but it was decided to stay at Marlow. A sum of £4,300 was approved for the construction of new buildings to accommodate a further one hundred cadets. Houses at different ends of the town were rented to serve as dormitories, although Le Marchant regarded this arrangement as unsatisfactory.

> In the long winter nights they [the cadets] have no access to their rooms in which they might employ some hours profitably and pleasantly. But they are kept in the principal Building, either collected together in great numbers in a room, or are wandering about the premises committing all sorts of dilapidations, or

> roaming about the streets, either with or in quest of companions of the most profligate description, whom it may be difficult to keep out of the College grounds at night.[13]

When he could find the time, Le Marchant continued with his favourite hobby of sketching and landscape painting, a pastime that he had started while in Gibraltar. At first, he took lessons from William Payne, one of the most sought-after painting teachers of the day, revered by both professional artists and aspiring enthusiasts. Before pursuing a career as an artist and drawing master, Payne worked as a draughtsman and civil engineer in the Board of Ordnance. Payne's step-by-step approach to watercolour landscapes was relatively easy for a skilled amateur to replicate, but he is perhaps best remembered by artists for developing the bluish-grey hue called Payne's Grey. The influence of Payne can be clearly seen in Le Marchant's landscapes.

Le Marchant later had lessons from one of Payne's pupils, John Glover, who taught in Lichfield before moving to London and eventually emigrating to Australia. Glover was renowned for his idyllic, romantic style of landscapes.

Given his military background, Le Marchant's artistic style evolved with an emphasis on simplicity and accuracy. He would often aim to finish his sketches and paintings on location, and the rolling countryside around High Wycombe offered ample opportunities for him to practise his artistic skills.

Le Marchant took a great interest in the recruitment of drawing masters for the Royal Military College. Joseph Farington, a landscape painter and member of the Royal Academy, wrote in his diary in July 1802: 'Coll Le Marchant called & I had a long conversation with him. The College is in want of a drawing master & He wished for my assistance in procuring one. The salary is £200 a year, besides allowance for lodging till the College intended to be built is completed, also fire & candle.'[14]

Following on from Farington's recommendation, Le Marchant appointed William Alexander as professor of drawing at Marlow. A position at the college offered artists a welcome guarantee of a regular salary, and this was certainly the case for Alexander: 'He feels the advantage of the situation as a relief from all anxiety about Income. After the lesson of the day is over He can sit down by his fire, without the reflection that the business of the day is interrupted, or the means of living not earned.'[15]

The novelty and convenience of a regular salary would eventually wear off. Joseph Farington noted in 1808: 'Alexander still finds His situation [as drawing master at the Royal Military College] irksome & that He has not spirits for it. After having attended the boys while at their lessons He feels incapable of any other effort beyond reading a newspaper.'[16] Alexander left the college that year to join the British Museum as the assistant keeper of antiquities.

Le Marchant developed a close friendship with another artist, William De La Motte. He was the son of a French refugee who, like Le Marchant, enjoyed the royal patronage of George III. After exhibiting at the Royal Academy, De La Motte became a drawing master at the Royal Military College in 1803 at the age of twenty-eight. He would remain at the college for many years. He was joined by his younger brother George, also a talented artist, who was employed as an assistant to the drawing department at the age of sixteen.

Not everyone was enthusiastic about taking up a position at the college. One aspiring artist, who would become one of the most famous of all English landscape painters, turned down the opportunity. John Constable told a friend, 'It would have been a death blow to all my prospects of perfection in the art I love.'[17] In addition to his artistic pursuits, Le Marchant also enjoyed music. He could play the flute and insisted that his daughters take up similar musical interests. Le Marchant settled down to a life of contentment at home, surrounded by his family, and contemplated the prospect of spending the rest of his military career at the college.

He was an early riser and tried to make the most of his time. His mornings were occupied with the business of the college and the study of military matters. He would enjoy a ride before dinner, during which he would stop and sketch. Evenings were devoted to his family, listening to his daughters play music and sing, but 'though tenderly attached to his wife and children, he did not take much part in their conversation'.[18] After everyone had retired to bed, he would catch up with his correspondence. Le Marchant could at times come across as quiet and shy, except when talking about subjects he knew well. He was determined to provide the best for his children, often impressing on them that 'Perseverance is the only sure road to success'.[19]

He had novel ways of dealing with indiscretions, both at the college and at home. His wife suspected that one of their domestic staff was stealing wine. The servant claimed she was innocent and there was insufficient evidence to take the matter further. Le Marchant's daughter, Katherine, takes up the story.

> An old cook who was in the habit of frequenting the cellaret [drinks cabinet] every night was corrected of her evil propensity by a happy expedient of the pencil. My father finding a daily diminution in the decanter, and suspecting the person, drew her figure suspended on a gallows, which he placed inside to meet her eye on opening it.[20]

Soon after, when the woman could no longer resist the lure of the bottle, she returned to the drinks cabinet. She saw the drawing and immediately confessed to her transgression.

Le Marchant would often welcome visitors to his house. As the Lieutenant-Governor, he was the highest-ranking officer residing at the Royal Military College, in the absence of General Harcourt, who was rarely there. He would entertain them at home at his own expense, his wife Mary a gracious and attentive host.

The Dukes of Cambridge, Clarence and Gloucester, and in particular Prince Edward, the Duke of Kent, were frequent guests at Le Marchant's residence. Le Marchant valued the support that the Duke of Kent had given during the early days of the college. When in March 1806 it appeared that the Duke would be leaving England to serve abroad, Le Marchant wrote to him expressing regret at his departure. At the same time, he took the opportunity of asking the Duke for help in promoting the college:

> The College will have to lament one of its most active and vigilant protectors at the Supreme Board, & I must in my own person feel most sensibly the loss of that encouragement & assistance which you have been so graciously pleased to bestow upon me. But I am not without hopes that before your departure your Royal Highness will be pleased to recommend to those high characters with whom you are connected the care of the Institution which is still in its infancy, and stands much in need of powerful support to enable it to reach that degree of perfection which the circumstance of the Country require in this as well as every other military arrangement.[21]

Le Marchant continued to develop his social network with influential individuals, important for his position and for the success of the college. He visited Robert Smith, 1st Baron Carrington, where he would occasionally cross paths with the Prime Minister. Lord Carrington lived close to the Senior Department having purchased Loakes house in 1798, renaming it Wycombe Abbey. He was Member of Parliament for Nottingham and an ally and close friend of William Pitt. As a partner in his father's banking firm and later the owner, Smith had helped bring some order to the Prime Minister's personal financial affairs.

Le Marchant also spent time with his good friend and patron George Grenville, Marquess of Buckingham, who lived within riding distance at Stowe in north Buckinghamshire. It was at Stowe that Le Marchant sometimes received invitations to meet with George, Prince of Wales, and other members of the Royal Family.

When not socialising, Le Marchant would invite students from the Senior Department to dinner, developing friendships that would continue after they had left the college. Many of these students would continue to write to Le Marchant from various locations while on active service. The high esteem in which Le Marchant was held is clearly evident in the words of Lieutenant-Colonel Samuel Ford Whittingham, who had attended the Senior Department. In October 1806, while awaiting departure from Falmouth for an ill-fated expedition to South America, Whittingham wrote to Le Marchant, 'I will not attempt to express how much I feel obliged by your kindness towards me. I hope to be again under your command & to merit your approbation by the strictest attention to my renewed studies. I am satisfied no absence however long will weaken or alter my determination on this head.'[22]

8

MUTINY AND REBELLION

Le Marchant observed that certain students in the Senior Department showed a greater interest in escaping from their regimental duties than in their own professional development. Others seemed unprepared for the level of discipline at the college, certainly not to the extent that Le Marchant would hand out when necessary. Some of the students became increasingly disobedient, primarily directed at the professors, with General Jarry seeming to bear the brunt of this behaviour. He was well into his sixties, hunched over with longish, straggly hair and was often the target of abuse because of his eccentric character.

Jarry was easy going and, surprisingly for an old soldier, found it difficult to discipline his pupils. He had a passion for cooking and often prepared meals for the students using his own produce. He would tell them: 'No man could be a good general without being a good cook, for a man could not know how to feed an army who did not know how to feed himself.'[1] Jarry spent most of his spare time tending to his garden and would shoot at any birds that attempted to feast on his fruit and vegetables.

At first, Jarry was not particularly offended by the insults and unruly behaviour of the students. But after a while, he stopped his lectures in protest and it took some time before Le Marchant could persuade him to continue. One student later wrote about an incident involving the French officer.

> General Jarry, in order to illustrate his able Lectures on Field Fortification, had himself constructed models, and placed them in the halls of study, and they had been found of the greatest use. Among other acts of insubordination of the junior officers was the total destruction of these models. The General felt indignant at such wanton mischief, and although he said little, he did not condescend again to exercise his ingenuity for the benefit of those so little worthy of it, and these valuable specimens were never restored. To counteract this more than irregularity, Colonel Le Marchant saw at once the necessity of some decisive step, or the Establishment would have dwindled into a mere excuse for idle officers to absent themselves from their regiments. He made himself acquainted with the characters of all, ascertained who the offending parties were, did not visit them with any punishment at the time, by which he avoided cabal and ill-will, but either caused them to be recalled to their regiments, or gave them intimation on the first vacation that they were not to return to the College. Nothing but this judicious and decisive step on the part of the Lieutenant-Governor would have prevented the ruin of the establishment at its earliest stage, although it was adopted to a certain degree at the hazard of his popularity. But a sense of duty and strict integrity operated on this, as in every other action of this upright officer through life. By dismissing the idle and ignorant, and retaining those in whom he discovered (in concert with General Jarry) a wish and ability to improve themselves, and in whom he could place confidence, he established the firm foundation of an establishment which has proved of so much real benefit to the army.[2]

Nor was the students' bad behaviour confined to the college premises. Le Marchant was called on to deal with an incident where two students, while walking along the banks of the river

Wye, came upon a farmer in a rowing boat. They asked him to take them over the river. But half-way across, they pushed him into the water and rowed away. Luckily for the farmer, the water was not too deep and he made it to the river bank, soaked through. The farmer went to the college to complain the following day. Le Marchant, furious at the students' actions, promised that they would face severe punishment, but the farmer did not want the culprits censured. When Le Marchant inquired why, in that case, he had reported the incident, the farmer replied that he just wanted to stop the same thing from happening again. The offending students were spared further punishment.

General Jarry's health was gradually deteriorating, and this started to have an impact on the quality of teaching at the college. In January 1804, Le Marchant wrote to Major-General Calvert, Adjutant-General to the Forces, seeking help for Jarry:

> General Jarry's health and infirmities have for the last two years prevented his giving instructions to officers in the field. His lectures that in the outset of the Establishment were read and explained by himself, are now simply given to copy without any means of elucidation to those who may find difficulty in comprehending them, and as the General has never taken the least responsibility in directing the Studies of the Junior classes, the Benefit to be derived in future from his very brilliant talents, must unfortunately be confined to a few occasional remarks on positions taken up in the course of the summer.[3]

Le Marchant identified what he believed to be the perfect candidate for the role of Superintendent in the Senior Department to assist Jarry. Major Benjamin D'Urban had joined the army as a Cornet in the 2nd Dragoon Guards in 1793 and served in the Netherlands and West Indies. In April 1800, he entered the Royal Military College on half pay. He showed such promise that in 1803 he was appointed Superintendent of the Junior Department when Lieutenant-Colonel Butler was promoted to Commandant.

Le Marchant's recommendation that Major D'Urban be appointed to the staff of the Senior Department made complete sense. After all, D'Urban was well known at the college and had proved himself most capable. However, General Harcourt opposed the idea. Le Marchant's proposal was dismissed, and D'Urban left the college soon after. He went on to serve with distinction and later became governor of Cape Colony in South Africa, with the city of Durban named in his honour. Le Marchant took this rebuttal personally: 'The appointment of Major D'Urban is to be opposed for no other reason than that it originated in me.'[4]

There may have been an ulterior motive as to why Harcourt had rejected Le Marchant's suggestion. With a capable officer like Major D'Urban at High Wycombe, then Le Marchant could spend more time at the Junior Department in Marlow, much to the displeasure of Lieutenant-Colonel Butler. Eventually, Captain Howard Douglas was appointed as Superintendent in the Senior Department. He had previously been a cadet at the Royal Military Academy for artillery at Woolwich.

In the spring of 1804, another instance of the growing tension between Harcourt and Le Marchant came to light. It began as a minor issue when Captain Peter Ryves, a junior officer on the staff of the Senior Department, requested two days' leave. Le Marchant, who planned to be away at the same time, rejected the request and offered Ryves alternative dates. Ryves refused, accusing Le Marchant of treating him unfairly. Le Marchant reported the incident to Harcourt, expressing his concern over Ryves' disrespectful behaviour. Simultaneously, Ryves had also lodged a complaint with Harcourt. The General overturned Le Marchant's decision, approving the Captain's leave. To make matters worse, Harcourt forwarded Le Marchant's report about Ryves to Prince Frederick, the Duke of York.

The response came in a letter from General William Wynard, Deputy Adjutant-General at the War Office. The Duke determined that Ryves had acted inappropriately and should be cautioned regarding his conduct. The comments about Le Marchant were notably more critical.

> But HRH observes with grief, that, in bringing forwards this complaint, the Lieutenant Governor has manifested a hastiness of disposition, & a want of deliberation, which must eventually prove detrimental to the discipline and harmony of the Establishment, and HRH is the more surprized at such conduct in the Lieutenant Governor.
>
> The Commander in Chief trusts that the Lieutenant Governor will deliberate before such complaints are again offered for HRH's consideration.[5]

Le Marchant arguably could have resolved the issue without involving Harcourt. There was certainly no need, on the other hand, for Harcourt to take such a small matter to the Duke of York, Commander-in-Chief of the army. Surely the Duke had far more important concerns that required his attention. The entire episode left Le Marchant deeply troubled; he felt his authority had been eroded.

In August 1804, Le Marchant's resolve would be further put to the test. A group of nine cadets from the Junior Department, taking exception to what they thought was excessive discipline from a new Captain, decided to take action. The plan involved setting fire to a haystack on the college grounds, raiding the armoury, arming themselves, then throwing the remaining weapons into a pond at the bottom of a nearby orchard. They would then wait for Le Marchant to arrive, and demand that he dismiss the Captain they considered too strict, and that the detested Black Hole cells, used for solitary confinement, be destroyed.

The plotters hid gunpowder and matches in the haystack, but the scheme was discovered. The cadets involved were rounded up and questioned by the Collegiate Board.

The conspiracy was reported to the Duke of York, then to His Majesty, George III, 'who immediately ordered, that the juvenile culprits should be expelled with every mark of military disgrace. Both departments of the Royal Military College were assembled, as the offenders having first had their swords broken over their heads, were stripped of their uniforms, and turned out of the College.'[6]

The punishment took place in front of every officer and student from both the Senior and Junior Departments. The young culprits were also warned that they could have been sentenced to transportation if they had appeared in a civilian court, while they might have faced the death penalty at a military tribunal.

There were no further serious outbreaks of trouble after the ill-fated mutiny in 1804, at least not for some time. Le Marchant was in the presence of George III one evening at Windsor when the King commented:

> I consider the Military College an object of the deepest national importance. The Duke of Cambridge has just given me a most favourable account of it, and I hear from scientific men, that your studies are conducted by very able masters, and according to an excellent system. I entirely approve of the measures you have pursued in the late disturbances, and I think the example must lead to the improvement of the Cadets. There was no expecting them to be docile at first, but the management of them will be, every day, less difficult. And you will all the while be raising a race of officers, who will make our army the finest in Europe. The country is greatly indebted to you.[7]

In July 1805, the Prime Minister William Pitt, Lord Carrington and a group of friends visited the Junior Department at Marlow. They were welcomed by Le Marchant, observed the cadets on manoeuvres and at study, and after dinner they inspected the cadets' dormitories. Later, they met with General Jarry, who provided a detailed explanation of the course of instruction. The Prime Minister was suitably impressed: 'Nothing could have the appearance of giving off better than the day did, as Mr Pitt examined into every part of the establishment and from the commencement till his going away he was full of encomiums & his approbation was unbounded.'[8] Le Marchant was promoted to Colonel in November, 1805.

By the end of the year, the cadets' behaviour had once more started to deteriorate. Le Marchant became increasingly concerned about the indiscipline at the Junior Department. He discussed the problem with Lieutenant-Colonel Butler and remarked that during a recent visit from the Duke of Kent, both he and the Duke had noticed the poor conduct of some of the cadets. He also noted that some of the correspondence concerning the Junior Department had gone missing, and asked Lieutenant-Colonel Butler to reinstate the missing letters. Butler, in turn, resented that Le Marchant had inspected the public correspondence of the Junior Department. Le Marchant wrote to Harcourt in January 1806, 'I have very lately, as well as on former occasions, experienced the difficulty of obtaining information from the Commandant of the Junior Department. The permission to withhold from me the perusal of his public correspondence will inevitably tend to leave me still more completely in the dark as to the transactions of that branch of the Establishment.'[9]

Le Marchant suspected that General Harcourt and Lieutenant-Colonel Butler were trying to undermine his authority. He expressed his concerns in a letter to his friend, Colonel Clinton, in April 1806.

> Your advice to be patient yet steady in my duty I have rigidly observed. I have issued no orders or made any communication on points of duty except in writing, by which means I have reduced those in command under me to some degree of order, as far as relates to outward appearance. But in effect the duties of the College are privately concerted between the Governor and the officers under me, so that I have no knowledge of what is intended till the orders of the Governor are sent to me to issue. I am prohibited from seeing the public correspondence of the two Departments, and in a great degree from issuing orders without

a previous reference to the Governor at St Leonards. Indeed of late he has commanded from Bath & Clifton, for he makes no difference in his command whether his residence is at a dozen or one hundred more miles from the College.

The Cadets are made Corporals, Sergeants, & Subalterns at the College by General Harcourt at the recommendation of Lieut. Col. Butler, & between them they determine upon those who are to be recommended to His Majesty for commission in the army. The first knowledge that I have of their choice is the Gazette. At the Senior Department it is much the same thing. The persons to be employed on the Staff owe their appointments more to Major Douglas's good word than any influence of mine.

Such is the state of things at the College. Mine is either a mortifying situation for any person to endure, but more especially for one who has done that little for the Institution that was necessary to its present organization, and that little it is attempted to give the merit of to others, who if they have done anything, have worked mischief.

I congratulate myself (considering the enemies against whom I have contended) that myself and my family are not entirely ruined, for the secret whispers by which their mischief has been levelled against me are the more dangerous, that it is utterly impossible to refute general insinuations privately circulated, and that never are suffered to appear openly and in a manner to be noted.[10]

Clinton wrote a consoling reply: 'Notwithstanding all the mortifications you may have endured, you must feel self-satisfaction in the share you have had in bringing forward the institution of which nothing can deprive you, and I trust that eventually you will find your merits have not been unobserved.'[11]

The atmosphere in the Junior Department continued to worsen with cadets expressing their dissatisfaction in a number of ways. In August 1806, Captain Charles Wright, on the staff of the Junior Department, reported that some cadets had been overheard plotting an insurrection. The words 'Let us Mutiny' and 'Rebel' appeared around the premises and 'the walls of the privies were covered with these Expressions of their discontent'.[12]

That month, Harcourt visited the Junior Department to assess the situation. He interviewed the officers on the department's staff. They reported that the cadets were happy, contrary to Le Marchant's opinion. But they did admit that disrespectful language had been scrawled on the college walls, which they believed might be the work of a single cadet. Instead of questioning possible suspects responsible for the graffiti, Harcourt chose to challenge the cadet who had provided information about the intended mutiny. He cautioned the cadet for telling stories about his fellow colleagues. Harcourt came to the conclusion that everything was in order and left the college.

Le Marchant did not agree. He wrote to his son Carey, 'The General is gone away well satisfied that the cadets are content and happy. But in this he is miserably mistaken. That what was written on the walls came from the same person, there was no proof of whatever, & was only a manoeuvre to weaken the grounds of apprehension.'[13]

Le Marchant observed that both the cadets' conduct and their appearance had deteriorated. If this was allowed to continue, it could have a lasting impact on their lives. He saw the need for clear and enforceable rules but felt constrained from taking corrective action. Le Marchant was growing increasingly despondent: 'When this anarchy will end it is difficult to determine, but it is not difficult to predict that unless speedily put down it will ruin the establishment.'[14]

He believed that an independent inspection was necessary, and this would quickly reveal the college's state of disarray. He was concerned that unless something was done soon, the cadets would start to tell their parents about the chaotic state of affairs within the college.

The relationship between Le Marchant and Harcourt continued to worsen, with Le Marchant writing in October to General Sir George Hewett, 'I have been so often reprimanded by General

Harcourt in cases where I have not been to blame, and my Character has been so frequently blackened and misrepresented to Higher powers that I am become timid in my own justification.'[15]

In the letter, Le Marchant also complained that Butler had become increasingly disobedient and had made changes to the Junior Department's curriculum without consulting him. The hostility between Le Marchant, Harcourt and Butler reached a climax just two months later.

A week before Christmas 1806, Le Marchant met with Harcourt in London prior to one of the quarterly meetings of the Supreme Board. While the initial conversation revolved around minor matters, it soon developed into a discussion about the general state of the college. In what he considered to be a private and confidential conversation, Le Marchant told Harcourt that there was a clear absence of discipline in the Junior Department which demanded attention. Professors and masters were frequently insulted by cadets, and there had been a second incident where a stone was thrown at one of the professors. Harcourt made no comment, asked no questions, nor did he seem surprised. The conversation between the two ended there.

On Christmas Eve at another meeting, this time at the College, Le Marchant was confronted by both General Harcourt and Lieutenant-Colonel Butler. Harcourt repeated the complaints that Le Marchant had raised privately the previous week regarding disciplinary issues in the Junior Department. In response, Butler became angry, accusing Le Marchant of spreading lies to tarnish his reputation. Butler argued that the discipline in the Junior Department was as good as ever and that the incident involving the throwing of a stone at a master had been thoroughly investigated and deemed an accident. Harcourt came to the support of Butler and asked Le Marchant whether he understood the seriousness of the accusations.

After a further heated exchange between Butler and Le Marchant, the latter accused Butler of being disrespectful and expressed his surprise that Harcourt had allowed Butler to speak to him in such a manner. Le Marchant moved towards the door and as he left the room he turned around and facing Harcourt and Butler, he said, 'Most extraordinary indeed.'[16]

The entire episode appeared to have been a premeditated, coordinated attack orchestrated by Harcourt and Butler and it caught Le Marchant completely off guard. It seemed that the two officers were attempting to exploit Le Marchant's sometimes volatile temperament. For although Le Marchant had generally kept his temper under control, there were times when it simmered just beneath the surface, ready to erupt.

Three days later, Le Marchant followed up on the explosive encounter with a letter to Harcourt where he repeated his initial concerns about the discipline in the Junior Department and the changes to the curriculum. He also reiterated that he had no intention of criticising anyone or tarnishing their reputation. However, if Harcourt interpreted it differently, then Le Marchant would have no choice but to defend himself at a public inquiry. Harcourt responded on 2 January 1807.

> Sir,
> I have to acknowledge your letter of the 27th December, requesting that an Enquiry may be made into your conduct in order that you may exculpate yourself from a reflection supposed to have been cast upon your character, in consequence of some expressions which you conceive were made use of by me in a conversation which passed between you and myself on the 24th of the same month in the presence of Lt. Col Butler and Major Douglas, the commandants of the two Departments of the Royal Military College. In reply to which I have to acquaint you, that the observations I made upon that occasion were not only general, but were also expressed in terms by no means bearing the same sense you seem to have conceived, as I never asserted or even considered you as the author of the Calumny against Col. Butler, tho' from the impression then in my mind, and which shall remain, I said that on one hand, if the supposed state of indiscipline of the

Junior Department had been proved true, it would afford very just cause of reprehension to Col. Butler, so on the other, if the instance of insubordination addressed, which was not only strongly contradicted by him, but explained also to have been formerly investigated & proved to be merely accidental. I certainly did declare and I still think that a charge resting upon such slender evidence as that of a person whose name has not been made known to me, was highly injurious to the Character of an old and very meritorious officer; & I must add that I am the most confirmed in that opinion, because not only from my frequent inspections of the Junior Department I am well satisfied with the general state of it. But I have also the satisfaction to find that opinion fully supported by the favourable testimonials of those members of the Supreme Board who have so lately visited the institution, and also by the very orderly manner in which the cadets quitted the College when they separated for the vacation.

Having now stated the substance of what passed from me in the conversation alluded to, I have only to ask that if you still adhere to the wish you expressed of having your conduct enquired into, I shall take the earliest opportunity of laying your request for that purpose before the Commander-in-Chief.[17]

Le Marchant's reply was, as expected, forthright.

It remains with you, Sir, to determine whether there be anything in the present state of the Junior Department of the R. M. College that calls for Enquiry. For I fear you deceive yourself when you suppose there exists no foundation for the report which my duty prompted me to make, and which I must here remark I had observed to Lieut. Col. Butler in general terms some days previous to my communication with you.[18]

There followed a further exchange of letters between the two before Harcourt took the matter to the Duke of York. Harcourt claimed that Le Marchant had made a malicious and ill-founded accusation against Lieutenant-Colonel Butler and that the Junior Department had no problems with discipline whatsoever. The Duke replied to Harcourt:

> Sir,
> I have to acknowledge the receipt of your letter of the 17th instant, enclosing a paper from Lieut. Col. Le Marchant expressing his wish to decline the office of a public accuser & wishing his report to you of the 27th of December be considered only as a private conversation & must desire you to acquaint him that it is totally out of my power consistently with my Duty to acquiesce in that opinion as I cannot but consider a report made by a person in his official situation as an accusation against those in whose Dept. the irregularity is alleged to be committed.
> I have therefore taken His Majesty's pleasure on the subject, and have appointed three general officers to investigate it and am to desire that the Lieut. Colonel will lay before them as Soon as Possible the Grounds upon which he founds the opinions which he has formed and reported to you, in order that the investigation may be immediately proceeded upon.[19]

The three general officers appointed by the Duke of York were General Sir David Dundas, as President, with the Duke of Cambridge and Major-General Calvert forming the committee. Le Marchant appeared in front of the senior officers at Horse Guards at the end of January 1807. He told the committee that he felt it was his duty to report his concerns about the Junior Department to the Governor. He described how before the mutiny at the Junior Department in 1804, he had shared his concerns with Lieutenant-Colonel Butler that something of the kind would occur. His warning was ignored, and the mutiny unfolded as he had predicted. Le Marchant believed that it would have been irresponsible of him had he not advised the Governor about the state of the Junior Department. After all, he had discussed his concerns with Butler weeks before bringing them to the attention of Harcourt. While Butler disagreed, Le Marchant argued that the Commandant did not take it as an accusation in any way.

He maintained throughout that it was not his intention to bring charges against or blame any one individual. This may have been rather naïve on Le Marchant's part, since any criticism of the discipline and conduct within the Junior Department would implicitly reflect on its Commandant, especially given the difficulties he was experiencing with Harcourt and Butler. On the other hand, Le Marchant had been the driving force behind the college, and it is understandable that he took action when he perceived that the college, especially the larger of the two departments, was in a state of decline.

It was now that Le Marchant's attention to detail came to his rescue. He had recorded everything in writing. He was able to produce a litany of dates and events that had happened, including 'verses and writings against the walls of the College, disrespectful towards the Officers, Major Bourke & myself. There were instances of the words "Rebellion" and "Mutiny" written in many parts of the College.'[20] The cadets had smashed windows in the study halls during lessons, fought in classes in the presence of teachers, and sent threatening letters to staff. In one instance a book had been thrown at the head of a French master. A professor who was returning home at night had to stop a group of cadets from abusing local women in town. And a tree in the college grounds had been set on fire.

Le Marchant told the committee that some of the cadets had thrown stones at their masters, to the point where the masters needed an escort while walking around the college. It had even become necessary to place sentries in classrooms during lessons to maintain order. Le Marchant continued: 'At night the Cadets were constantly in the streets in search of female companions of the most profligate description, and I might have added, that no less than eight had been infected with a venereal disorder, during the last three months, whilst for two years before scarcely an instance of the kind had occurred.'[21]

Le Marchant counted up to twenty incidents of indiscipline that had taken place during those three months, compared with only four minor incidents in the previous nine months. He produced copies of letters that he had sent to General Harcourt about the situation in the Junior Department, and a letter from one of the French masters outlining how he had been hit from behind by a stone as he was leaving a lesson. The cadet claimed that he was playing with one of his colleagues and had not seen the teacher. A mathematics teacher noted how 'a degree of laxity in subordination did pretty generally pervade the cadets'.[22]

During the course of the inquiry, it came out that Le Marchant had been prevented from issuing orders related to discipline, and from reviewing the correspondence of staff officers under his supervision in both the Senior and Junior Departments of the college. He presented letters and orders from both Harcourt and Butler to support his case.

In addition to the question of discipline, the inquiry also considered the second of Le Marchant's grievances. The curriculum of the Junior Department had been changed without his knowledge. He suggested that the committee should interview some of the teachers, since it was from their complaints that he had formed his opinion. He told the inquiry, 'I am confident that if the masters both of Arithmetic & French were heard upon this point, the Committee would be satisfied that the studies are not carried on with all the advantage to the public that they are susceptible of.'[23] The committee referred to the professors and masters, who confirmed that the new curriculum was indeed unworkable, and that they wished to revert to the original syllabus.

Le Marchant contrasted the challenges he had faced at the college with his previous service in the army. He had held command of three regiments of cavalry at various times and had never experienced any issues with fellow officers. He even referred the committee to three commanding officers under whom he had served, who could vouch for his conduct. He added that he had trained up to 150 officers from various regiments in his sword exercise without the slightest difficulty.

Le Marchant described the whole affair with some bitterness in a lengthy letter to Lieutenant-Colonel Robert Long, one of the early students at the Senior Department. They became life-long friends. Lieutenant-Colonel Long was an intelligent and capable officer but could be even more volatile and unconventional than Le Marchant. Long was frequently involved in disagreements with his superiors.

> It was a vile and cruel prosecution in those who brought it forward. I acquit the Duke of York of intending me any harm and he, no doubt, acted in consequence of the representation that had been made to him of my conduct. The conduct of the Committee appeared to me to be not only liberal, but feeling and impartial. I have not the slightest doubt but that the committee saw into the malicious intention that was entertained against me.
>
> I have no doubt that my ruin was aimed at by the loss of Character, appointments & professional prospects. How unfeeling was this conduct towards one who had been the founder of the institution, and above all, as coming from the very persons who reap the greatest emoluments and advantages from my labours, without having contributed themselves in the smallest degree to the edifice.
>
> A month has elapsed since the enquiry closed and I know as yet nothing of the result. I however feel easy on the subject, being conscious that I have done my duty, & that my report had been substantiated by facts clearly proved.[24]

Le Marchant thanked Colonel Clinton for his support and advice. In the end no action was taken against Le Marchant. He was congratulated on the outcome by Lieutenant-General Sir William Stewart: 'I rejoice at the victory you gained. 'Tis shocking that your zeal & honest endeavours should thus be thwarted. Your written documents were masked batteries, & pounded down your antagonist's loose columns.'[25]

9
RECONCILIATION

The entire episode had been unpleasant for everyone involved, but perhaps it was necessary to clear the air between Le Marchant, Harcourt and Butler. After the committee had taken evidence from all sides, there were significant diplomatic efforts behind the scenes to mend the strained relationship between the three individuals. Lieutenant-Colonel Sir Herbert Taylor, private secretary to George III, attempted to play the role of peacemaker as he advised Le Marchant on steps he could take to improve the relationship with Harcourt.

> My Dear Le Marchant,
> I have long lamented that any Difference should ever have presided between yourself & General Harcourt, aware as I was how distressing it must be to both and how injurious in many respects to the important & valuable establishment at Wycombe & Marlow. I think you cannot act more than in using every possible means of conciliation which can alone ensure your mutual comfort both at present and in future, and I am convinced you will find General Harcourt disposed to meet you half way for he is not only a respectable honorable man, but also a good tempered man, and

when you consider his Rank & Age and the favor which he has ever enjoyed with the King, you will admit that it is natural that he should expect as Governor of the Establishment a degree of Deference & Attention which is due to him.

When once an amicable intercourse is established between yourself and him, I am persuaded that harmony will be soon restored in every Branch of the Departments.[1]

Taking Lieutenant-Colonel Taylor's advice on board, Le Marchant set aside his distrust of Harcourt and Butler. It is highly likely that Harcourt and Butler were also spoken to, for when Le Marchant next visited Harcourt, he found the General's attitude had changed completely towards him. Le Marchant responded to Lieutenant-Colonel Taylor.

My Dear Taylor
I owe too much to your kindness not to inform you of the result of my visit yesterday at St. Leonards.

Gen. Harcourt received me in a most conciliatory manner, and spoke on affairs of the College with a degree of Confidence and candour that leave not the slightest doubt of a good understanding subsisting between us in future.

I cannot sufficiently thank you for the kind advice that confirmed me in the propriety of calling on the General, & I have only to entreat a continuance of your good offices.[2]

Le Marchant began to receive reports and correspondence from Butler, which he would in turn review and forward to Harcourt. 'Lieut. Col. Butler's conduct is considerably changed for the better since the enquiry. He is paying greater attention to the duties of the College, than he had ever done before, so that I am not without hopes that the Establishment will derive benefit from what has happened.'[3] And Harcourt's instructions concerning the Junior Department would first go to Le Marchant before reaching Butler.

The rules governing discipline, particularly in the case of the Junior Department, were revised. Le Marchant was tasked with putting together regulations to address poor behaviour and inattention to studies. Le Marchant gave the parents of offenders a straightforward choice: either remove their son from the college or consent to the cadet's suspension and placement in a local private school nearby, at the parents' own expense, for between three to six months. At the end of the period, the cadet would take an exam and if there was an improvement in both studies and conduct, they could be readmitted to the Junior Department.

Le Marchant found that it was typically the orphan sons of officers that were the most likely to be expelled, since they would have previously suffered from a neglected education, putting them at a disadvantage. Le Marchant proposed that for some of these orphans, the college could fund their attendance at a local private school, since the government already covered the cost of their education at the Royal Military College anyway.

It was a time when hundreds of new, small private schools emerged across the country. Several of these sprang up in the surrounding area of Marlow, with the blessing of the college. These schools offered preparatory education in classics and military studies for those young boys aspiring to enter the Junior Department. One such school, established with the college's sanction, was run by the Reverend James Knollis, a former classical and history professor at the Royal Military College, and a fellow of Lincoln College, Cambridge. The school used the same textbooks as the Junior Department and followed the same vacation schedule.

Le Marchant's approach did not always succeed. Some cadets sent to private schools because of ill-discipline remained unreformed, and never returned. In other instances, cadets who had spent a considerable time in the Junior Department without making any progress, even after several warnings, were removed from the college.

General Jarry, facing old age and declining health, had offered his resignation two years earlier. Although he did agree to remain until a successor had been appointed. Le Marchant assumed the role of the primary intermediary between the students and Jarry. In August 1806, Jarry announced his intention of retiring at the end of the year, citing his deteriorating health as the reason behind the decision. Le Marchant expressed concern that the college, without an experienced officer as a replacement, would 'soon dwindle' and 'ultimately shut up'.[4]

Jarry's resignation was accepted, but he was informed that he would be unable to leave the country while Britain was at war with France. He left the college in December. Early the following year, his health had deteriorated to such an extent that he asked Le Marchant to take care of his family in the event of his death. General Jarry passed away shortly afterwards. Le Marchant made arrangements for the General's funeral and instructed a local undertaker for Jarry to be buried in an oak coffin with the following inscription.

Francis Jarry
A General Officer
Knight of the Military Order of St. Lewis
&
Inspector General of Instruction
At the
Royal Military College
Died
On the 15th of March 1807
Aged 75

General Jarry was buried in the parish church at High Wycombe. The fondness and gratitude that Le Marchant felt towards General Jarry were evident in the notice he wrote that appeared in local newspapers:

> On Sunday last, in the 75th year of his age, after a long and painful illness, General Jarry, much regretted by the Officers and

> Members of the Royal Military College, of which he was Inspector-General of Instruction. He was a man of distinguished abilities and great professional knowledge; he possessed a cultivated mind, and as an Officer had the benefit of long experience under the particular orders of that great Master of modern warfare, Frederick the Second, whom he accompanied during the whole of the seven years' war, in which he received many severe wounds. The last years of his life were successfully devoted to the improvement of the British service, for which he was eminently qualified.[5]

Shortly after the funeral, Le Marchant wrote in a letter to Colonel Clinton, 'Poor Jarry is at length gone – he suffered a lingering illness but retained his mental faculties to the last moment. He made a present before his death of all his private papers upon military subjects which are voluminous & invaluable. The country was never fully aware of his abilities, nor did we make the most of them.'[6]

In the preface of a translation of General Jarry's *Treatise on the Marches and Movements of Armies*, completed in early 1807, shortly before Jarry's death, Captain Richard Rochfort commented that in spite of Jarry's advanced age, 'his mind is a lamp that throws lustre wherever it reaches'.[7]

Le Marchant was appointed a trustee responsible for the pension to be paid to General Jarry's family. He arranged for the widow and two daughters to receive £100 each a year, while they remained in the United Kingdom. One year later, the pension had still not been paid, and the Jarry family had almost exhausted the small amount of money they had been left on the General's death. Le Marchant took it upon himself to escalate matters, entering into correspondence with Sir James Pulteney, Secretary at War, and writing to Lord William Bentinck, a former private pupil of Jarry, asking for help.

> General Jarry has been dead nearly twelve months during which time his Widow and Daughter have subsisted on a trifling sum that

> was left at the General's death, but which if not entirely expended is nearly so. I had hoped that the pension which your Lordship had obtained the promise of for them would have come opportunely to their aid, but I learnt yesterday with extreme regret by a note from Sir Pulteney that the pension in question could be granted "only when the funds of the Treasury would admit to it".
>
> Their situation, without your Lordship's assistance, will be distressing to the extreme, and such as would discredit His Majesty's Government to suffer, considering the Services that General Jarry is allowed to have rendered to the British army.
>
> I trust that your Lordship's influence with his Grace the Duke of Portland, will lead to some immediate steps being taken to save Madame Jarry & her Daughter from Penury, which otherwise awaits them.[8]

Madame Jarry, originally from Poznan in Poland, would frequently amuse visitors by telling stories about a member of the Bonaparte family she employed as a dressmaker while living in Paris. Madame Jarry died in November 1808, not long after the first payment of her pension had been made. Their daughter, Theresa, married an adjutant from the Royal Military College in August 1809. A second daughter married and emigrated to Canada.

Following General Jarry's resignation in late 1806, the initial plan was to replace him with another French émigré officer, General Charles Dumouriez, who had led the French *Armée du Nord* at the beginning of the Flanders campaign. Dumouriez, like Jarry, had fallen out of favour with the French revolutionaries and had defected to the allies. He settled in England in 1804 and became an advisor to the War Office. During negotiations for Jarry's replacement, Dumouriez wanted a higher rank in the British army than the government felt appropriate.

Jarry's duties were taken over by Captain Howard Douglas, who was promoted from Superintendent to Commandant of the Senior Department, with the rank of Lieutenant-Colonel in the army. He would leave High Wycombe in the autumn of 1808 to join General Sir John Moore's army in Spain during the Peninsular War, but later returned to the Royal Military College.

Le Marchant became a reference point for several officers who, like him, were interested in reforming the army. He shared his thoughts with others, among them Lieutenant-General Sir William Stewart of the 95th (Rifle) Regiment of Foot. Stewart published *Outlines of a Plan for the General Reform of the British Land Forces*. Le Marchant, impressed by Stewart's work, sent him some of his own thoughts on the subject, including copies of his own work. Stewart replied: 'I have wished to read over your work with some little attention, & as you kindly suggested, to accompany the perusal by a few remarks. I have reflected much on what I have read & am prepared as well as anxious to have a full conversation with you on the subject, & without which interview I shall still be feeling my way, as it were, in the dark.'[9]

After all that had happened, Le Marchant took a well-deserved break in Guernsey from July to September 1807, joining his wife and children who were already on the island. They attended the wedding of his wife's sister, Sophy, to Peter Mourant on 17 August. Whenever he returned to Guernsey, he travelled around the island, capturing the beautiful coastal scenery on canvas at every opportunity. From the gardens at Candie House, the home of the newlywed Peter and Sophy Mourant, Le Marchant would sit and paint the enchanting view of St Peter Port harbour and Castle Cornet, with the smaller islands of Sark and Herm in the distance. To the north of the island, he drew the picturesque harbour at Bordeaux, while in the south, he painted Fermain Bay from high on the surrounding cliffs that were covered in gorse and bracken.

During this particular stay, he visited Sark where he painted La Coupée, the narrow path some eighty metres above the sea, with a sheer drop on either side, that connects the main part of the island to Little Sark. He also spent a few days in Jersey where he produced a sketch of Mont Orgueil Castle, and a watercolour painting of the main town of St Helier, with Elizabeth Castle in the background.

As he made his way around Guernsey, Le Marchant would have observed the changes that had taken place. Due to its proximity to France, the island was at risk of invasion following the French Revolution. In 1787, the Duke of Richmond, as Master-General of the Ordnance, had commissioned William Gardner to produce an Ordnance Survey map of the island, detailing the roads and military positions. Le Marchant had previously warned Mary of the danger facing the Channel Islands back in 1794:

> At present, and I may add the public in general, are of the opinion the Islands will be attacked. I mentioned my fears that the principal inhabitants would be made to give up their fortunes, and that I had advised my friends to leave it. They all said I had done well, for it would certainly be the ruin of those who might be taken. I hope and do trust your father will not delay any longer coming over, for in all circles you are talked of as being in danger. I think so myself, and if your father is still likely to continue some time longer, my advice to you is by all means come to Southampton, as depend on it the consequences of an Invasion are Terrible. You cannot come away too soon, in your next [letter] after the receipt of this, I hope to find you at the eve of a departure for no time should be lost.[10]

The threat to the Channel Islands increased after Napoleon had seized power in 1799. Hundreds of wealthy French people, fearing the worst, fled to Jersey and Guernsey.

Soon after his arrival in 1803, Lieutenant-General Sir John Doyle, the new Lieutenant-Governor of Guernsey, declared a state of emergency. He began strengthening the defences of the island. Fort Doyle, on the north-eastern tip of the island, named after Sir John, was completed in 1805. Fort Le Marchant, an extension of an existing fortification and named after a member of the family and Bailiff of Guernsey, was also completed that year. Fort George served as the military headquarters and barracks for a garrison of the British army tasked with protecting the island from a possible French invasion. Doyle also reclaimed land between the northern parish of the Vale and the rest of the island to make the area easier to defend. He constructed new roads, including *Route Militaire*, still one of the principal roads in the north of the island, to enable faster troop deployments.

In the end, Napoleon's army never made an attempt to invade the Channel Islands, and it was not until the Second World War that the islands would face occupation by enemy troops.

Le Marchant must have been delighted when, in August 1808, George, Prince of Wales, together with Prince William, the Duke of Clarence, visited the Royal Military College and were most complimentary about what they had seen.

> His Royal Highness the Prince of Wales has been pleased to express to the Governor in the strongest terms, his approbation of the precision and intelligence with which the Plans and Drawings were executed by the officers of the Senior Dept. that shows much zeal and application to the object of the institution. His Royal Highness is pleased also to express equal approbation on the headings and military appearance of the Junior Department under arms, and the regularity with which they performed their military movements.
>
> His Royal Highness likewise observes with satisfaction that the reports which he has received of the discipline of the Department is not less creditable to the institution than the application of the Gentlemen Cadets to their studies.
>
> It is His Royal Highness's request that there be no studies this afternoon.[11]

The Marquess of Buckingham offered Le Marchant a seat in parliament, with the incentive that he might be considered for a position at the War Office, but he declined due to his duties at the college. He was eventually persuaded to become a county magistrate, and soon after was nominated and appointed as a Deputy Lieutenant of the county of Buckingham.

In his role as magistrate, Le Marchant found himself involved in a case concerning several thefts at the Junior Department. When the culprit was detained – the miscreant was not a cadet at the college – Le Marchant suggested that his relatives persuade the boy that he should join the navy. The magistrates had no power to send him to sea against his wishes. Yet, if the boy was willing to go on his own free will, then he would avoid the alternative where the thefts might be considered as a capital crime. Le Marchant thought that 'by this means the object of mercy will be attained and he may become useful to King and Country'.[12]

The overall situation at the college had improved, along with Le Marchant's relationship with Harcourt and Butler. It would not be long, though, before Le Marchant and the Royal Military College became entangled in a scandal that would have far reaching consequences.

10

A SEMINARY OF VICE

The tradition of publishing pamphlets dates back to the introduction of the printing press. By the eighteenth and nineteenth centuries, pamphlets had become popular as a vehicle for public debate and voicing opinions – sometimes seditious – on politics, society, religion, in fact on any topic the author wished to champion or attack. Content varied from well thought out arguments to unfounded accusations.

Members of Parliament would often publish their speeches, and individuals would use pamphlets as a way of conducting ongoing arguments in public, sometimes referred to as pamphlet wars. Satire and cartoons were common. Some were distributed free, others sold. It was not unusual for pamphlets to be read out aloud in taverns or on street corners.

In November 1808, a pamphlet of near on seventy pages appeared at a cost of two shillings and two pence. It had the rather lengthy title of *Observations on H.R.H. The Duke of Kent's Shameful Persecution since his Recal from Gibraltar, together with an Enquiry into the Abuses of The Royal Military College*. The author, Pierre Franc McCallum, was a radical journalist, a political writer and a man of letters. While in

Trinidad and Tobago, he had been imprisoned by the Governor, General Sir Thomas Picton, for supporting those fighting for constitutional rights on the island. He was expelled from the island and returned to England.

In the first section of the pamphlet, McCallum expressed disgust at the harsh treatment of Prince Edward, the Duke of Kent, by his brother Prince Frederick, the Duke of York and Commander-in-Chief of the army. The Duke of Kent was the fourth son of George III and later the father of Queen Victoria. He had been appointed Governor of Gibraltar in March 1802. Upon arrival, he had set about restoring discipline amongst the drunken and disorderly garrison, resulting in a mutiny within his own regiment on Christmas Eve. In response, he executed the four mutinous ringleaders. He was recalled from Gibraltar in May 1803 by the Duke of York, effectively ending Prince Edward's military career, even though he was later promoted to Field Marshal and made ranger of Hampton Court Park.

McCallum was convinced that while in the West Indies he had been severely dealt with by Picton, and he drew parallels with the treatment of the Duke of Kent in Gibraltar. McCallum began his pamphlet with the following:

> He who has felt the force of tyranny and oppression, is ever ready to sympathise with other victims who have had the misfortune to be placed in the like situation. I have, myself, suffered more oppressive cruelty in a distant quarter of the British dominions than commonly falls the lot of an individual, from a man who has been shamefully protected by those who have persecuted his Royal Highness the Duke of Kent.[1]

McCallum then launched into a vigorous defence of the Duke of Kent. He argued that the military establishment had worked against Prince Edward, even though he had in fact brought discipline to the garrison in Gibraltar. The execution of the ringleaders, according to McCallum, was at the instigation of a number of senior officers against Edward's wishes. McCallum believed that the real reason behind the recall of Prince Edward was the Duke of York's jealousy of his brother's growing military reputation, which McCallum referred to as a 'cruel, unbrotherly, and dirty business'.[2] He continued to vilify the state of the army under the Duke of York's leadership as Commander-in-Chief, claiming that it would soon be reduced to a state of ruin.

In the second part of the pamphlet, McCallum was highly critical of the college. After all, it had been founded with the full support of the Duke of York.

> A ROYAL MILITARY COLLEGE, professedly established, a few years ago, for the improvement of this army, [was] rendered totally useless through the grossest mismanagement. For its establishment, we understand our WORTHY generalissimo affects to claim much credit with the public. But we know to a certainty, that he has never so much as once been near it, either to enquire into the internal management of its affairs, or to rectify the abuses that evidently exist in it. If he is at all acquainted with its situation at present, he must know that it is a shameful JOB, from the governor down to the laundress, who was his servant: that the system of education carried on is not only erroneous, but that it is an absolute mockery of everything like military instruction.[3]

It continued with a damning reflection on the management of the college, sparing only Le Marchant from reproach: 'The selection of men for superintending, conducting, and managing it, is, with the exception of the lieutenant-governor, the most injudicious that could possibly have been made.'[4]

The criticism of Harcourt was equally damaging. 'We have no hesitation in saying, that whilst it continues under the government of General Harcourt, and is managed as it is at present, it never can prosper, or produce a good officer.'[5] As for Lieutenant-Colonel Butler, 'The commandant of the junior department, where all the cadets are, is, if possible, still less qualified; and is moreover so purblind, that he cannot distinguish a cow from a cadet at the distance of twenty paces.'[6]

The publication implied that there had been corruption relating to a contract providing clothes to cadets, where the supplier involved had made significant profits. McCallum also claimed that there had been several cases of embezzlement of funds within the college. In fact, earlier that year Le Marchant had led an investigation after allegations of fraud were made by a local coal merchant against a storekeeper at the Junior Department. Le Marchant had promptly addressed the issue and taken steps to prevent such occurrences happening again.

McCallum alleged that Harcourt had been receiving expenses for a private secretary even though the post did not exist. The laundress at the college, who had previously been a maid to Harcourt's wife, was accused of incorrectly charging cadets for laundry.

Finally, McCallum claimed of the college, 'Is it not more a seminary of vice, pollution, and immorality, than a profitable military institution? Is it not better calculated for polluting, depraving, and injuring the army, than for ameliorating or improving it?'[7]

The Supreme Board of the college met in December when the pamphlet was read out. The Board concluded that the author should be prosecuted for libel. At the end of the meeting the Duke of Cumberland remarked to Le Marchant, 'One would think that you were the author of the libel, as you are the only person of the College who is not abused.'

Le Marchant replied, 'I take no merit to myself in being exempted from abuse in so scurrilous a production.'[8] The exchange was passed off as a joke, the participants laughing as the meeting broke up.

A few days later, Le Marchant was summoned to a meeting with General Harcourt and Lieutenant-Colonel Taylor at the Queen's Lodge in Windsor. It emerged that after the Supreme Board meeting, the Duke of Cumberland and Harcourt had decided that as Le Marchant was the only person belonging to the Royal Military College who had not been criticised in the pamphlet, he should issue a public statement denouncing the pamphlet's contents. Harcourt and Taylor accepted that Le Marchant had not been involved in the publication itself, nor contributed to it in any way. Nevertheless, a public announcement by Le Marchant would remove any doubt that he concurred with the criticism of the college and staff.

Le Marchant agreed that the pamphlet was libellous, however he was reluctant to write anything on such a sensitive subject that would appear in public. Taylor attempted to persuade him that it was in his best interest. After all, Taylor argued, even if Le Marchant might incur McCallum's anger and resentment, it was crucial to demonstrate that there was no basis for the accusations against the college, and that there was no animosity between Le Marchant and Harcourt. Le Marchant still refused to condemn the pamphlet in writing.

It was at this point that Taylor produced a draft outline of a letter he had prepared. Taylor suggested that Le Marchant send this letter to Harcourt, and it would then be published in the press. The draft letter 'contained assurances of the horror & detestation in which I held Mr McCallum's pamphlet as a libel on the College & then followed assurances on my part that I had been in no manner privy to the publication or inconsiderately furnished the grounds to any person, unworthy of my confidence, & who had abused the same'.[9]

There was a suspicion amongst some that one of the contributors to the pamphlet was a certain James Glenie. Glenie, who had attended the Royal Military Academy at Woolwich and served as an artillery officer during the American War of Independence, was under the patronage of the Duke of Kent. In early 1806, the Duke proposed Glenie as an instructor of gunnery and fortification at the Royal Military College. Le Marchant invited Glenie to High Wycombe to discuss his appointment and show him around the college. James Glenie was never appointed to the staff of the Royal

Military College since the Duke of York 'would not hear of him as a master, that he was certainly a very sensible man, but likewise a most troublesome and unpredictable one'.[10]

Glenie had previously been involved in a dispute with the Duke of Richmond. When Glenie was asked to comment on the Duke's scheme to establish defensive lines along the English coast, he claimed that the plans were foolish and impractical. This led to a drawn-out argument and a series of pamphlets between the two. Harcourt and Taylor suspected that when Le Marchant had met with Glenie two years earlier, he may have inadvertently expressed his irritation with the situation at the college and this was then used as a basis for the pamphlet.

Le Marchant countered by noting that it had been some time since he had been introduced to Glenie by the Duke of Kent, and he referred to several letters that the Duke had written to him on the subject. The conversation then turned to two other members of staff, a former housekeeper at the Junior Department and a master who had been dismissed, both close associates of Glenie, who might have provided him with information about the college.

Le Marchant was also wary of starting a pamphlet war with McCallum. Publishing a letter would, he thought, 'place me in an awkward situation with respect to Mr McCallum if my letter be considered by him to be an aggression. It was difficult to know in what manner he might be disposed to resent it, whether by overwhelming me with abuse, or making it personal by sending me a message.'[11]

Le Marchant eventually wrote a letter to Harcourt, and two additional letters were drafted and signed by a number of officers and staff from the college, explicitly refuting the allegations made in the pamphlet. Le Marchant was asked to sign the two additional letters but declined to do so. He disagreed with the content of the two letters and believed that the officers who had signed them had done so under duress.

Although Le Marchant considered most of the pamphlet's content to be libellous and untrue, he thought that some of the accusations were accurate. He felt that by prosecuting McCallum, everything, both good and bad, about the college would be brought out into the public domain. The three letters, all addressed to Harcourt, were published in various newspapers, including the *Morning Post* and the *Morning Chronicle*, in early February 1809. The first letter, that of Le Marchant, was the shortest of the three:

> Royal Military College, High Wycombe
> 31st December 1808
> Sir – As I trust that you are thoroughly convinced of the interest I take in everything that concerns this establishment, you will, I am sure, give me credit for no small share of indignation at the most unfounded attack lately made on its reputation by Mr McCallum; yet, as this Gentlemen has thought proper to except me from the marked abuse which he has so liberally and unmeritedly bestowed on yourself and others, I am anxious to assure you, that I feel the malignity of the libel, even more than I should have done, had it been directed against myself; and I take the earliest opportunity of assuring you that I shall be most happy to co-operate under your command, with any Members of the College, in such measures as may be thought required for vindicating the honour and character of the establishment.
>
> I have the honour to be, Sir,
> Your very obedient servant
> J. G. Le Marchant
> Col. and Lieut.-Gov. R.M.C.[12]

The second letter, signed by Lieutenant-Colonel Butler, the college chaplain, the surgeon and several other members of staff, was much longer and went much further. All of the accusations in the publication were 'infamous fabrications' and the signatories called for the prosecution of the author, editor and publisher of the pamphlet. The letter lavished praise on General Harcourt, commending his 'equitable administration of everything connected with the affairs for the College'.[13]

The third letter, signed by another group of staff and officers, rallied to the defence of Butler, explaining that he had introduced the necessary level of discipline and regulations 'so as to preclude any embezzlement, or untrue consumption of provisions by any person whatever'.[14]

A further pamphlet was published in February 1809 written by Lewis Peithmann, a German master at the college, denouncing the claims made by McCallum and 'proving that institution to be a most salutary, useful, and excellent Establishment, reflecting the greatest honor on H.R.H. The Duke of York'.[15]

The Government's solicitors were of the opinion that McCallum's pamphlet was a scandalous libel against the Duke of York, the Governor and other officers of the Royal Military College. They believed that there was sufficient evidence to take McCallum to court. In the end, no prosecution took place. In fact, McCallum's publication, which had singled out the Royal Military College for severe criticism, was orchestrated by the enemies of the Duke of York. Their attempts to bring him down did not stop there.

In 1803, Prince Frederick, the Duke of York, had taken a mistress, Mrs Mary Ann Clarke, whom he installed in a house in Gloucester Place, fairly close to Buckingham Palace. Mrs Clarke had financial difficulties and devised a scheme to make money. As Commander-in-Chief, it was the Duke who could approve by favour the purchase of commissions in the army. And Mary had influence over the Duke, which she intended to exploit. She submitted recommendations for promotions to the Duke and in return received unofficial payments from the officers involved.

Gwyllym Lloyd Wardle, a former army colonel and now Member of Parliament for Oakhampton, assisted by Major Thomas Dodd, military secretary to the Duke of Kent, and James Glenie, took Mrs Clarke on a journey to the coast in the autumn of 1808, supposedly for a seaside trip. But the real objective was to get as much information about how much the Duke of York knew about her money-making scheme. And Mrs Clarke was happy to oblige, no doubt intent on revenge. The Duke had discarded his lover two years earlier.

In January 1809, Gwyllym Wardle stood up in the House of Commons and outlined a string of cases where Mrs Clarke had allegedly secured promotions for her clients with the Duke of York's full knowledge. At the end of his speech, the House agreed to establish an inquiry to investigate the extent of the Duke's involvement. Mrs Clarke appeared and gave evidence at the inquiry, and such was her spirited performance and responses to questions that she became a celebrity.

In March, Wardle moved an address in the House for the Duke's dismissal as Commander-in-Chief of the army. The debate on the conduct of the Duke of York raged on for several days. Eventually, the Duke was found not guilty of corruption, although the house did take note of his negligence in the matter. Some felt he escaped sanction because of his royal status. Although the Duke continuously denied having known of his mistress's scheme, he submitted his resignation to the King. He was replaced by General Sir David Dundas.

In February 1811, The Duke was reinstated as the Commander-in-Chief by his brother, the Prince of Wales, who had assumed the role of Prince Regent after their father had suffered from another bout of illness. As for Mrs Clarke, she published her memoirs titled *The Authentic and Impartial Life of Mrs Mary Anne Clarke*. She was also paid several thousand pounds and offered a pension by the Duke of York to prevent her publishing his love letters. Mrs Clarke was later imprisoned for nine months for libel, after which she spent the rest of her life in France.

Over the years, Le Marchant's name became well known for his work with the Royal Military College, and others sought to learn from his experience and follow his blueprint. Lieutenant-Colonel Samuel Whittingham, an alumnus of the Senior Department, consulted Le Marchant when planning a military college at

Majorca. The East India Company, whose cadets had attended the Junior Department at Marlow, established a military school at Addiscombe near Croydon, with input from Le Marchant. By this time, the East India Company's army had grown to a formidable 250,000 troops, led by British officers, although the majority of the soldiers were Indian.

Government ministers continued to call upon Le Marchant for advice on military matters. In 1806, William Windham, who had recently been appointed Secretary of State for War and the Colonies, asked Le Marchant to prepare a report on how best to defend the country in case of invasion. Le Marchant replied:

> I am just returned from having had a conversation with General Jarry on the subject of a military organisation adapted to the political situation of this Country. His very extensive conception of the question and the order in which he places under observation the different heads of arrangement appear to me worthy of your notice, more especially as he considers the subject differently from any person I had before met with. Knowing the good opinion you entertain of the General's abilities added to his great experience of military measures, I presume to take the liberty of calling him to your recollection. He would feel flattered by your notice, at the same time that as a foreigner he thinks it might be deemed an intrusion were he to offer his opinion on points of such importance unasked.
>
> I have the honor to transmit herewith for your consideration some additional articles and alterations proposed to be made to the act of Parliament relating to a general enrolment, & I shall be happy to attend your commands in Town whenever you may please to require it. I propose being in London shortly, & will take the liberty of calling in Downing Street, in case you might wish to speak with me.[16]

Le Marchant, in his usual thorough and detailed manner, produced an *Outline of a General Organization of the Military Establishment of Great Britain*. In his report, he proposed a significant reform in which the army should be raised through voluntary enlistment for a limited term of years, and that the militia should become second battalions of established regiments under the command of regular officers. He also included a strategy for mobilising the population in the event of an invasion.

At the same time, Le Marchant was actively engaged in efforts to secure the release of his elderly uncle, Thomas Le Marchant, who was held prisoner at Lyons, France. When war broke out in 1803, British citizens aged between eighteen and sixty in France were detained and classed as enemy aliens. Napoleon considered all British prisoners, whether military personnel or civilians, as potential threats to France.

Le Marchant identified a Swiss national, a prisoner of war in England, as a possible candidate for exchange. With assistance from a relative of his wife in Switzerland, Le Marchant established direct contact with the family of the Swiss prisoner. In July 1809, Le Marchant wrote to Thomas with encouraging news about the negotiations for his release.

> It will give me sincere pleasure to see you return, and I flatter myself with a belief that your exchange will be brought about. I have many friends capable of insuring to you the indulgence that other Englishmen have obtained and that you will not be refused leave to embark suiting your convenience. I expect to be able very shortly to write to you a report of progress stating the detenues who are endeavouring to effect your release.[17]

Regrettably, these efforts came to nothing. The British government was adamant that a civilian held by the French could not be considered as a prisoner of war and that the exchange of non-military persons was extremely unlikely.

Le Marchant persevered. He contacted his friends and acquaintances in government, including Edward Cooke, Under-Secretary of State for War and the Colonies. He wrote to the Duke of Northumberland, who was unable to help. The Duke was also trying to secure the release of his own brother and nephew who were being held prisoners in France.

While the relationship with Harcourt and Butler had improved, Le Marchant was still not satisfied with the discipline in the Junior Department. He would have welcomed the newspaper reports that appeared in January 1810. General Harcourt might be leaving the Royal Military College to replace Lord William Howe, Governor of Plymouth, who was seriously ill. Harcourt remained at the college, much to Le Marchant's disappointment. This was not the first time that there had been rumours that Harcourt might be replaced as Governor. Each time Le Marchant's hopes were dashed. In the early summer of 1810, Le Marchant wrote to Major-General Robert Craufurd:

> Sir,
> I cannot refuse myself the secret satisfaction of stating to you what I feel most heavily at the present moment. The situation of the Junior Dept. of the R M College becomes daily more critical. Since I spoke with you on the subject several circumstances have occurred exceedingly discreditable to its discipline. The Cadets have continued to Lampoon their masters, whom they turn into the greatest ridicule. Others have committed acts of open resistance.
> The parents of the Cadets complain of a mismanagement in the direction of the studies, and this morning not less than eight of the masters decline attending their duty, with those cadets who remain at the college during the vacation on a plea that they cannot justify. Three cadets have been expelled within the month for acts of insubordination, and yet these examples appear not to have deterred others from the same course. Unhappily my hands are tied, for I dare not express my opinion to Lord Harcourt without again incurring the risk of being brought forward as a prosecutor. All that I can do is to state facts to his Lordship, which I have done for years past to no good purpose. I think it is quite impossible, that the institution should exist for another twelve months in its present state and unless something occurs to remove Lord

Harcourt, I do not see anything likely to occasion any reform of the establishment.

If an Enquiry could be brought about, and which the present state of things renders urgently necessary, the first thing to be done would be to remove those who are the cause of the evil, and to examine into the power and responsibility of each individual in command, in order to establish discipline. The masters should be consulted in respect to the mode of conducting the studies.

General Clinton was here the other day. He expressed his surprise at the unmilitary appearance of the Cadets, and if you have seen Sir Charles Craufurd lately, I suspect his report generally of what he has seen, will not have been more favourable.[18]

11
SANDHURST

As Le Marchant was refining his plan for the Royal Military College, attention turned to potential locations for a permanent institution. Early newspaper reports even suggested that it was intended to convert the royal palace at Hampton Court into a military college. Another of the initial sites considered was Nottingham Castle, belonging to Henry Pelham-Clinton, the 4th Duke of Newcastle, who had inherited the title at the tender age of ten.

At the end of 1799, William Huskisson had written advising Le Marchant that the Prime Minister, William Pitt, was looking very favourably towards the plan and that 'he desires you ... procure Him particulars of the Duke of Newcastle's House, as it appears to Him very desirable it should be purchased immediately, if upon investigation it should be found to answer, & can be purchased on reasonable Terms.'[1]

Le Marchant turned to Colonel Charles Craufurd, asking him to assess the Castle as a suitable location for the military college. Craufurd provided highly favourable feedback. The extensive estate at Nottingham Castle, spanning almost 150 acres, was an ideal size for the military college, offering ample room for additional buildings, while still leaving sufficient space for exercises, manoeuvres, temporary fortifications and field works. The house itself was in good condition. Located in the East Midlands, it seemed ideal and it was convenient for northern England and Scotland. Yet it was far enough from London so that students would not be tempted by the fleshpots of the capital city. Craufurd ended his report: 'I am convinced that no situation can be found in the Kingdom which combines more advantages than Nottingham Castle.'[2]

In spite of the positive report, alternative locations were sought, and in November 1800 Colonel Henry Calvert, Adjutant-General to the Forces, wrote to Huskisson explaining that 'a suitable piece of ground has been found near Blackwater consisting of 125 Acres of enclosed land, and the manor extending over about 200 more, with a considerable quantity of timber and some good materials on the premises, and that the Proprietor was disposed to enter into agreements to sell the same for about £8,000'.[3]

Major-General Delancey, in his role as Barrack-Master General, was given the task of acquiring the Blackwater estate as soon as possible. Interestingly, the above letter did not disclose the owner's name, perhaps understandably since it turned out to be none other than Prime Minister William Pitt. He had recently purchased the land from his niece, Lady Griselda Tickell, and her husband. The exact amount that Pitt paid his niece remains uncertain, although there were some reports that the estate was valued at around £2,600.

Pitt had accrued significant debts and no doubt the sale of the land for just over £8,000 eased his personal financial problems. The location, straddling the Surrey and Berkshire border, was far enough from a city or large town so the students would not get distracted. There was enough space for students to practise military movements and the area was frequently used for temporary encampments at the time. Soon after the acquisition, additional land of 153 acres, adjacent to the site, was purchased at a public auction for £1,500.

As part of the gradual industrialisation throughout the country, the eighteenth century witnessed substantial growth in infrastructure and improved communications. The development of turnpike roads was significant, with local trusts taking on responsibility for the development and upkeep of highways for which they would levy a toll. At the same time, the construction of canals was gaining in popularity, backed by private investors in what was sometimes referred to as 'canal mania', and was now the cheapest and easiest way of transporting goods. The Basingstoke canal was completed in 1794. The proximity of the Sandhurst estate to the turnpike running through Bagshot, and in particular the canals in the area, would have been considered a great advantage for transporting building materials for the new college.

James Wyatt from the Board of Ordnance was chosen as the architect, with a brief to design buildings for both the Senior and Junior Departments of the Royal Military College. Wyatt was at the forefront of the then fashionable Greek revival style of architecture, notable for its simplicity, symmetry and the use of columns. He was well known to the royal family having previously worked on alterations to Frogmore House in Windsor Great Park for Queen Charlotte, and to Windsor Castle itself. He had also designed the buildings for the Royal Military Academy at Woolwich. His initial cost estimates for the new college amounted to £118,956. When pressed, he reduced the costs by £14,735 through replacing civilian labourers with troops to dig and move earth and for transporting materials.

In March 1802, Edward Bracebridge was appointed to reside on site and manage the estate, overseeing all expenditure. His role also included landscaping of the grounds. He particularly admired the work of the landscape designer Lancelot 'Capability' Brown whose designs featured large sweeping lawns and lakes, still evident at Sandhurst today. By August 1802, the design of the landscape had been completed and would include the planting of a variety of trees including copper beech, Spanish chestnut, oak, lime and silver birch.

Alexander Copland was awarded the contract for construction. He had cornered the market in military buildings due to his innovative approach, erecting barracks in the shortest possible time, sometimes using prefabricated huts, although not always of the highest quality. This he achieved by using a multi-skilled workforce which he would move around from site to site, supplying them with the necessary equipment, contrary to the normal practice at the time of employing local craftsmen who provided their own tools. He amassed a small fortune.

His reputation for speed, however, seemed to have deserted him when it came to Sandhurst, and it is not clear whether there was a delivery date specified in his contract. In an attempt to save costs and increase profit, he decided to make his own bricks, renting part of the Sandhurst estate from the government for this purpose. By the end of 1804, little progress had been made. Copland continued making bricks, and two years later, building work had still not started.

The lack of progress at Sandhurst resulted in the Supreme Board looking at other possible sites. In November 1805, a delegation consisting of the Duke of Kent, the Duke of Cumberland, the Earl of Harrington, Harcourt and Le Marchant visited an estate between Marlow and Henley. It was deemed unsuitable since there was insufficient housing for professors and masters. Another option, the Military Hospital at Chatham, only had enough capacity for 250 cadets, with no further room for staff and professors.

Faced with the risk of overrunning the budget that had been originally approved by Parliament, it was decided to construct the buildings at Sandhurst in stages. Priority was given to the Junior Department, the largest of the two departments. There was little doubt that the current premises at Marlow were too small, and not fit for purpose. In March 1806, Le Marchant, not known for his patience, wrote to William Windham, Secretary for War and the Colonies.

> It is to the Junior Department to which I wish particularly to direct your attention. The number of Gentlemen Cadets rated in the

Estimate of this year is altogether but 300, of which number 72 are cadets intended for the Artillery whose Education is finished at Woolwich, and 16 destined for the Company's service in the East Indies. After deducting these numbers there are left only 214 for the supply of officers for the service at large, & of this number there are probably some who will not enter into the army. It requires between 3 & 4 years to educate a Cadet for a commission, consequently of the 200 not more than from 25 to 30 can be sent annually from the college into the army, which considering the present very extensive Military Establishment will not afford an officer per Regiment in four or five years. It is therefore evident that a Military College on so confined a scale can have no immediate influence on the discipline and improvement of the British army.

The accommodation at Marlow has been already stated to be altogether unworthy of a national institution & inadequate even to our present confined number. The most extravagant prices for houses are demanded by the proprietors & paid by the officers & Professors belonging to the Establishment, for which they receive but a very trifling compensation. Many also for want of means of residing in the Town are obliged to live a distance from the College, some even as far as 5 miles. The Cadets are dispersed over the Town in separate buildings to the great prejudice of their Health & Morals.

In addition to the propriety & economy of placing the College in a natural building such as Winchester Palace it is worthy of remark that it might be prepared for its reception by the month of February next, whilst on the other hand, an entire new building could not be completed in less than two or 3 years.

The objection urged against placing the College at Winchester is stated to arise from His Majesty having expressed a dislike to that plan, but if by a reference to competent authority it should be found that the balance on the score of economy and expediency is so decided in favor of Winchester, might it not be an object worthy of the Ministers attention to ascertain whether such a report is well founded, and whether His Majesty's objection might not be removed.[4]

The King's House at Winchester had been designed by Christopher Wren for Charles II. The building, on the site of Winchester Castle, had fallen out of favour as a royal residence and remained empty. In 1792, it was used to house religious refugees fleeing from the French Revolution, and then served as an army barracks for British troops.

The notion of relocating the entire Royal Military College to Winchester was not new. At the beginning of 1804, the Secretary at War had plans and estimates drawn up. The King's House was in disrepair, it had been reported that the house was full of vermin, yet the cost of £19,560 for refurbishment would be much cheaper than erecting a new building, and the house could be ready in one year.

In any event, George III's reluctance to consider the King's House at Winchester either as a temporary or permanent site for the college held sway. The idea was abandoned. Le Marchant suspected that it was General Harcourt, a close associate of the King, who was the principal objector.

> The Supreme Board has determined upon the removal of the institution, and the King's House at Winchester is considered to be the most eligible place for that purpose. The Governor is the only dissenting voice. He thinks it too distant from St. Leonards for him to exercise the species of command that he has established, nevertheless I believe we shall remove, and without delay.[5]

The Senior and Junior Departments of the Royal Military College would remain at High Wycombe and Marlow respectively for another five years.

Since the opening of the Senior Department, 137 commissioned officers had attended at High Wycombe, of which fifty had been appointed to various positions on the staff of the army, and a further fifty had returned to their regiments. As for the Junior Department, 628 cadets had been admitted of which seventy-three had received commissions, 215 had gone on to the artillery college at Woolwich, twenty-nine to the East India Company, the remainder still studying at the college. The success of Le Marchant's Royal Military College was not in doubt.

By this point, the Supreme Board, as well as Le Marchant, had grown impatient. They suggested abandoning the whole scheme at Sandhurst altogether, selling the estate along with the materials and bricks, and looking for a new site. It would be better to choose a site nearer to a town where staff and professors could readily find accommodation. Le Marchant favoured Reading, especially since there might be a possibility of transporting the building materials from Sandhurst by canal. Winchester was, once again, under serious consideration. When the Sandhurst site was valued, it was significantly below the amount previously paid to Pitt, who had passed away in January 1806. As a result, it was considered impractical to proceed with a sale of the estate.

Finally, in May 1808, over seven years after Alexander Copland had been awarded the initial building contract, the decision was taken to proceed with the original site at Sandhurst. Copland was asked for an updated estimate for the Junior Department, with a capacity for 400 cadets, and new houses for Harcourt and Le Marchant. Five months later, the Treasury approved Copland's revised estimate of £89,770. The Supreme Board would later go back to the Treasury for a further £35,000 for additional accommodation and buildings.

Shortly afterwards the Duke of York, Harcourt and Le Marchant visited the estate at Sandhurst 'and after viewing several positions proposed for the site of the intended building, decided that the north-west area would be the most eligible spot'.[6] They directed Copland to start on the foundations.

Even then, progress was slow. When Lieutenant-General Sir Robert Brownrigg, Quartermaster-General to the Forces, visited the site during the early summer of 1809, he found no more than twenty to twenty-five men at work. Copland was advised in no uncertain terms to ensure that 'this great National Work is forthwith entered upon with that energy which its importance demands, and that the number of Workmen employed be such as to give a reasonable expectation that a very considerable progress be made in the Work during this Season'.[7]

To speed up construction, Copland's solution was to increase the rate at which he made bricks, by building additional kilns and using the clay earth on the adjoining land. He also asked for some fifty troops to assist with ground works, as well as repairing roads. In the end, many of the homemade bricks that he had amassed over time turned out to be of such poor quality that they could not be used, necessitating the purchase of new bricks at an additional cost.

In the early summer of 1811, Le Marchant stood and scrutinized the building works at Sandhurst. He had gone to the site in the company of the Duke of Cambridge, General Harcourt and Lieutenant-General Sir Harry Burrard for the purpose of deciding where the professors' and masters' houses should be located. After a slow start, the construction was now progressing well. Le Marchant saw several hundred labourers, masons, carpenters and blacksmiths going about their work. The challenges that he had encountered in terms of space and accommodation, especially for the Junior Department, would soon be at an end.

He had anticipated remaining at Sandhurst for the rest of his military career, with his family by his side, where he could see the realisation of the plans that had kept him occupied for many years. He returned to High Wycombe in an extremely happy state of mind. Just prior to the visit to Sandhurst, Le Marchant's efforts had once more been recognised with a promotion, this time from Lieutenant-Colonel to Major-General.

Then, in an instant, everything changed. For not long after, he received a communication from Lieutenant-General Henry Calvert, Adjutant-General to the Forces. As he read the letter, his heart sank. It contained the most unwelcome news that would change his fortunes and those of his family forever.

12

ON ACTIVE SERVICE

Le Marchant was to stand down immediately from the college. The Prince of Wales, who had now assumed the rôle of Prince Regent, along with Prince Frederick, the Duke of York, considered Le Marchant's new rank of Major-General to be too high for him to remain as Lieutenant-Governor of the Royal Military College.

In spite of the difficulties he had faced along the way, Le Marchant considered the founding of the college as the most fulfilling years of his life. Not only was he to give up his position as Lieutenant-Governor of the college, he was also concerned that the possible loss of £500 a year in income resulting from his new role might have an adverse effect on his family.

On 9 June 1811, Le Marchant replied to Lieutenant-General Calvert with sadness and perhaps a hint of bitterness.

> My Dear Sir,
>
> Allow me to thank you for the early intimation that you have had the goodness to give me of my intended removal from the Military College. I would have answered your letter immediately and without hesitation, to the same effect as I am now about to do, but unfortunately there was yesterday no post.

I cannot disguise from you that this change in my situation will make a very sensible difference in my income, which must unavoidably be heavily felt by a numerous and growing family. I had certainly (though without sufficient consideration) looked forward to my continuance at the College, as the more natural course that my military life would have taken, under the particular circumstances of my having given rise to an establishment, which is admitted to have been of essential service to the army, & of my having devoted my best military years to its advancement and improvement, during which time I have unavoidably lost every opportunity of distinguishing myself in common with those of my own standing, by active service in the field. But as the appointment of Lieutenant-Governor is deemed incompatible with my present rank in the army, I hope that I need not say to you, that these thoughts shall never occupy me a moment, and I shall thank you to assure his Royal Highness the Commander-in-Chief, that I never can have any other object in view as to my professional employment, than that of showing myself worthy of that situation, (whatever it may be) in which His Royal Highness may be pleased to think my humble services may be most useful & acceptable.

Of course, I do not know whether it is to you alone that I am indebted for this early communication of what is intended, if so pray allow me to repeat my best thanks, but if you have done it with the permission of His Royal Highness, may I beg that you will express in the strongest terms my humble acknowledgement of this mark of his condescension and kindness.[1]

The disappointment that he felt was heightened by the prospect that he might have to uproot or even leave his family behind, with most of his eight children still at a tender age and his wife heavily pregnant. Le Marchant wrote to Lieutenant-Colonel Taylor, Secretary to the King, 'I have broken to Mrs Le Marchant the change that is made in our situation, which she bears with becoming fortitude, relying confidently on the justice & humanity of the Commander in Chief.'[2]

Le Marchant had expected to be placed under the command of General Charles Stanhope, 3rd Earl of Harrington, the Commander-in-Chief of the British forces in Ireland. But Ireland was not to be his destination. Just over three weeks later, Le Marchant received his orders from the army headquarters at Horse Guards:

My Dear General
A brigade of cavalry is ordered for immediate service in Portugal, & the Commander-in-Chief has selected you to take the command of it. I am persuaded that you will be gratified by this preference on the part of His Royal Highness, but I delay the official communication, till you inform me whether there are any cogent reasons that would render this mark of distinction unacceptable to you at present.

Let me hear from you as soon as you can, in the course of tomorrow if it is in your power.

I remain yours faithfully
H Calvert[3]

Le Marchant replied to Calvert the very next day. He would serve wherever His Royal Highness, the Commander-in-Chief, thought proper. After all, the command of a heavy cavalry brigade was a highly sought after position.

On 6 July, Le Marchant issued an order to the staff and students at the Royal Military College.

His Royal Highness the Prince Regent, having been graciously pleased to appoint Major-General Le Marchant to the command of a Brigade of Cavalry, under immediate orders of embarkation to serve in Portugal; he desires, that until further orders, all reports may be made to Colonel Butler, as senior officer at the College.

The Lieutenant-Governor cannot resign his command of an institution which he had the good fortune to be instrumental in forming, & to the advancement of which he has devoted so many

> years, without expressing his ardent wishes for the welfare of its members, & his sincere hope & conviction that it will completely fulfil the just expectations of the army & the public, from so important an establishment.[4]

A delegation of officers asked that he set a date for a farewell dinner, but his departure from the College was so swift that he did not have time. Le Marchant's disappointment at having to leave the college was shared by his friends. Lieutenant-Colonel Robert Ballard Long wrote to his brother, Charles:

> I have just received a letter from Le Marchant announcing to his displacement from the Lt. Governorship of the College over whose interests he has so long and faithfully presided, and in whose establishment he was so instrumental. I wish to God I could see in such an act recompense for public services, a mark indicating that it arose from patriotism and a sense of public interests, rather than from that spirit of intrigue, jobbing and persecution which mark the abuse of power.[5]

Le Marchant attended a meeting of the Supreme Board of the Royal Military College for the last time on 16 July, at Horse Guards in London. Following his departure, it was deemed no longer necessary for the Lieutenant-Governor of the college to attend the Supreme Board meetings in future.

Immediately, he began preparations for his new role, writing to the commanding officers of the three cavalry regiments that would make up his brigade. First of all, Le Marchant sought the opinions of several cavalry officers who had served on the Peninsula regarding the equipment that his brigade should take with them. He shared that advice with his regimental commanders, advising them to bring all clothing and equipment to Lisbon, where a depot would be set up to store items not immediately needed in the field. Each regiment should carry two full sets of horseshoes, with one set for immediate use and the other in a shoe-case. The two sets would be enough to last for two months. He recommended that eight men per troop should be trained to shoe the horses. Finally, every officer should bring a good telescope and a map of Portugal. Le Marchant also contacted the ordnance department of the army to ensure that all his troops and horses were properly equipped. And he gave six months' notice to the landlord of the house he had been renting in High Wycombe.

Still, the overriding concern as Le Marchant prepared to take up his new post in Portugal was the plight of his family. He continued to make the case that they would be affected by the loss of income as a result of him leaving the Royal Military College. He wrote to the Duke of York:

> Sir,
> I hope that I am incapable of troubling your Royal Highness with pretensions which are altogether unfounded, and I am sure that your Royal Highness' known justice and attention to the Service will secure even as indulgent consideration of that which the particular circumstances of my situation encourage me respectfully to submit to your Royal Highness' decision.
>
> When I first had the honor to propose a plan for the improvement of the British Army by establishing a Military College, the Cavalry was at home without a prospect of being called on Service, from which I was led to believe, that under the circumstances of the moment I was engaging in a measure of all others the best calculated to benefit my country, and procure to me the approbation & favour of my Sovereign.
>
> I had the advantage of having served under the Orders of your Royal Highness in Flanders, and was Lieut. Colonel of one of the finest regiments of Dragoons in the army, a commission that I felt considerable pride in receiving from his Majesty in consideration of the sword exercise, which I introduced with your Royal Highness' approbation into the practice of the Cavalry.
>
> When the College began to assume some consistency and bore an appearance of ultimate success, I was required to relinquish my

Lieut. Colonelcy in the 2nd Dragoon Guards for one unattached, being told that I could not be called upon to join a regiment, as my services were more beneficially employed in the direction of the College, of which I was Lieut. Governor & Superintendent General.

Your Royal Highness is no stranger to the fruitless endeavours of the Duke of Richmond some years before to establish a similar Institution, nor to the difference of opinion which existed as well in parliament as in the Service at the time when I first was honoured with your Royal Highness' support, respecting the expediency of Military Instruction as a measure of national utility. Notwithstanding which I came forward out of the immediate line of my duty to carry into effect an innovation not sanctioned by public opinion, that in the event of failure would have proved injurious both to my credit & professional prospects. For twelve years I devoted myself to the accomplishment of this important object, under the most harassing circumstances to the injury of my health, firmly believing that if I succeeded in rendering the College a national establishment, both myself & my family would participate in that success by the enjoyment of a permanent Lieutenant Government, waiting such mark of favor as my anxious & zealous services might be thought to merit.

At the moment that the College was on the point of removing into a magnificent building suited to the Good Government of such an Establishment, when the difficulties under which it was established were done away, a recent Regulation in the Service has made the appointment of Lieut. Governor incompatible with my present rank in the army. I have not hesitated on such a trying occasion to prefer my duty to every other consideration in cheerfully retiring from my Lieut. Government into the pursuing of more active service, and it shall be my earnest endeavour to acquit myself with credit in the very flattering command to which your Royal Highness had been most graciously pleased to appoint me, in anxious desire (that if they deserve it) my past services will be marked with your Royal Highness' approbation. Whilst in compassion to pressing claims of a numerous & growing family who are chiefly dependent on my professional success, I am compelled for your Royal Highness' consideration for the loss of income that is occasioned by my unexpected removal. My salary & allowances as Lt. Governor of the College amounted to little short of 1500 per annum in which my family participating, whereby I was enabled to give my Children an education suitable for my rank. But at present my staff appointments are not only considerably less than those of the College, but they will be requisite to the support of my establishment abroad as Major General, to the exclusion of my Family who all experience great pecuniary difficulties, unless relieved through the humanity & justice of your Royal Highness in procuring for them some remuneration in acknowledgement of my zealous services at the College, having not yet received any permanent benefit there from, whilst there is not an individual of the establishment besides myself who had not received Military Rank, or been otherwise benefitted either in being brought back into the service after having sold out, or promoted without purchase.

I have the honor to be, etc.

J G Le Marchant[6]

Just a few weeks after receiving notice of his departure from the college, he left his family home in High Wycombe and travelled to London before sailing for Portugal. While in the capital, Le Marchant visited Lord Henry William Paget to pay his respects and seek his advice. Le Marchant had previously served under Lord Paget and held him in high regard. Since their days together in the 7th Light Dragoons, Lord Paget had become a Lieutenant-General and a distinguished cavalry officer who had already seen action in Portugal and Spain. He was given overall command of the cavalry under General Sir John Moore in Spain, achieving success against the French cavalry at the battles of Sahagun and Benavente in December 1808.

Lord Paget's involvement in the Peninsular War came to an abrupt end. He had been engaged in an affair and then eloped with Lady Charlotte, the wife of Arthur Wellesley's younger brother Henry, and mother of their young children. It was now impossible for him to serve under Wellesley. The British army on the Peninsula had lost one of their most capable cavalry officers.

When Le Marchant asked for some guidance on leadership, Lord Paget replied, 'The best advice that I can give to a cavalry General is to inspire his men as early as possible with the most perfect confidence in his personal gallantry. Let him but lead, they are sure to follow and I believe hardly anything will stop them.'[7]

Le Marchant set off on his journey from London to Portsmouth, where he would board the troop ship bound for Portugal. Meanwhile, the new buildings at Sandhurst, at least for the Junior Department, were nearing completion.

The departure of Le Marchant from the college was not the only change to take place that year. In July 1811, General Harcourt stepped down as Governor, making way for Lieutenant-General Sir Alexander Hope, who had been serving as Deputy Quartermaster-General at Horse Guards. Hope would continue as Governor until 1819, choosing to reside at Marlow to be near the Royal Military College, unlike his predecessor. And in August, Lieutenant-Colonel James Butler, Commandant of the Junior Department, was appointed Lieutenant-Governor of the college, succeeding Le Marchant.

On his arrival at Portsmouth, Le Marchant lodged at the George Inn, High Street, a popular spot for army and naval officers about to set off overseas. Lord Nelson had stopped at the inn before he set sail in September 1805, prior to the Battle of Trafalgar.

13

THE PENINSULAR WAR

The Treaty of Amiens between Britain and France, signed in March 1802, brought an end to the French Revolutionary Wars after ten years of hostilities. The peace did not last for long. A breakdown in the relationship occurred over the terms of the treaty, leading Britain to declare war on France in May 1803. Napoleon gathered an invasion force, *L'armée d'Angleterre*, across the English Channel. The invasion of England never took place due to Napoleon's inability to establish naval supremacy. Instead, he diverted his army to counter the threat from Russia and Austria. In late 1806, Napoleon sought to damage the British economy by imposing an embargo, known as the Continental System, preventing any European country from trading with Britain. Enforcing the blockade proved difficult.

Portugal stood out as one of the few European countries to reject participation in the Continental System. In response, France, along with its ally Spain, insisted that Portugal abandon its alliance with Britain, seize all British ships in its ports, and detain all British subjects in the country. Portugal refused to comply. In October 1807, Napoleon and King Carlos IV of Spain signed the Treaty of Fontainebleau, in which they agreed to divide Portugal between their two nations.

In November, a French army under General Jean-Andoche Junot marched into Lisbon shortly after the Portuguese royal family had fled to Brazil. Portugal was occupied and its army disbanded. By February of the following year, the French had gained control of four key fortresses in Spain: Barcelona, Figueras, Pamplona and San Sebastian. The French troops then advanced towards Madrid. In April 1808, Napoleon invited Carlos IV and his son Ferdinand to Bayonne, where they were effectively held captive and forced to abdicate. Napoleon promptly declared his elder brother, Joseph Bonaparte, as the new King of Spain.

The French army was initially welcomed as they went through Spain, but that soon changed. The turning point came with the *Dos de Mayo* uprising in Madrid in May, where an insurrection by the Spanish against the French garrison was brutally suppressed. Hundreds of protesters were executed. This sparked further uprisings throughout the country. In response, the Spanish sent a delegation to London to ask for Britain's help, followed shortly after by the Portuguese. By the summer of 1808, the Iberian Peninsula stood on the brink of war.

An army of 9,000 under Arthur Wellesley had assembled in Cork, Ireland, preparing for an expedition to South America in support of Venezuelan nationalists seeking independence from Spain. The government decided to divert Wellesley's force to Portugal with the aim of removing General Junot and the French. The British army reached the broad sandy beach at the mouth of the Mondego river in Portugal and began to disembark amid the thunderous Atlantic waves. The landing proved difficult and slow, with some drowning as they attempted to make their way ashore, and equipment was lost. Within a few days a further 5,000 infantry had arrived, and the army set off southwards for Lisbon, a hundred miles away.

Former officers and students from the Senior Department were to play a prominent role during the Peninsular War, eager for a chance to engage in action. For one Wycombite, there was disappointment. Major Thomas Birch, who had served so successfully in Egypt, expressed his frustration to Le Marchant, complaining that he had not been selected to go to Portugal. Le Marchant replied with a letter of consolation, while also highlighting the achievements of some of the students from High Wycombe who had already gone out to the Peninsula:

> You have not occasion to feel disconcerted at not going out with the late Expedition, it acquires much interest & solicitation at the Horse Guards to get on Service, it is therefore not expected that you will be preferred to those who are more important – there is a season for all things. When you had seen no service, you were urgent as any of those who now assail Head Quarters, since then you have served in the most glorious Campaign that this Country has to boast of & the Credit of those achievements is a sufficient guaranty of your honor & character as a soldier not to require your being a volunteer upon every occasion that offers. Our friend Carey is a Bachelor, & he cannot do better, or be more profitably employed than on actual service. You are married & the case is quite different therefore rest satisfied in coming forward when called upon.
>
> I receive frequent accounts from Wycombites now in Spain & Portugal, that are most gratifying, as holding out the fullish assurance of a glorious struggle in the cause of independence. Captain Whittingham has from the commencement been with General Castanos, in whose confidence he is, & the letters that have been received from him in this Country have recommended him to the notice & approbation of the highest powers. Captain Patrick, a Wycombite, is accompanying Sir Thomas Dyer, he informs me that recruits are coming in from all parts of the country, & that it is impossible to convey an adequate idea of the zeal shown by the patriots in forming their armies & providing an effectual resistance to the enemy.
>
> I have the fullest confidence that the patriots will be ultimately successful, which must lead to the complete overthrow of

> Bonaparte. God grant that this may be the case, for without it, England will be shut out from the Continent, and owing to an absence of trade, our finances ruined.
>
> P.S. It is not generally thought that the Duke of York will go out in command of the forces in Spain, tho' it appears to have been at one time in contemplation.[1]

Wellesley received word that another 15,000 men were being sent to confront the French army in Portugal. While this might have seemed to be a positive move, for Wellesley it signalled unwelcome news. A Lieutenant-General at the age of just thirty-nine, Wellesley was considered too junior an officer to lead such a sizeable force. General Sir Hew Dalrymple was appointed to assume overall command of the British army in Portugal, with Lieutenant-General Sir Harry Burrard his second-in-command. General Sir John Moore, of higher rank than Wellesley, was also en route to Portugal.

Sir Hew Dalrymple's only active service had been during the disastrous Flanders campaign, followed by roles as Lieutenant-Governor of Guernsey from 1796 to 1803, then taking up a similar position in Gibraltar. Sir Harry Burrard had entered the Royal Military Academy in Woolwich as a cadet and later joined the Royal Artillery. In 1798, he had commanded a brigade on an expedition to the low countries, during which he surrendered to the French. He was held as a prisoner of war for six months until he was exchanged. Both Dalrymple and Burrard, perhaps because of his time in French captivity, were considered to be rather cautious in nature.

Wellesley hoped to defeat Junot before any of the senior officers arrived. The first battle of the Peninsular War took place at Roliça, where Wellesley triumphed over the French and continued south towards Lisbon. Sir Harry Burrard had now arrived and instructed Wellesley to halt further progress until additional resources had been brought in. Neither Burrard nor Wellesley anticipated what the French would do next.

The French army under General Junot moved north from Lisbon and attacked Wellesley at Vimeiro on 21 August 1808. By midday, Wellesley had, once again, defeated the enemy and was eager to pursue the French. He felt it was a great opportunity to crush the French army in Portugal and advance on Lisbon. The French had suffered significant losses, with 2,000 killed, wounded, prisoners or missing, out of a total force of 14,000 men. The British, in contrast, lost 720 out of a total of around 20,000. Sir Harry Burrard, however, disagreed and ordered the troops back to camp. The following day, General Sir Hew Dalrymple arrived from Gibraltar, shared Burrard's reluctance to continue the fight, and prevented Wellesley from following up on his victory.

After the defeat at Vimeiro, Junot sought a truce with the British. An armistice was negotiated culminating in the Convention of Sintra, signed on 30 August. According to the terms of the agreement, the French army was granted safe passage from Portugal back to France aboard British naval ships, taking with them all their possessions, arms and spoils.

The objective of forcing the French from Portugal had been accomplished, but there was outrage back home. The fact that British ships had transported the enemy back to France was deemed unacceptable, and widely seen as a humiliation. It prompted the government to set up a military court of inquiry to examine the circumstances surrounding the Convention. Dalrymple, Burrard and Wellesley sailed home to give evidence.

Speculation was rife about the possible outcome of the inquiry. Le Marchant had his own opinion, which he shared with Lieutenant-Colonel Long: 'It will turn out that Sir Harry Burrard rendered a convention necessary in not following up the advantages gained over the enemy by Sir Arthur Wellesley. But under the circumstances of being obliged to act, Sir Hugh gave terms for which as yet we see no excuse. I think both will be in a scrape.'[2]

In the end, the committee charged with the inquiry ruled in favour of the terms of the Convention given to the French. Wellesley was congratulated in Parliament for the success at Vimeiro. Wellesley returned to Ireland, while both Sir Hew Dalrymple and Sir Harry Burrard were never given another command.

Meanwhile, the British government set about reorganising the Portuguese army. The task was entrusted to John Charles Villiers, now the British Ambassador at Lisbon, who had been instrumental in helping Le Marchant establish the Royal Military College. Villiers suggested that Le Marchant should come over to Portugal as his temporary military advisor, a choice backed by the Secretary of State for War. Le Marchant received notice of the proposed appointment in a letter from Villiers dated 26 October 1808.

> My Dear Sir,
> I much wish to know whether you think that you could retain your important situation at the College, if you undertook a temporary service of 2 or 3 months which would take you abroad with me for that time. If you cannot, as a friend of yours I shall never mention your name for the object in question. If you can, I should like to submit the idea to your consideration. In the meantime pray consider this letter as most strictly confidential.[3]

While Le Marchant remained committed to his role at the college, he expressed an interest in going to Portugal, even if only for a brief period. Given his experience at the college, he would be an ideal candidate to train the Portuguese army. Villiers, who appeared to be making progress with his attempts to facilitate Le Marchant's release, contacted him again just two weeks later.

> I am rejoiced to think that I shall have both your company & your assistance. I will not on any account have you miss the meeting at

> Sandhurst. I will acquaint you as soon as I know the time when I am likely to go.
>
> If everything goes perfectly well and cheerfully at Sandhurst perhaps you may find the means of getting your work settled, as a matter of course. Do not miss an opportunity if it occurs, but do not force or require anything, for it may be proposed regardless when I can be prepared sufficiently to have the Duke of York's commands taken on the subject. By the by, in speaking of the subject either to the Duke or to General Harcourt, take care to impress them with the idea that though I must go prepared to enable the Portuguese Government to do something & that consequently several Individual officers may know how they are likely to be employed, yet to prevent jealousy with a very jealous people, it is extremely important that this object should be as secret as possible until the Portuguese Government is a little better settled, after which not a minutes time should be lost.
>
> Pray tell General Harcourt that though I cannot suppose that he consents to your absence on any account but your own, & the public service, yet I am willing to believe that the idea of contributing to the success of so old a friend (I may say of two generations) is not disagreeable to him & that I take his indulgence to you as a kindness.[4]

The appointment seemed to be progressing steadily towards a satisfactory conclusion. Harcourt raised no objections. Perhaps he found the idea of removing his sometimes troublesome subordinate from the college appealing.

At Villiers' suggestion, Le Marchant met with Lieutenant-General Sir John Cradock, recently appointed as commander of the British garrison in Lisbon. Cradock held a very low opinion of the state of the Portuguese army, and wholeheartedly supported the idea of Le Marchant's appointment. In fact, he could think of no one he would prefer for the role and agreed to recommend Le Marchant to the relevant ministers. During

John Gaspard Le Marchant.

Le Marchant's wife, Mary (*née* Carey).

Le Marchant's father, John.

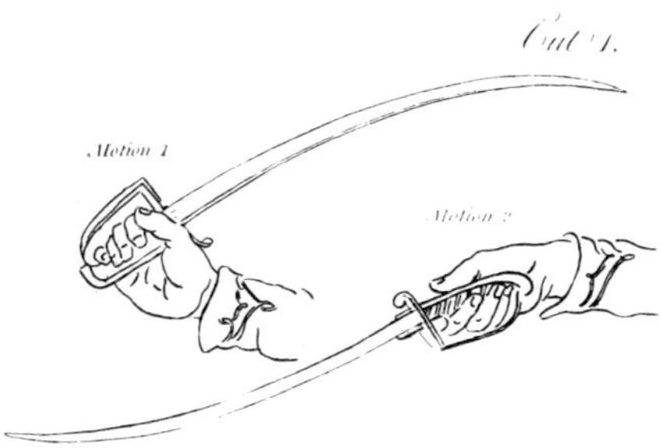

Above left and left: Illustrations from Le Marchant's *Rules and Regulations for the Sword Exercise of the Cavalry.*

1796 pattern light cavalry sword designed by Le Marchant.

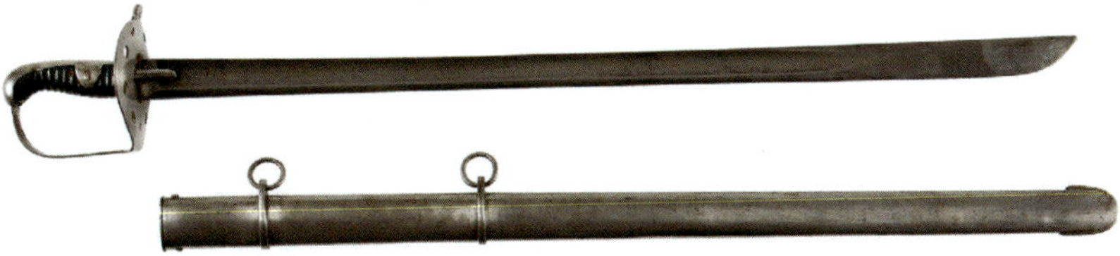

1796 pattern heavy cavalry sword similar to that used by the Austrian cavalry.

St Peter Port and Castle Cornet, Guernsey, artist J G Le Marchant.

Bordeaux Harbour, Guernsey, artist J G Le Marchant.

La Coupée, Sark, artist J G Le Marchant.

Above left: General Jarry, Director of Instruction at the Royal Military College.

Above right: Issac Dalby, Professor of Mathematics at the Royal Military College.

High Wycombe, home of the Senior Department of the Royal Military College, artist J G Le Marchant.

Military review at the Junior Department of the Royal Military College, Marlow.

Above left: Plaque at the site of the Senior Department, High Street, High Wycombe.

Above right: Plaque at the site of the Junior Department, West Street, Marlow.

Belem Tower, Lisbon, artist J G Le Marchant.

Sintra, Portugal, artist J G Le Marchant.

Lord Wellington's Quarters at Santarem, Portugal, artist J G Le Marchant.

Salamanca from Cabrerizos, before the Battle of Salamanca, sketch by Le Marchant.

View of the battlefield at Salamanca from the ridge near the village of Calvarrasa de Arriba with the Greater Arapile on the left and the Lesser Arapile on the right.

Mural illustrating Le Marchant's cavalry charge decorates the wall of the municipal sports hall in Los Arapiles, painted in 2022 to commemorate the anniversary of the Battle of Salamanca. The left column features an account of Le Marchant's charge in Spanish.

their discussion, Le Marchant made it clear to Cradock that while he was interested in the position, he wanted everyone to understand that he had never actively sought the opportunity nor taken any measures whatsoever to secure it. The college remained Le Marchant's primary focus, and he wanted to return as Lieutenant-Governor once the temporary assignment was over.

Villiers began to finalise arrangements with Le Marchant, preparing for their journey together to Portugal.

> My dear Sir,
>
> I flatter myself that nothing can disappoint me of the pleasure & assistance which I shall derive from your accompanying me to Portugal. I think I must leave London on Monday at latest, though certainly unexpected delays may happen.
>
> My baggage will go from hence on Friday morning. Perhaps you had better come to town immediately to make your own definitive arrangements. You might join me on the road or at the place of embarkation & may rely upon hearing from me the day before I actually start. But I think you had better come to town without delay.
>
> I see no objection myself to your Adjutant & much utility in having him, but will it be prudent to ask his absence likewise from the Colleges? If he wishes to go, & you wish to take him, let him hold himself in readiness to start at short notice, & let us discuss the subject when you come to town. Bring your trunk with you if you wish it to go with my baggage.[5]

An article appeared in *The Times* at the end of November, reporting that the Lieutenant-Governor had set out on a special military commission to Portugal.

Le Marchant never made the trip to Portugal; there was a last-minute change in plans. The Duke of York considered Le Marchant too important to the running of the Royal Military College, informing Lord Castlereagh, the Secretary of State for War and the Colonies, that Le Marchant could not be spared.

Villiers may have been correct that jealousy at Le Marchant's appointment might influence the outcome.

Le Marchant had been eager to take a break from the college, even if only briefly, especially since the appointment in Portugal would have been beneficial to his career. He expressed his annoyance at the outcome in a letter to his friend, Lieutenant-Colonel Robert Long: 'I was nearly going out to Portugal with Mr Villiers who is sent there as minister. What I was to have done there, & the cause of my being disappointed you shall know hereafter. All is going quietly at the college. The old humdrum routine. I am heartily tired of it but it must be born with for nine good reasons, a wife & eight children.'[6]

In Wellesley's absence, command of the 30,000-strong British army in Portugal fell to General Sir John Moore. Moore advanced into Spain, heading for Burgos, but before he had gone too far, he received intelligence that Napoleon had crossed the Pyrenees with a force of 200,000 troops. Recognising that he was going to be heavily outnumbered, Moore withdrew back towards the Spanish coast. He faced the French forces at Corunna, where he was fatally wounded by a cannonball to the chest on 16 January 1809. He was buried in the ramparts of the town, and the British army sailed home from Corunna the following day.

Wellesley, having been exonerated by the inquiry into the Convention of Sintra, returned to Portugal in April 1809 as Commander-in-Chief of the British army, just three months after the setback at Corunna. He was also appointed as Commander-in-Chief of the Portuguese army to form a combined Anglo-Portuguese force. Wellesley's friend, General William Beresford, took charge of the Portuguese army. Beresford was a strict disciplinarian and set about reorganising and instructing the Portuguese troops. He would later serve as Wellington's second-in-command.

The training of Portuguese troops in the methods of the British army continued. In May 1809, Villiers, who had been so eager to enlist Le Marchant's help the previous year, was still seeking his support:

You will learn how much we have suffered from the want of your assistance. I was not likely to prove in the wrong in any advice founded on my opinion of you but I can hardly tell you what the difference of our force would have been, had my opinions been followed, & had you, with a sufficient number of assistants, accompanied me when I first came to this place.

I have seen so little reason to change my ideas of the importance of your assistance that I have even restated them lately.

I am however extremely glad of the caution which I observed as soon as ever I saw the jealousy which was likely to attend your appointment & should have been extremely unhappy, if you had ultimately suffered as was too probable, by a recommendation founded entirely on your merit.

I shall be much obliged if you will have the goodness to send me the Statutes of the College & a plan of its Institution. The Government here are likely to adopt it & it is indeed the only chance of permanent improvement in their army.

You know my notions about the Sword Exercise & my ideas of its utility. I intend to have it taught here. If there are the means of having the book translated into Portuguese in England & if it could be printed there by Government, it would be very acceptable & be much quicker done than here.

I had a very small abstract made & printed (merely the words of command through the whole exercise). Perhaps a copy may be found in one of the open drawers under the left hand window in my library – but if not you could in half an hour make the abstract & it would be very useful. It was small enough for a waistcoat pocket & I gave one to every non-commissioned officer who was employed in the drill.

Pray excuse all this trouble. You know that we are neither of us of a temper to be indifferent to the success of what we engage in & therefore you must not wonder at my wishing to profit by your assistance.

You must not quote my opinions but we are here in the most intricate & critical situation imaginable in great immediate danger, but not without the greatest & most extensive hope.[7]

Le Marchant arranged for the translation of a shortened version of the sword exercise in London, and he sent it over to Villiers in Portugal.

In the summer of 1809, Wellesley led his army into Spain with the intention of confronting the French forces in Madrid. The decisive encounter took place at Talavera on 27 and 28 July, where the French were forced to retreat. The victory earned Wellesley the title of Viscount Wellington of Talavera. But he was soon to withdraw back into Portugal where he set up a series of defensive positions, the lines of Torres Vedras, just north of Lisbon.

There was a belief among some officers and men that the British army might well return to England. In August 1810, Le Marchant received a letter from Captain Haverfield, a graduate from the Senior Department of the Royal Military College, who was now based at Horse Guards, the headquarters of the British army.

> With respect to Portugal, I still adhere to my first opinion that the latter end of the Summer or Autumn would bring the troops home. I now think a short time will determine the fate of Portugal. But whether we shall maintain it or not is impossible to calculate without better information of the strength of the respective armies, but I am inclined to think the Peninsula Country will be abandoned, that is excepting perhaps Cadiz & Corunna. However if the French do not do it before three months have elapsed, we shall keep it another year. So much for speculation.[8]

The cavalry faced arduous and exhausting conditions in the rugged, sometimes mountainous terrain of the Portuguese countryside. The summers were extremely hot, the winters wet and cold. The roads were rough, in some cases non-existent. The difficulty in finding forage for the horses added to the hardship, with some of the cavalrymen resorting to selling forage for brandy or wine.

Wellington had never served as a cavalry officer. Yet he was an accomplished horseman, a skill he had learned at school in Angers, and he had personally led a successful charge of dragoons in India. He was aware of the limitations and exercised caution when deploying cavalry during the Peninsular campaign. He believed in keeping the cavalry in reserve in support of infantry. Wellington summarised how he intended to use the cavalry at his disposal in a letter to Marshal Beresford:

> I have always considered the cavalry to be the most delicate arm that we possess. We have few Officers who have practical knowledge of the mode of using it. Or who have ever seen more than two regiments together; and all our troops, cavalry as well as infantry, are a little inclined to get out of order in battle. To these circumstances add, that the defeat of, or any great loss sustained by, our cavalry, in these open grounds, would be a misfortune amounting almost to a defeat of the whole; and you will see the necessity of keeping the cavalry as much as possible en masse, and in reserve, to be thrown in at the moment when an opportunity may offer of striking a decisive blow.[9]

Wellington had encountered problems with cavalry operations during his time in Portugal and Spain. At the Battle of Vimeiro in August 1808, the first major engagement after Wellington's arrival, the 20th Light Dragoons launched a successful attack on French infantry, causing them to retreat. The Dragoons, in their excitement, continued their charge for over half a mile without a clear purpose or objective. It was then that the French cavalry, held in reserve, cut them to pieces, the Dragoons losing half of their men. Although the Battle of Vimeiro was a British victory, that particular cavalry charge proved costly. Out of a total of 720 British casualties during the battle, over half were from the 20th Light Dragoons.

On 28 July 1809 at Talavera, Major-General George Anson led a light brigade comprising the 23rd Light Dragoons and the

1st Hussars of the King's German Legion. Their mission was to attack a French infantry division on what appeared to be a flat plain, ideal for a cavalry charge. Despite coming under fire from French artillery, the light brigade accelerated from a canter to a full gallop. The French infantry had formed up into squares. All seemed in order until the British cavalry hit a ditch, partially concealed by long grass.

The speed of their charge was such that the men were unable to pull up their horses in time. Over half the brigade crashed into the ditch, with both men and horses suffering broken necks and limbs. Those who survived pressed on but were beaten back by the French infantry. The 23rd Light Dragoons suffered substantial losses. Out of an initial strength of 480 troopers that set out that day, 207 were killed, wounded or missing, with 224 horses lost.

During the Battle of Campo Maior in March 1811, a force of 2,000 cavalry, led by the 13th Light Dragoons, attacked a French siege train protected by enemy cavalry. Taken by surprise, the French cavalry scattered, leaving eighteen siege guns unattended. Instead of securing the enemy artillery, the British cavalry chose to pursue the retreating French for over six miles, in what seemed more akin to a fox hunt. The pursuit ultimately led them to Badajoz. In the excitement of the chase, the British cavalry had forgotten about the siege guns, which had been left unguarded. Those same guns were retaken by French infantry. Wellington was less than impressed.

> Their conduct was that of a rabble, galloping as fast as their horses could carry them over a plain, after an enemy to whom they could do no mischief when they were broken. If the 13th dragoons are again guilty of this conduct I shall take their horses from them and send their officers and men to do duty in Lisbon.[10]

Le Marchant's friend, Lieutenant-Colonel Long, bore the brunt of the criticism for the chaos at Campo Maior, although some considered Wellington's remarks to be unjust. The 13th Light

Dragoons argued that they had destroyed some of the French cavalry. They contended that the problem lay in the absence of support from the heavy cavalry, which had been held in reserve by General Beresford, Wellington's trusted ally and friend.

In any event, the examples above highlight the challenges of managing a cavalry unit during battle. The intensity of combat could often lead to a situation where both the riders and their horses, caught up in the excitement, would transform into an uncontrollable mass hurtling forward at breakneck speeds.

In spite of Wellington's reservations about the cavalry's absence of self-control and their ability to adapt to the challenging terrain, he welcomed the arrival of additional troops and horses in the summer of 1811.

> At the same time I am of opinion that we cannot have too much British cavalry. We can certainly do nothing without them in a general action out of our mountains; and, from all that I can learn, the expense of feeding the horses is not greater than it is in England. An augmentation of cavalry, therefore, should the season be favorable, and the country which is the scene of our operations should produce forage, will give us great advantages; and even if we should be obliged to keep part of our cavalry in the rear, from the want of forage, it will enable us to relieve those in front occasionally, and thus always to have a body of cavalry in good condition. I am therefore very glad that you have sent Le Marchant's brigade.[11]

14

AN INCOMPARABLE LOSS

A 148-foot French frigate was captured by the Royal Navy in 1794 and converted into a troop ship, HMS *Melpomene*. On 1 August 1811, it left Portsmouth harbour with Major-General Le Marchant and his staff on board for the short journey down to St Helens on the eastern side of the Isle of Wight. Anchoring offshore, they waited for a favourable easterly wind that would propel them down to Portugal. Accompanying Le Marchant was Sir John Vandeleur, also recently promoted to Major-General, in command of a brigade of infantry.

They set sail for Portugal on the afternoon of 10 August, with a convoy of some twenty transports carrying a division of the British cavalry. Also aboard the convoy were the cavalry and infantry from the King's German Legion, comprising officers and soldiers who had sought refuge in England after the French had occupied Hanover in 1803.

As HMS *Melpomene* approached Lisbon, Le Marchant was greeted by the spectacular sight of the imposing Fort of Saint Julian on the north side of the entrance to the estuary of the river Tagus. Just three years earlier, the fort had served as the headquarters and barracks for Napoleon's army of occupation.

It was now in British hands; an evacuation point for the British army in case of a reverse.

Sailing past several smaller forts scattered along the coastline, Le Marchant landed at Belem on the north bank of the river, with its ornate tower, ramparts and small turrets. It was here that sailors and explorers would return after their adventures overseas during the Portuguese Golden Age, flaunting their treasures and sharing tales. It was also from Belem that the Portuguese royal family had fled for Brazil in 1807 as the French army advanced towards Lisbon. The Portuguese royals were assisted, coincidentally, by Admiral William Sidney Smith of the Royal Navy, Le Marchant's old school friend from King Edward's at Bath.

The appearance of the British contingent caused quite a stir. Even though the local inhabitants had grown accustomed to the coming and going of armies over recent years, crowds gathered at the dockside to witness the arrival of the cavalry. While in Lisbon, Le Marchant was able to keep in close contact with his family back home, with the Falmouth-Lisbon packet ships carrying letters to and from England every week. He waited anxiously for news from his wife who was entering the later stages of pregnancy. The news he received was positive, the most recent letters indicating that everything was progressing well.

During late August and early September, Le Marchant's heavy brigade continued to assemble in Lisbon. The brigade consisted of the 3rd (King's Own) Dragoons under the command of Lieutenant-Colonel Godfrey Mundy, the 4th Dragoon Guards under Lieutenant-Colonel Francis Sherlock, and the 5th (Princess Charlotte of Wales) Dragoon Guards under Lieutenant-Colonel William Ponsonby. The 4th Dragoon Guards were the first to arrive, taking up quarters in Sacavém.

Next to arrive was the 3rd Dragoons. Prior to leaving England, they had been stationed at Guildford for the best part of a year. On 9 June 1811, they, together with other cavalry and infantry regiments, paraded in front of the Prince Regent and 200,000 spectators on Wimbledon Common.

The journey to Lisbon could take anything from two to three weeks, occasionally extending up to five weeks. Delays were not uncommon, transport ships sometimes becalmed for several days with no wind. This, though, was nothing compared to the rough seas of the Bay of Biscay during violent storms, requiring ships to adopt the practice of 'running under bare poles'[1] when sails would be stowed away.

The combination of the weather conditions and the monotony of the voyage heightened the feeling of relief when the troops could finally set foot on dry land. Captain William Bragge of the 3rd Dragoons provided a first-hand account of his passage to Portugal in a letter to his father:

> I saw two Whales spouting Water close to the Vessel, a Number of large Sharks and Multitudes of Porpoise, whose clumsy sport in the Water is truly laughable. Sea and Sky, Sky and sea were the only objects to look at during the Days these Watery Monsters remained below and as reading and writing is not easily managed by a Landsman at Sea, I found the Voyage tedious, tho' never sick or the least unwell.[2]

The 5th Dragoon Guards were the last to arrive having suffered a tortuous journey on their way to Portugal. Originally stationed in Colchester, they were ordered to Kingston-upon-Thames in June 1811. Like the 3rd Dragoons, the 5th took part in the review on Wimbledon Common. Their next stop was at Chichester, while their troop ships were readied. Those men considered unfit for duty were discharged, and a great many horses were sold off at auction.

Then there was the spectacle of the drawing of lots to determine which of the soldiers' wives would accompany their husbands on campaign. In 1800, the Duke of York had issued a Standing Order which allowed a ratio of six wives to a hundred men to travel with their husband's regiment, although many more would travel in practice. It was not uncommon for a woman to become a widow more than once during a campaign, since there was never a shortage of offers of marriage from other soldiers. Officers' wives would usually stay at home, although there were some notable exceptions.

On 12 August, the 5th Dragoon Guards marched to Portsmouth, ready to board their troop ships. The local inhabitants, showing their support, lined the streets, cheering on the troops as they embarked on their journey. The convoy consisted of three frigates and twenty-seven troop ships. It was not long before the ships were dispersed by a violent storm as they sailed down the English Channel towards the Bay of Biscay. A few ships ended up perilously close to the coast of Holland.

The fleet reassembled at Falmouth and resumed its journey, but once again ran into a storm. The ships scattered and headed back to Torbay for repairs, before eventually departing for Portugal. On arrival at Lisbon, several ships from the convoy ran aground on the sand banks at the entrance to the river Tagus. The ships were freed with the help of the crew of a British navy warship anchored off the Fort of Saint Julian. They landed at Lisbon on 12 September, precisely one month after departing from Portsmouth. Thirteen horses were lost during the voyage.

Le Marchant's brigade once assembled must have presented an impressive sight, comprising nearly 2,000 men, doubling the number of heavy cavalry regiments on the Iberian Peninsula. Captain Lord Charles Fitzroy and Captain Gabriel were Le Marchant's aide-de-camps, Captain Thomas Hutchins of the 3rd Dragoons his Brigade-Major.

The city of Lisbon, seen from a distance, appeared to be equally impressive. Its narrow streets and whitewashed houses climbed up the north bank of the river Tagus, with its splendid palaces and churches, 'the harbour and river, crowded almost with sails and boats, presents a scene truly grand and beautiful'.[3] Once in the city, the troops found the sights and smells unpleasant, heightened by the stifling summer heat. The population had grown, thousands of peasants from the countryside had flocked to the city seeking refuge as the French made their way towards Lisbon, reaching as far as Wellington's defensive lines of Torres Vedras. One of Le Marchant's officers described the scene:

> The city abounds in splendid buildings and chapels which are chiefly built of white stone, which gives them a lively appearance but the streets and houses occupied by the lower class are filthy and inconvenient, the streets narrow and badly paved, all the filth and slops thrown out of the windows of the upper storeys unto the street so that people passing along must be very watchful & sharp to avoid the contents of a vessel of greasy slops.[4]

The conditions in the horse's stables were far better than in the men's barracks. The stables were clean and contained racks, mangers and cisterns for drinking water. In contrast, the men slept on a basic wooden platform riddled with holes. They had to put up with a multitude of bugs, fleas, mosquitoes and 'whole squadrons of rats which often left the marks of their teeth upon the faces of those who lay down top heavy overnight'.[5]

Illness continued to be a problem, partly as a result of the poor conditions but also because of the excessive consumption of food and wine, in spite of repeated warnings from army doctors. By the beginning of September, the number of British soldiers falling ill had exceeded 12,000, and deaths in army hospitals averaged more than seventy per week. One cavalry officer took precautions: 'Rheumatism and Diarrhoeas are the usual complaints of the country but I trust by living temperately, wearing Flannels and avoiding Fruit to escape two Disorders which have already carried off Numbers.'[6]

Nevertheless, the city made a favourable impression on Le Marchant, as he received a warm welcome from officers who had attended the Senior Department at High Wycombe. They were able to introduce him to the city and its local dignitaries. Le Marchant was particularly fascinated by the area of Sintra, situated to the northwest of Lisbon, renowned for its stunning medieval royal palace. He took to his sketch pad.

It was not long before Le Marchant received the sudden, devastating news that left him inconsolable, a loss from which he would never fully recover. His dear wife, Mary, had died in childbirth on 21 August, while he was aboard the troop ship on its way to Portugal. Mary had retired to bed in good health, had gone into labour during the night, but after delivering a boy suffered from an internal haemorrhage. She was forty-six years old. The household servants woke Denis, second son and just sixteen years old at the time, who hurried to fetch the doctor. Mary's brother, Colonel Thomas Carey, quickly made his way from Colchester to High Wycombe, in spite of his ill health. Lord Carrington, Sir John Dashwood-King, Member of Parliament for Wycombe, and other friends and neighbours called and offered to take in the children. Tom declined. He thought it better that the younger children should be cared for by members of the family.

The same packet ship that had brought the disastrous news also carried a letter from Lieutenant-General Calvert, on behalf of the Duke of York. The Duke had written to Wellington recommending that Le Marchant return home to take care of his children. The rumour amongst his officers was that Le Marchant was about to leave Portugal. Lieutenant-Colonel Long, commanding officer of a light brigade, wrote to his brother Charles, 'A most melancholy circumstance, the recent death of his wife, will likewise deprive us of the services of my friend Le Marchant, from whom I yesterday received a sad epistle announcing his misfortune. Thus circumstanced, I have advised his not returning to this Country, to risk the existence so important and essential to his Family.'[7]

Le Marchant stayed in Portugal. Colonel Thomas Carey made arrangements for the three eldest children to continue with their education in England, while the five youngest would be cared for by Mary's sister, Mrs Sophy Mourant, at her home at Candie House in Guernsey. Tom proposed that Le Marchant stay on the Peninsula to advance his career, a suggestion to which Le Marchant agreed.

Mary Le Marchant was laid to rest in All Saints Parish Church, High Wycombe. The funeral was attended by many officers, friends and neighbours. Colonel Thomas Carey and Denis were the chief mourners. The following day, Denis, Mary, Caroline, Helen, Anna Maria and the baby, his nurse, and the governess, left for Guernsey. The eldest son, Carey, stayed with his regiment. Katherine continued her studies with her private tutor in Marlow, while John remained with Charles Stanhope until it was time for him to return to school.

Le Marchant wrote to Lord Wellington on 15 September from Lisbon, expressing gratitude for the offer to return to England to attend to his children. He withdrew his application for leave, now that they had been placed in proper care.

Le Marchant would never forget the debt that he owed to his sister-in-law, Sophy. He later explained to his son Carey:

> God knows our obligations to her are boundless. We never can repay her great generosity & kindness in taking your brother and sisters in the moment of our distress. I have insisted that her noble heart may not lead her to make sacrifices beyond what are reasonable sacrifices to friendship. She wants to keep the five children, governess & servants in her house, as her own. This was quite inadvisable, I have desired that accommodation may be obtained in the way of a cottage or lodgings near to Candie, where Sophy may give them her superintendence.
>
> It is by far better that they should be in Guernsey under the care of friends, tho' without good masters, than near London left to a governess. They are at that early age when the best masters are not indispensable, and by the time that such masters are required it is probable that I should have returned home as the war in this country cannot be of many years duration, owing to the enormous expense of Blood that it is to Both Parties.[8]

15

JOURNEY THROUGH PORTUGAL

Le Marchant and his heavy brigade left Lisbon to join Wellington's main army in winter quarters in northern Portugal. The men were delighted to have exchanged the poor conditions of the barracks in Lisbon for the fresh air of the countryside, and the relative luxury of resting under a tree on a bed of soft grass. They had now reached a beautiful area of Portugal in the shadow of the Serra de Estrela, the highest mountain range in the country. 'The surrounding is very pleasant, being diversified with woods, rivers, shrubs and vineyards, everything smelt sweet and refreshing after so long on board of ship annoyed by the disagreeable stench from the horses and the polluted and filthy streets of Lisbon.'[1]

As the brigade pressed deeper into Portugal, they began to see the desolation left behind by the French army. After a ten-day march, during which they were delayed by persistent heavy rainfall, they reached Abrantes on 17 September 1811. Abrantes, a fortified town situated on a hillside, provided commanding views over the river Tagus and the surrounding countryside. Captain William Bragge, a junior officer in the 3rd Dragoons, vividly described the devastation they encountered:

> Whole Villages without any Inhabitant and Towns, which were two Years ago in the utmost Prosperity, are now the residence of a few wretched Inhabitants whose countenances betray the greatest Misery. At Santarem 11 Convents and 8 Churches fell a Victim to the French, who have been guilty of the most wanton Mischief, such as tearing down Altar Pieces and Tombs so perfectly useless to them.[2]

In mid-October, Le Marchant accompanied the 3rd Dragoons as they moved from Abrantes to Castelo Branco, close to Wellington's main army. They settled into winter quarters and would remain there for the rest of the year. While acknowledging Le Marchant's achievement in founding the Royal Military College, some of his officers harboured doubts about his ability to lead them in battle. Captain Bragge wrote to his father, 'General Le Marchant marched part of the Way hither with our Squadron and regularly treated us with dinners. He is a pleasant Man, highly accomplished and a great Theoretical Warrior, but I greatly fear we shall in him experience how very much Practise exceeds Theory.'[3]

While stationed at Castelo Branco, Le Marchant became acquainted with some of the local dignitaries, including the Portuguese General Carlos Frederico Lecor, the military governor of the area. He also became friends with the Spanish General Don Miguel de Alava. Remarkably, General Alava had fought for the French against the British at Trafalgar in 1805, and then for the British against the French in both the Peninsular War and the Battle of Waterloo in 1815.

Amidst the demands of his day-to-day activities, Le Marchant continued to mourn the loss of his dear wife, and he remained deeply concerned about the well-being of his children. In early October, he wrote a letter to his daughter, Katherine:

> My Dear Katherine,
>
> I have not been able to write to you before this, the melancholy & incomparable loss that we have experienced rendered me utterly

unfit to write, or for any occupation which required the smallest attention.

Your several letters have reached me up to the 6th of last month. I am obliged to you for your punctuality in writing, & I hope that you will continue to let me hear from you regularly, as I have no pleasure equal to that of corresponding with my children.

No misfortune could have befallen us equal to that of losing your excellent mother. Her conduct would have been an example for you to follow in riper years, but unhappily you are deprived of the blessing of such a mother, & must now depend upon your own industry & good sense in attaining those qualifications of the heart & mind that are necessary to render you deserving and good.

It is thro' the means of a religious & sound education alone that you can hope to reap any of those advantages that are denied you by the want of the example & advice of such a mother.

All that I have said so often to you of the necessity there was to profit of the moment, in devoting yourself to your studies is become more than ever deserving your attention. I intreat my dear girl that you will make every exertion in your power to improve your mind, by reading & study, and that you may also excel in the accomplishments of music & drawing. Recollect that time passes rapidly on, and when I return to England you will be the only one of the family to whom I can look as a companion.[4]

After her mother's passing, Katherine continued to reside in Marlow as a boarder under the private tuition of Mrs De Minibus, a very accomplished musician. She was the wife of a French émigré teaching in the Junior Department. Professor De Minibus had an intriguing connection. He had once served in the same company of engineers in the French army as Napoleon, who was then a Lieutenant. The professor described Napoleon as a 'dark designing uncompanionable youth'.[5]

Le Marchant would often emphasise the importance of education and personal development to his children, especially to Katherine. He was convinced that she could do no better in that respect than with her present tutor, Mrs De Minibus. He discouraged Katherine from too much socialising, which he considered a distraction, with the exception of visits to Lady Anne Carrington, the wife of Robert Smith, Lord Carrington, who lived in High Wycombe. The Carringtons had one son and eleven daughters, and Katherine would stay with them on occasions, sometimes for extended periods. Le Marchant ended his letter to Katherine with, 'Mine is a melancholy situation, & the good conduct of my children is the only consolation that I can hope to receive: do not disappoint me in this expectation, let me find you well informed & accomplished. It is by great application steadily directed that you can attain this end. Your affection for me will I trust carry you thro' all difficulties that you may meet with.'[6]

Le Marchant persisted with his drawings and sent them back to England. On one occasion he dispatched a package containing two small books and 30 additional sketches. He asked Katherine to share the drawings with William De La Motte at the Royal Military College, seeking the drawing master's opinion of his work. In return, De La Motte sent sketching pencils and paper out to Le Marchant.

Le Marchant's eldest son Carey was stationed with the 1st Foot Guards on the Isla de Leon, the island that connected Cadiz with the mainland of Spain at that time. Carey was born in St Peter Port on Guernsey, at the house of his maternal grandfather. He was sent as a boarder to a school in Berkhamsted, but after a year he returned home in poor health. When Le Marchant looked into what had happened, he found that his son, along with several other students, was suffering from malnourishment. The school was closed down.

Carey subsequently went to Eton and was then admitted to the Junior Department of the Royal Military College in April 1806 at the age of fourteen, when his father still held the position of Lieutenant-Governor. Carey passed his examination in November 1807 and later served with the 1st Foot Guards as an aide-de-camp to Lieutenant-General Sir Harry Burrard.

Le Marchant arranged a year's leave for Carey to accompany his uncle, Major Octavius Carey, who went with his regiment, the 10th Foot, to Sicily. The young man took the opportunity to visit Greece, Turkey and the Middle East, during which he spent time at the villa of Lady Hester Stanhope, the sister of William Pitt. Carey brought his father up to date in a letter from Malta in February 1811:

> The way that I pass my time is as follows. At seven in the morning my Italian master comes, and stays until eight, at nine we breakfast, from ten to twelve I read, and from that hour till one I draw or write. Should an opportunity offer for Constantinople, a place so few Englishmen have visited, I think I should be almost tempted to accept of it, and a prolongation of my leave of absence for two to three months while the Regiment remains in its present quarters might I imagine be easily procured. The money that I drew from you in Sicily I expended when there. The reason for my not drawing until the last moment was on account of the exchange which I was in hopes would lower. I have now drawn for £20 more. I hope you will not think that I have been extravagant.[7]

The trip was not all plain sailing, however, for while in Sicily he contracted malaria, took to his bed for ten days and was 'bled, blistered & had twelve leaches applied to my temples'.[8] That summer, he rejoined his regiment in the south of Spain.

Major-General Le Marchant was a prolific writer of letters and expected his older children to do the same. He would scold them if he had not heard from them in a while, even though it was not uncommon for letters to go astray on their way to the Peninsula. Katherine frequently wrote long letters that brought comfort to her father, while Denis was less communicative. Carey found writing a chore, but his father insisted that a willingness to write was essential for a position as an aide-de-camp or on the general staff, and in maintaining a social network. Otherwise, he would quickly find himself without friends.

The young man found life with his regiment at Cadiz monotonous, especially after the adventures he had experienced on tour. He complained that very little new or exciting seemed to occur there. He was desperate to join his father in Portugal. On 17 November he wrote to his father:

> I spoke to the adjutant on the subject of my going to Portugal. He says that if I serve as an A.D.C. or in any situation without receiving pay, three months leave of absence may be granted from the General at this place, without applying to Lord Wellington, through which means I shall be kept on the strength of this army. If on the other hand I am to hold a situation with pay, an application must be made to Lord Wellington in order that I may be put on the strength of this army. In one of your letters you mention that in the first instance you will get me appointed to the staff of one of your friends. If you could manage it I should wish to go with General Long, however just as you choose, the sooner I leave this place the better.[9]

Carey surely felt disappointed upon receiving the following forthright response.

> I told you my reason for not naming you to my staff. The money that would be saved to me by it is no light consideration. But I have never thro' life hazarded my credit for the sake of temporary advantages, & in this instance in taking you I should have involved your good name with the regiment which I am as jealous of as my own. I had likewise (by laying by for so many years) greater cause to seek intelligent and experienced staff. I repeat this to show that other men can & must naturally be actuated by similar motives in the appointment of their staff. Therefore the first & principal recommendation in a young officer is the faculty of rendering himself useful. You have not had the means of experience, but you have had opportunities of cultivating languages, the French, Italian & now the Spanish. I hope I am correct in the opinion that

you are tolerably strong in your knowledge of the two former, and are making considerable progress in the latter. As soon as you write to me that you speak and write Spanish, French & Italian sufficiently to interpret & be serviceable to a General, I can ensure you an appointment on the staff of this army. The means are in your power. Study hard, by it you will acquire the means of seeing service in a manner creditably to yourself, and of relieving me from the expense on your account which I am confident your affection for me must make you desirous of for the sake of the appropriation of that sum for the benefit of your Brothers & Sisters.

As my getting you on the staff would be upon the grounds of your knowledge of languages, do not deceive yourself in believing yourself more perfect than you may happen to be when you report yourself qualified as we should look silly were you otherwise.

Life, my dear son, is short and uncertain. You see yourself now with only one support left. How soon that may be taken from you it is impossible to anticipate. What a different situation yours, would you be left without parents. My ambition was and is to see you left in a line of service in which you might put to your way with advantage. With this view I gave you the education that you have received, & for this reason I encounter the expense attendant on the Guards. You have had advantages that very few young men possess in adding the experience and knowledge of other countries & cultivating the living languages.[10]

Le Marchant's insistence that Carey improve his language skills, particularly Spanish, might seem harsh. Yet the advice was well-founded since there was a shortage of officers in the army who could speak Portuguese or Spanish. It was especially important for officers on the staff, particularly those in the Quartermaster-General's department or as aide-de-camps, who would have most contact with local inhabitants. Some officers had set out from England with the best of intentions and tried to learn these languages during the journey to Lisbon. Others who had overestimated their ability were quickly found out as soon as they came into contact with the local population.

The winter months saw little activity. The brigade spent their time on patrol, escort and outpost duties ahead of the main army, keeping watch for enemy movements. Those out on patrol had a most interesting way of signalling the presence of the enemy as described by one cavalry officer:

> When the enemy appeared, the vedette put his cap on his carbine. When he only saw cavalry, he turned his horse round in a circle to the left; when infantry, to the right. If the enemy advanced quick, he cantered his horse in a circle, and if not noticed, fired his carbine. He held his post until the enemy came close to him, and in retiring kept firing.[11]

Gathering forage for the horses proved to be a particularly challenging task during the inhospitable Portuguese winter. Detachments of cavalry would leave their quarters shortly after daybreak, sometimes travelling over ten miles in search of food for their horses, and return after dark.

The local inhabitants were adept at keeping their straw hidden, after all it was the only source of food for their livestock during those winter months. Dragoons could spend several hours searching a farm, sometimes finding straw hidden under beds or having to move stores of wood only to find just a few days' supply for their horses. As the forage became even more scarce towards the end of winter, straw would be taken from inside the beds themselves.

As the winter wore on, the dragoons became ever more familiar with where forage might be hidden. And of course, having discovered a hidden cache, they would have to face the protests and complaints of the women. The men would often have gone into hiding, afraid of being taken as guides or being threatened to disclose where straw was hidden.

Le Marchant recognised the importance of securing an ample supply of feed for his brigade's horses and considered it to be as critical, if not more so, as providing his men with enough food. They could not fight effectively if their horses were not well fed. He appeared to be in good spirits when writing to his daughter Katherine from Fundao at the end of November.

> I always thought you a good girl, and the affection that I have seen from you has been unbounded. Your attentions for me convince me that I have not been mistaken either in the qualities of your heart or mind & with such qualities. Education alone is requisite to insure to you the situation in society to which you were intended by your Birth, and the rank which I hold in the army.
>
> An improved understanding obtains for you the esteem of your acquaintances & friends, and at all times a bad introduction into the best society, any other than the best, would be worse than none...
>
> I must tell you my dear Katherine that you write too much in a hurry in consequence of which you are incorrect in things being much within the compass of your knowledge which to strangers would operate to your disadvantage. To write correctly is requisite to every one above the common walk of life, in saying this I do not mean to find fault, because I am much pleased with your improvement, but it is to place you on your guard, that you might take more time in writing as well in respect to the hand as to the correctness of style.
>
> I had hoped to hear from you in French. It is now that you should acquire the practice of speaking it constantly.
>
> I rely on your readiness to attend to my advice and I look forward to your society hereafter as of the greatest comfort that I shall have possession of at home.
>
> My health thank God is good. The climate in Portugal at this season of the year is delightful, I am writing with my door & windows open without fire. The chestnuts are all fattened, the oranges are arriving at their full size, tho' not ripe. The olives are fattening.

> You would oblige me by doing your duty to your Grandmother to write to her occasionally, once in a couple of months. Tell her when you hear from me & of what I say on common subjects. Write to her of the children. It is an affection that she has the right to expect of you. I should add that you must write in French as she does not understand English.[12]

Besides commanding the heavy brigade, Le Marchant was given an additional responsibility as the President of the Board of Claims. The first meeting of the board took place at Fundao in December. The position of president required sound decision making and objectivity on his part. The Board of Claims was responsible for assessing all requests for compensation arising from the loss of horses, mules, and equipment. Le Marchant, as president, had the final decision on all cases.

Claims resulting from disobedience of orders, neglect or wear and tear would be rejected. Similarly, compensation for the deaths of horses and mules during the course of those frequent lengthy marches, or made on behalf of deceased officers and soldiers, would also be refused. And even in cases where a claim was successful, the applicant would only receive two-thirds of the total amount of the loss. Le Marchant would often sit down to this additional work after a full day's march.

Christmas of 1811 proved to be a difficult time for Le Marchant. Yet, he appeared to have come to terms with the misfortune that had touched his life and that of his children. In a letter to Katherine from Castelo Branco on Christmas Day, he concluded, 'This day is one of more than usual melancholy to me. Last year at this time you were all around me, & I was happy in the enjoyment of my Family. We all dined together & if you recollect our toasts, we were wishing to be all together on that day, twelve months. But alas what a difference! But God's will be done.'[13]

On the same day, he wrote to his son Denis expressing similar sentiments. After his mother's death, Denis had left High

Wycombe for Guernsey, but was now in London studying law at Lincoln's Inn. In his letter, Le Marchant began by admonishing the young man for not writing to his father often enough: 'I feel great affection towards my children, and consequently I am doubly mortified and distressed when anything appears like neglect or indifference on their part.'[14]

Over the space of three months, Le Marchant had received just two letters from Denis, a fact he was at pains to contrast with the frequent letters he received from Katherine. 'As long as I live, you will be certain of my most affectionate support in every rational undertaking, but let me entreat of you to make the most of the time present.'[15] In fact, Denis had written several letters to his father, but instead of using the normal packet service to send his letters, he had entrusted them to an officer for delivery. Le Marchant later apologised to his son, 'Your last letters have come to hand. I am sorry to have given you pain on this head.'[16]

As the end of the year approached, Wellington started to think about his next move. A cautious man, Wellington kept his plans to himself. Le Marchant added in his letter to Denis, 'Tomorrow I shall remove my quarters to Thomar, where a regiment of my brigade is stationed, and there I shall pass the rainy season, unless actively employed. Of this we know nothing, so properly are all Lord Wellington's movements kept secret.'[17]

16

SIEGE OF CIUDAD RODRIGO

During those winter months, Le Marchant made his way over to Wellington's headquarters at Freineda, a modest Portuguese town near the Spanish border. It was a poor, rundown village with a population of 200 people, located about fifteen miles from the French-held fortress at Ciudad Rodrigo in Spain. Le Marchant's quarters, although not the worst in the village, lacked windows and furniture, and had a leaking roof.

It was here that Le Marchant had the chance to meet up with several of his old friends and acquaintances on Wellington's staff, some of whom had attended the college. One of them observed:

> I found the General as active and energetic as when I had first known him fourteen years before. I was happy, also, to perceive that his temper had greatly improved, and indeed he seemed to have spared no pains to get it under his control. He once said to me, 'I have been all my life squabbling and quarrelling, and unable to get out of troubled waters. I am determined henceforward that no one shall have any just ground of complaint against me.' I thought this was being too hard upon himself, and could not help telling him, that it was not so much from defect of temper that he

> had fallen into these difficulties, as from expecting all men to be as eager and able to do their duty as himself, and treating them, in case he happened to be disappointed, as if they were the very reverse of what he had supposed them. If he would but adopt a more humble standard, he would form a more accurate estimate. I afterwards observed that my advice had not been thrown away. For no general could show more judicious indulgence than he did to his officers and men, or in return be more beloved by them.[1]

The winter months normally brought a temporary halt to the fighting. January 1812 would prove to be the exception. As Napoleon started to remove his most experienced troops from Spain in preparation for the Russian invasion and diverted others to support a French assault on Valencia, Wellington seized the opportunity to go on the offensive.

Sitting astride a rocky, oval-shaped hill, the old town of Ciudad Rodrigo towers over the river Agueda and its Roman bridge. The town is surrounded by medieval walls that were strengthened during the seventeenth century. This fortress was of significant strategic importance as it controlled the northern route from Portugal into Spain. Captured by the French in 1810, it was defended by a well-armed garrison of 1,800 men, under the command of General Jean Barrié.

The siege of Ciudad Rodrigo began on the night of 8 January. The allies first assault was on a small fort on top of the Grand Teson, a hill situated outside the walls of the city. The ground was covered in deep snow, yet the allies managed to capture the stronghold within twenty minutes. This gave a vantage point from where they had a clear view of the town and its defences.

Le Marchant had by now rejoined his men at Castelo Branco. On 12 January, he received orders to move his heavy brigade forward to support the army's operations and provide cover for the siege. Setting out from Castelo Branco early in the morning, the march to Ciudad Rodrigo lasted a challenging five days. The conditions were harsh, the snow and ice rendered the roads treacherous as they made their way through desolate landscapes and deserted villages. There were very few inhabitants, the houses derelict. The soldiers' water froze in their canteens.

The brigade established its headquarters in the village of Aldea de Ponte, still in Portugal and approximately twenty-six miles from Ciudad Rodrigo. The brigade carried rations and bundles of straw, which soon ran out. The hostile nature of the countryside made foraging difficult. The horses resorted to eating oak leaves and some of them died.

Faced with the prospect of spending long winter evenings in such discomfort, the troops set about improving their quarters. They built chimneys and fireplaces and repaired doors and windows, provided they could find wood. For much of the timber had been taken from roofs, along with the doors and window shutters, to make fires. In some towns and villages, residents would remove and conceal doors and shutters before the arrival of troops, to replace them once the army had moved on.

The conditions certainly gave ample cause for complaint, and the troops' only source of comfort was to be found in their efforts to stay warm. One of Le Marchant's officers described their efforts: 'The Village itself is truly wretched, but some heretic Soldiers having built a Chimney and Fire Place in the corner of almost every Room, it is during the present severe Frost by far the most agreeable Place after Sunset that we have seen in Portugal.'[2]

The home improvements made by their uninvited tenants were not always appreciated by their landlords. One was far from pleased when he found a new fireplace in the corner of a room: 'He said it was not the custom to have chimneys in their houses and that he would have the trouble of pulling it down when we were gone, or people would laugh at him for having two Kitchins.'[3]

The French had dispatched reinforcements to relieve the siege. Marshal Auguste Marmont, an experienced artillery officer and aide-de-camp to Napoleon, had been given command of the French army in northern Spain. Marmont, with a contingent of around 12,000 men, had just reached Salamanca. Wellington was well aware that he needed to take Ciudad Rodrigo before they got any closer. Spanish irregular soldiers, the first to be labelled as *guerrillas,* a diminutive of the Spanish word for war, *guerra,* played a crucial role in providing intelligence about French army movements. They formed a network of spies, and their role in intercepting communications between French generals proved invaluable to the allied army. It soon became apparent that French relief was only two days away.

The allies continued to dig trenches under cover of night as close to the walls as possible, braving the extreme cold. At least it was dry. The enemy responded by hurling fireballs down from the ramparts to illuminate the area while keeping up a relentless barrage of musket fire. A cavalry officer described the scene: 'The weather was particularly favourable, the frost continued the whole time. This made the trenches dry and the men worked hard to keep themselves warm. Some of the Portuguese lost their fingers through cold.'[4]

On 18 January, Le Marchant carried out a reconnaissance of the area, in case the cavalry were called upon to shield the infantry from the advancing French army. His brigade took up positions on the plains below the town.

That evening, Le Marchant dined with Wellington, General Sir Thomas Graham, who was in overall command of the siege, and other divisional commanders. Plans were made for an assault on the walls the next day. Wellington thought it unlikely that the cavalry would be needed and ordered Le Marchant to stay by his side as they readied themselves for the offensive.

On the 19th, eleven days into the siege, two breaches had been blasted in the city walls. The order to begin the assault was given at seven o'clock that evening. Major-General Henry McKinnon's brigade led the attack on the larger breach, to the northwest of the town. Major-General Robert Craufurd was in command of the assault on the smaller breach to the north, while Portuguese troops attempted to scale the walls on the other side of town as a diversion. By nightfall the French had surrendered. The walls of the city still bear the scars of the cannon shot, as does the cathedral, and the repairs to the breaches made after the siege remain visible to this day.

Between 500 and 600 French were killed or wounded and over 1,000 enemy prisoners taken, along with 150 cannon and a significant quantity of ammunition. The allies lost up to 1,000 men killed or wounded. Major-General McKinnon was among the 150 casualties who were caught in the explosion of an enemy mine in the great breach. He was buried in the main square of the nearby village of Espeja. Those killed in battle were generally buried in consecrated ground only if they were Catholics. Major-General Craufurd's back had been broken by a musket shot. He died four days later and was laid to rest in the breach of the wall where he had fallen.

Le Marchant accompanied Wellington as they entered the town and was witness to the excesses of the allied troops as they ransacked the city. It took until the following day for the men to be brought back under control. He attended Wellington's interview with General Barrié, commander of the defeated forces. Le Marchant wrote to Katherine from Spain in late January.

> I am now in Spain where the manners & customs are so different from those in Portugal as the English are from the French. Tho' only on the frontier it is astonishing the marked difference that reigns.
>
> The Spaniards are cleanly in their houses & persons. The women tidy & domestic. Nothing can be more singular than the dress of Spanish women. In the next drawings that I send home you shall see what they are.
>
> We have been four months in Portugal & I recollect but two decidedly raining days. You will observe by the date of my letter that we are bordering on spring. The wet weather however will come & when it does it will be incessant rain.

I came here to the siege of Ciudad Rodrigo. It has been taken, & the army is to return to its former cantonments in Portugal. How happy should I be to have you my companion this winter. You would be my greatest delight because I am confident I should find in you all the information, virtue, & accomplishments that your years are susceptible of.

Countenance my dear Girl to improve yourself that I may have a motive to return to domestic life whenever my professional duties permit it.[5]

He was particularly happy that Katherine continued to enjoy the patronage of Lady Carrington.

Lady Carrington's notice of you is very kind in her, yet I am proud in believing that the attentions which she in the first instance showed you on account of our forlorn situation, she continues to pursue out of regard to your good & amiable qualities, the only certain means of possessing friends. She may have many opportunities of being kind to you, and you cannot be too studious in cultivating her esteem which is by improving yourself & satisfying her by your conduct that you are worthy of the society of her daughters, with whom she would never allow you to associate if she once discovered any defects. If you were idle she would fear that you would communicate the evil to her children. If vulgar or unladylike she would have the same apprehension. To be wanting in improvement & knowledge would be either presumptive proof of idleness or incapacity, considering the opportunities you have of being advanced in both. I mention this to show you how Parents reason in respect to with whom they allow their children to associate & cultivate.

You have a kind friend in her Ladyship, and I trust you will never lose that advantage.[6]

From Ciudad Rodrigo, Le Marchant's brigade returned to their winter quarters in Portugal, once again hampered by a scarcity of forage. Upon reaching Fundao, they found it to be a particularly charming town, little affected by the ravages of war.

The month of February was uneventful, as both armies hesitated to engage in combat. The 4th Dragoon Guards suffered from sickness and the relentless marching had taken its toll. Wellington had inspected the regiment the previous October, shortly after their arrival, commenting, 'I yesterday saw the 4th dragoon guards. Of 470 men, they could produce only 230 mounted; and these looked more like men come out of the hospitals than troops just arrived from England.'[7]

They were replaced by the 4th Dragoons commanded by Lieutenant-Colonel Robert Edward Somerset. Captain Bragge noted: 'We are all much pleased with a recent change in the Brigade, by which we lose the Fourth or Royal Irish Dragoon Guards and get the Fourth or Queen's Own Dragoons, the Regt with which we Brigaded for 3 Years at Canterbury.'[8]

Le Marchant found time to explore the area, providing him with a respite from the harsh realities of war and the concerns for his family. In a letter to Katherine dated 22 February, he captures the wild beauty of the countryside with the perception and appreciation of an artist.

> I am just returned from a tour, the object of which was to visit that beautiful mountain the Estrela. I was five hours in reaching Manteigas, the principal town in the Sierra, the greater part of which time was employed in ascending, such is its extraordinary height. The wildness of the scene exceeds all description. The tops of the mountains are seldom visible from below, being usually capped with clouds. The road is narrow, and only fit for mules, indeed horses would be unsafe. I can only compare it to riding on the cliffs at Serk, where a false step, as you know, would not be without its consequences. On my journey there it was a clear day, and generally the whole of the mountain was visible, and the view from it could be supposed scarcely to have an equal. The valley below, the beautiful river, the Zezere, and an immense extent

of country, were brought together in one *coup-d'oeuil*, where the largest hills and features of ground were apparently lost in regard to size, owing to the height from which they were seen, and the vast expanse of the horizon embraced. You who have never been on the Continent can form no idea of the different scale of country between England and this. There is not a greater contrast between our little islands and England.

The Zezere, the most beautiful, though not the largest river in Portugal, takes its rise in the Estrela. It is not supplied so much by springs as by the mountain streams, arising from rain. Half an hour's heavy rain having been known to sweep away above forty houses situated on the banks of the river. The rapidity of the current is quite wonderful, and in consequence, its ravages are great, and the country it passes through bears ample proof of its ruinous effects. Innumerable are the cascades that I passed in my journey, falling from very considerable heights among rocks and forest-trees the most majestic be imagined. Indeed, for miles are seen continual cascades from the summit of the mountain to the Zezere, into which the water comes rolling down with a tremendous roar...

Many parts of the mountain are of massive rocks, covered with moss of different colours. The heath and aromatic plants are in the greatest variety and abundance. Chestnut trees self-sown, growing to an enormous size on spots where there seems hardly soil enough for the most slender shrubs, the evergreen oak, the firs, and the mountain ash are scattered about in equal quantity and luxuriance.

The woods and caverns are frequented by wild boars, who feed on the chestnut; wolves, and foxes, as well as a small tiger. I have bought a skin of the latter, which I will send you as a curiosity. I saw none of these animals, but in very cold weather, when they are pinched for food, they descend from their haunts to the great annoyance of the villagers, and carry off cattle, and any domestic animals that have the misfortune to be within their reach.

Manteigas is the principal town in the Estrela. The houses are all cottage roofs, and only one story high. No regularity, no two in the

> same line on the same level. The streets are so ill paved, that you cannot walk and look another way without being tripped up by the large stones that are strewed about in all directions.
>
> On my return from Manteigas the day was not very clear, so that in the course of an hour I got sufficiently high into the mountain to lose sight of the valley, the clouds being very low. The weather continued very hazy for three hours, and I pursued my way in a thick fog, along a route covered with snow, until I approached the Zezere, when the mist suddenly broke, and I again came in sight of the surrounding country. It was like looking upon another world. Standing as I was in a region of the most dreary winter, a forward spring burst upon my view with all its gay and beautiful accompaniments. The climate and vegetation here on the 20th of February are as advanced as you have them in the month of May.[9]

Marshal Marmont, having learned of the fall of Ciudad Rodrigo, moved north from Salamanca towards Valladolid. Now that the threat of Marmont had been removed, at least for the time being, Wellington turned his attention to the fortress at Badajoz that controlled the southern route from Portugal into Spain. This was to prove extremely challenging.

The river Guadiana made an approach from the northwest difficult, and Badajoz was more heavily fortified than Ciudad Rodrigo, with thick, low-profile walls that offered the smallest possible target for artillery. The French garrison of 4,000 to 5,000 men had resisted two previous attempts by the allies to seize the town.

Le Marchant's brigade left Castelo Branco and arrived at Vila Vicosa on 5 March, a pleasant Portuguese town just across the border from Badajoz. It had previously been a summer residence for the Portuguese Royal family. The palace had since suffered at the hands of opposing armies that had in turn occupied the town. Even then, it was still in good enough condition to be used as a barracks.

The brigade took up quarters in the neighbouring villages. Le Marchant remained at Vila Vicosa while preparations were made for the siege of Badajoz. He used the time productively for training and drill of his brigade. Suffice to say, not everyone was ecstatic at the prospect. Captain William Bragge shared his feelings in a letter to his father:

> General Le Marchant has his whole Brigade within reach of him and has therefore begun playing Soldiers in order to prove the efficiency of some miserable awkward Manoeuvres which has himself been coining. I have no doubt they all occurred to Sir David [Dundas] but were rejected for others infinitely superior. Be that as it may, our Schoolmaster had the three Regiments out yesterday and would I have no doubt treat us with more Field Days should opportunities offer themselves.
>
> I sincerely wish the French could see the 5th Dragoon Guards in their present condition. They have scarcely a Horse under 15 Hands 2 Ins and their Men are nearly as tall as the Life Guards, the whole in as good order as when they left England and as they have never Trimmed or cut their Horses' Tails since that Time, every Horse had the exact appearance of a West Country Stallion. The Regiment at present has a most Formidable Look but a little Starvation and Work will I fear soon reduce them.[10]

The manoeuvres, discipline and practice imposed on his troops by Le Marchant would soon prove to be invaluable.

Le Marchant kept himself busy and while he concealed his emotions from those around him, he clearly had not forgotten about the tragedy that had befallen his family. He wrote to Major Birch on the 10 March:

> As for myself, my days have been woefully embittered by misfortune, and discouraged by disappointment, I have now little to look forward to. From Carey [Colonel Thomas Carey, brother-in-law] you will have learnt how my poor Children have been disposed of, it is

impossible to express what I owe to his friendly care of them, added to the unexampled kindness of his sister, Mrs Mourant. Whenever I allow myself to think of my family in their present dispersed & dependent state, I am made truly wretched. Still, whatever may be my lot I feel that I shall have done my duty to my country & to my family, and if I have not been more successful it will not be owing to any want of exertion on my part to merit a more fortunate issue. But I will not my dear Birch dwell on this gloomy topic, you know already everything that relates to my most private concerns, and I am confident no one participates more than yourself in my grief. I have now been six months in Portugal, during which I have constantly been on the march. I am now just arrived here from the North, having been present at the storming of Rodrigo, the most spirited enterprise that has been undertaken this war, & nothing could exceed the good order and judgment with which it was carried.

The troops are collecting fast on the left Bank of the Tagus, with a view to the attack of Badajoz. It is expected that we shall find the works considerably strengthened since we last sat down before it, added to the probability of a general action. I am in command of what is considered the finest Brigade of Cavalry in this army, consisting of nine large squadrons, rely upon it, they will make a hole wherever their exertions are directed.

I expect my son Carey to join me from Cadiz. I have not seen him since his tour in the Mediterranean, it is two years since we parted. What unforeseen events have occurred since we parted!! My time is exceedingly taken up between the duties of my Brigade & the Board of Claims of which I am president, and this is not to be regretted. I meet with great kindness from all quarters, not a single controling hand from any in this army, and I have reason to hope & believe that I shall make it out well with all whom I have any concerns with, which is no small degree of consolation and comfort. In the course of a few days it is supposed that the Cavalry will be posted forward, beyond the Guadiana as far as Villa Franca. I am told it is a fine country for the movements of that army, where it probably will have much to do.[11]

The siege of Badajoz began on 16 March, with Wellington's men wielding pickaxes and shovels, the muddy trenches inundated with heavy rain that would persist for nearly two weeks.

Before the siege started, Wellington had received intelligence that Marshal Nicolas Soult, one of Napoleon's most trusted commanders, was leading a French army north from Seville in the direction of Badajoz. Wellington dispatched General Sir Thomas Graham with a force consisting of three infantry divisions and two brigades of cavalry southward to Llerena to confront the advancing French army.

Those two cavalry brigades included the three regiments of Le Marchant's heavy brigade and the light brigade commanded by Lieutenant-Colonel Frederick Ponsonby, under the overall command of Lieutenant-General Sir Stapleton Cotton. Stapleton Cotton was thirty-eight years old, of medium build with a dark complexion. He took great pride in being immaculately dressed, even in the heat of battle.

It was as part of Graham's corps that Le Marchant's brigade forded the Guadiana river along the Portuguese and Spanish border. They headed to Zafra in northern Estremadura, southeast of Badajoz, from where Le Marchant wrote to his daughter Katherine, 'I am quite pleased with this country, it is in all respects superior to Portugal. The Houses & its inhabitants are cleanly, the cultivation & soil are to be preferred & the ensemble affords a pleasing contrast to what I had been accustomed to for some months before. Carey is arrived at Lisbon & on his way here.'[12]

The brigade remained at Zafra until the 25 March, then moved on to Bienvenida. That night, they advanced as far as Llerena with the intention of surprising the enemy. They were close to reaching the town undetected when one of their horses broke loose and during the ensuing confusion, shots were fired. The French, now aware of the presence of the British, withdrew. Le Marchant returned to Villagarcia. Over the next two days, his brigade was engaged in several skirmishes with the French, the rolling plains of the surrounding countryside a perfect stage for cavalry engagements.

On 1 April, one squadron from the 3rd Dragoons and one from the 5th Dragoon Guards, both belonging to Le Marchant's brigade, were sent on outpost duties in a wood near to Usagre. A private from the 3rd Dragoons deserted and shared their position with the French. That morning, the squadron's lookout reported that a sizeable enemy force was moving forward, with approximately 600 cavalry ahead of an estimated 1,500 infantry.

The two squadrons from Le Marchant's brigade advanced to confront the French cavalry. The order was given to charge, at which the enemy cavalry withdrew back towards their infantry. The retreating French cavalry then turned on the British, forcing Le Marchant's men to fall back several miles, where they regrouped with the remainder of the brigade.

As the sun began to set over the horizon, the French, facing superior numbers, withdrew. Le Marchant ordered his men to remain vigilant for enemy movements throughout the night. The encounter with the French cavalry had left its mark on the 5th Dragoon Guards. They lost twenty-eight men killed with thirteen wounded. The 3rd Dragoons suffered the loss of one man with twelve taken prisoner. Two days later, the regiments under Le Marchant were relieved from outpost duties by the 16th Light Dragoons and withdrew for a well-earned rest: 'For six Days our Horses have been constantly saddled and during the whole Time have not received a Mouthful of Corn.'[13]

The French army under Marshal Soult pressed on and reached Villafranca de los Barros, just two days march from Badajoz. In response, the allied force fell back to take up a defensive position at La Albuera, the site of one of the bloodiest battles of the Peninsular War in May 1811. Le Marchant's brigade 'passed the day on the fatal plain of Albuera, still white with the skeletons of last year's battle'.[14]

Wellington took Badajoz on the night of 6 April. After several days of relentless bombardment, the allied guns fell silent at eight o'clock that evening. A mist, accompanied by an eerie hush, enveloped the city for nearly an hour before the attack began.

The unrelenting rain and resolute defence thwarted numerous attempts to overcome the French garrison. Eventually, the allied troops resorted to scaling ladders to reach the ramparts, and then surged through the breaches in the city walls. The allied losses were severe with nearly 5,000 killed or wounded. Once the city had been taken, there followed a period of seventy-four hours marked by violence and looting directed at both the town and its local inhabitants. A cavalry officer observed:

> As soon as the troops entered the town, such a scene that night, and for the whole of the 7th, took place as was never before witnessed. The men got drunk, fired their muskets in the streets, wounding and killing many people, as well as their own comrades. Every house was plundered, and most of the doors opened by firing at the locks. The men had not the least respect for their officers, and if not of the same regiment, would as soon shoot them as no. All interference on their part was quite out of the question.[15]

In the aftermath, Wellington found it necessary to take severe measures to restore discipline. He directed a Portuguese brigade to enter the town and erect gallows in the main square. The worst offenders were strung up and flogged, prompting the others to swiftly vacate the town.

It was while at Villafranca that Soult learned Badajoz had fallen. Local inhabitants reported that he had vented his frustration by breaking all the plates in the house in which he was staying. Since his forces were insufficient to challenge the allies at Badajoz and unable to join up with Marmont's army to the north near Salamanca, Soult turned back south towards Seville via Llerena, followed by Le Marchant and the British cavalry.

17

SUCCESS AT VILLAGARCIA

On 10 April 1812, Lieutenant-General Sir Stapleton Cotton rode to the small town of Bienvenida where he received intelligence, most probably from Spanish guerillas, that the French were still at Llerena.

The French infantry, led by General Jean-Baptiste Drouet, Comte D'Erlon, numbered between 10,000 and 12,000. Drouet was a capable officer with a distinguished service record in several major battles during the French Revolutionary and Napoleonic Wars. They were accompanied by just over 2,000 cavalry under the command of General François Lallemand, a close associate of Napoleon. Stapleton Cotton's cavalry division included a heavy cavalry brigade led by Major-General John Slade, a light cavalry brigade under Lieutenant-Colonel Frederick Ponsonby, and Le Marchant's heavy brigade consisting of the 3rd Dragoons, 4th Dragoons and 5th Dragoon Guards.

Stapleton Cotton resolved to attack the French cavalry, which had advanced as far as Villagarcia. The plan was for Ponsonby's light brigade to charge the French from the front, while Le Marchant would circle around to attack from the side, aiming to cut off the enemy's retreat. Slade's heavy brigade was to be held in reserve. The success of the plan relied heavily on the element of surprise, depending entirely on a simultaneous attack from Ponsonby and Le Marchant.

Le Marchant and his brigade set off that night. Their route covered five miles of rocky terrain, forcing the troops to advance slowly forward in single file through the olive groves. It was not long before the 3rd and 4th Dragoons had fallen behind Le Marchant at the head of the 5th Dragoon Guards.

The element of surprise was lost when Ponsonby's light brigade initiated the attack before Le Marchant was in position. The French withdrew, regrouped and, realising that they outnumbered the light dragoons by two to one, turned and drove the British cavalry back towards Villagarcia. Le Marchant's heavy brigade was still out of sight.

Ponsonby's light cavalry retreated into a ravine enclosed by low stone walls, with the French in pursuit, sensing victory. As they closed in, the French commander, General Lallemand, caught sight of a small number of red coats from Le Marchant's 5th Dragoon Guards amongst the olive trees. Lallemand, appreciating the danger, reported back to his commander, General Peyremmont, that he had seen additional British cavalry and asked what he should do. Peyremmont, who had a low opinion of British cavalry and their officers, ordered Lallemand to continue with the attack – 'The officer commanding the British detachment must be a blockhead, and was throwing himself upon certain destruction.'[1]

The French resumed their pursuit of Ponsonby's light dragoons. Le Marchant lined his men up, then charged down from the olive grove at the left of the enemy. The French turned to face Le Marchant. Stapleton Cotton and the 16th Light Dragoons then leapt over a low wall and approached the French from the front. Ponsonby's light brigade, which had been so close to defeat, turned and joined in with the attack. Lieutenant-Colonel William Tomkinson of the 16th Light Dragoons described the action.

> We came down the hill in a trot, took the wall in line, and were in the act of charging when the 5th Dragoon Guards came down on

> our right, charged, and completely upset the left flank of the enemy, and the 12th, 14th, and 16th advancing at the same moment, the success was complete. The view of the enemy from the top of the hill, the quickness of the advance on the enemy, with the spirit of the men in leaping the wall, and the charge immediately afterwards, was one of the finest things I ever saw.[2]

The British cavalry pursued the enemy, who turned and formed half-way between Villagarcia and Llerena. It was on the plains of Llerena that Le Marchant led the 5th Dragoon Guards on a second charge, supported by the 3rd and 4th Dragoons and the light brigade. Tomkinson continued: 'They received us with a sharp fire from their carbines and pistols, and I had the misfortune to have my horse shot under me, but by dint of exertion I soon procured another belonging to a French Dragoon.' The enemy fled in the direction of Llerena, four miles away, with the British cavalry on their tails. The encounter had been brutal and fought at close quarters, 'The prisoners were dreadfully cut, and some will not recover. A French dragoon had his head nearer cut off than I ever saw before. It was by a sabre cut at the back of the neck.'[3]

Le Marchant was well aware that his cavalry could, at times, let success go to their heads. He knew from experience that it could be difficult to control their excitement, sometimes verging on recklessness. His brigade had marched fifty miles from Nogales before the battle, with only a brief pause where the horses remained saddled and constantly on the alert. Although Le Marchant wanted to halt the charge, Lieutenant-Colonel Tomkinson wanted to press on. Le Marchant did not stand in his way.

> The desire of General Le Marchant to halt after the charge, my urging the men on, the enemy being in confusion, and his acknowledgement that I was right.
>
> He said, 'Halt, and form your men.'
>
> I said 'The enemy are in greater confusion.'

'You must halt.'

'Must I call out, Halt?' I asked.

Seeing the general hesitated (he would not give the order), I called to the men to come on, and we drove the enemy a mile, in the greatest confusion, into Llerena.[4]

As the cavalry approached Llerena in pursuit, the French artillery opened fire, their cannon shot sailing over the heads of the combatants for fear of killing their own men. The British cavalry drew up and made their way back to Villagarcia with prisoners in tow, exhausted after a contest that had lasted five hours. One cavalry officer described the whole affair as 'the finest chevy I ever had in my life'.[5]

Le Marchant later wrote to Lieutenant-Colonel Long, 'To the credit of the 5th Dr Grds not a man remained behind during the pursuit, either in attendance of the wounded or to secure the enemy's horse, on the contrary the difficulty was to curb their impetuosity.'[6]

That evening, Major-General Le Marchant's brigade returned to Bienvenida and the following day set off for Santa Marta. His commanding officer, Lieutenant-General Sir Stapleton Cotton, hosted a ball that continued until daylight the next morning, after which the officers saddled their horses and proceeded on their march. The charge of the 5th Dragoon Guards, at the moment that Ponsonby's light brigade faced almost certain defeat, enhanced Le Marchant's reputation as a daring and decisive officer. The encounter was included in Lord Wellington's dispatches: 'I have only to add my commendation of the conduct of Lieut. General Sir S. Cotton, Major-General Le Marchant, and the officers and troops under their command.'[7] It was unusual for an officer to be commended in the same dispatch as his overall commander.

Le Marchant downplayed the whole episode, 'The affair tho' of no great consequence has brought myself & my Brigade acquainted with each other in essential points & I have reason to believe that we are naturally pleased with each other & the Division orders of this day contains the Lieutenant-General's thanks for the gallantry with which the troops were led on the charge.'[8]

Yet, he also felt that the 5th Dragoon Guards did not get the full credit they deserved for the part they played in the attack. He was disappointed with Stapleton Cotton's description of the battle which appeared in the *Lisbon Gazette*, and the report from the War Department published in several national newspapers. Le Marchant expressed his opinion in a letter to Lieutenant-Colonel Long.

> Sir Stapleton's account does not convey a correct notion of the attack, for you would suppose that the enemy were charged in front & flank by the Light Brigade & one regiment of heavy. When as far as my observation went, & from all whom I have spoken with on the subject, it appeared that the 5th Dragoon Guards broke the enemy by its charge, & the light cavalry then joined in the pursuit. By implication & not otherwise can you judge of the regiments most engaged. The 5th Dragoon Guards having 43 killed & wounded besides two officers, whilst the three regiments of light cavalry had only one man killed & eleven wounded.[9]

Le Marchant gave credit to Stapleton Cotton that the omission was not deliberate. Perhaps Le Marchant had learned from the disagreements with his superiors that occasionally marked his tenure as Lieutenant-Governor of the Royal Military College. 'I think him [Stapleton Cotton], too much a man of honor to commit these mistakes otherwise than thro' inadvertency. I have said nothing on the subject to him, we are the best friends possible, & I hope that the next time (should it ever occur) matters will be better told.'[10]

He also wrote to his brother James, giving his version of the battle at Villagarcia, one which again differed from the official narrative, to which he added, 'I trust to your prudence in not showing this account, as nothing can be more injurious to an officer than having any other account made known than the one transmitted officially. All others are always supposed,

& very properly, to be a puff of the individual in favour of himself.'[11]

Le Marchant was wise in asking his brother to keep his views of the battle confidential. Certainly, in the early days of the Peninsular campaign, some officers included too much information or criticised their superiors or fellow officers when writing to family and friends back home, a practice that was referred to as 'croaking'. Wellington was fully aware of the problem: 'As soon as an accident happens, every man who can write, and has a friend who can read, sits down to write his account of what he does not know.'[12]

Sometimes, the details from those letters would end up in the national press. Then there was the risk that French warships would intercept the Lisbon Falmouth packet ship. Even though Wellington was opposed to censoring letters sent back home, he did issue an order directing officers to refrain from including specifics about the army's size, positions, or upcoming plans in their letters. Wellington had written to the British Ambassador in Lisbon in September 1810:

> I must devise some means of putting an end to it, or it will put an end to us. Officers have a right to form their own opinions upon events and transactions, but officers of high rank or situation ought to keep their opinions to themselves: if they do not approve of the system of operations of their commanders, they ought to withdraw from the army.[13]

Aside from the disappointment in how the battle had been reported, the success of his brigade during the encounter had lifted his spirits. Le Marchant was undeniably delighted when his son Carey arrived at Zafra. Carey was a modest, calm, and gentle young man, with an oval face and a tanned complexion from his time in southern Spain. He shared his father's stature, standing at just over six feet.

Le Marchant and Carey left Zafra, heading north back to Portugal. Due to heavy rains, they had to pass through Badajoz to cross the river Guadiana. The siege had left an indelible scar on the town. Most of Badajoz had been destroyed with houses left in ruins. It made for a distressing sight. After crossing the Guadiana they arrived at Elvas in Portugal. The heavy rain persisted, causing flooding in the town as the water flowed down the steep, narrow streets. They continued on to Estremoz, a walled town dominated by a castle, then headed north in the direction of Niza, arriving on 21 April.

While at Niza, Captain William Bragge noted how the constant marching was beginning to have an impact on Le Marchant's men: 'Never were Troops so harassed with Marching as we have been since the first of January, having in that Time gone nearly 800 Miles and have now no prospect of a Halt although our Horses are worn to Skeletons and our Backsides to Thread Paper.'[14]

Moving north, Le Marchant took up quarters in the house of a vicar in Castelo Branco. Wellington had received intelligence that the French might threaten Ciudad Rodrigo, and that Marshal Marmont was consolidating his army in northern Portugal. Le Marchant's brigade was ordered to head further north to confront the enemy and continued until they reached Zebras, described by Carey as 'a pretty little village, standing on a hill covered with cork-trees; every cottage having its own vine, which formed a shady seat before the cottage door'.[15] On closer inspection, they found that the insides of the houses in the village had been destroyed. In any event, they went no further. The French army under Marmont had withdrawn into Spain.

Le Marchant then returned to Castelo Branco. After weeks of continuous marching, he caught up on correspondence with his children. He wrote to Katherine on 25 April.

> It is now ten months since I took leave of you. Time passes rapidly & whenever I may return it will appear to be a dream that I have been ever absent. It may not be long before that time comes, tho' I am not aware that it will be so, yet you should be prepared whenever it arises to join me as my companion & friend, for which you can be qualified but by an improved mind & lady like accomplishments…

> Carey is at length with me, and is now my aide-de-camp. He will prove very useful to me, perhaps more so than any other I could have met with, for he speaks & writes three languages well, namely French, Italian & Spanish. You perceive by this that he has not lost his time, and he feels the advantage of having attended to my advice.[16]

In a letter to his son Denis, Le Marchant expressed his distress at the state in which he found the local population.

> My return to the North of Portugal is accompanied with the deepest regret at the melancholy effects of the ravages committed by the enemy on the helpless inhabitants during our absence. Not a vestige of clothing, furniture, meat, grain, wine, or oil, have they left them, everything carried away or destroyed. Little do you, who have never witnessed the horrors of war, comprehend its destructive effects. I returned yesterday from my old quarters at Fundao, where I went to see the Lieutenant Governor of the district. He and his family had just come back from their emigration to the mountains, and found nothing but an empty house perfectly gutted, their cattle driven away, and, in fact, themselves left entirely destitute. A respectable inhabitant apologized, through a friend, for not calling upon me, having no clothes. Others of the most opulent proprietors, my acquaintance and friends, are I am afraid, equally sufferers. Whole villages emigrated, indeed, not a soul remained wherever the enemy advanced. The distress of these poor people during their emigration, from want of provisions, as well as on their return, cannot be expressed. I have not been more melancholy throughout the whole campaign than at beholding these scenes.
>
> The enemy has retired, and we are provisioning Almeida. What is to follow no one knows, to conjecture would be a waste of time.
>
> Carey gets on famously, and will make me a most useful aide-de-camp. We both enjoy health and strength, and stand well the fatigues of active service.[17]

18

DESTINATION SALAMANCA

The victories at Ciudad Rodrigo and at Badajoz meant that Wellington controlled the two main routes from Portugal into Spain. He now set his sights on Salamanca, which would provide a gateway to Madrid, then on to the Pyrenees.

Le Marchant received orders to take his brigade south. In early May, he reached Crato, a small town between Castelo Branco and Estremoz. Crato became his brigade headquarters, while his regiments were billeted nearby at Cabeco de Vide and Fronteira. And there they stayed for the rest of the month, allowing both men and horses to rest and refit.

The month of May turned out to be very quiet, offering a welcome reprieve from the exertions at Villagarcia in southern Spain, and the weeks of marching back to Portugal. Le Marchant took time out to sketch and write letters to family and friends. He wrote to Katherine from Crato on the 19 May 1812. It is interesting to note that Le Marchant once again stressed the importance of reading to his daughter. Like many of his contemporaries, he believed that children, including women from the middle and upper classes, should be well-read. This, he believed, would help them to participate in conversations on various topics and be accepted in social situations.

You have improved considerably in the style of your letters but I do not think you devote sufficient time to reading. I may be mistaken, but from your own account of what you have read it does not appear much, for the time that I have been absent nearly twelve months. You would feel mortified at finding yourself deficient in this respect with the young women whom you will meet with in life, bear this in mind I entreat you...

I hope that Denis will take care of my sketches, as I shall be much vexed to have them soiled or defaced. When he has done with them they are to be in your keeping.

It begins to be very warm here the windows & doors are constantly open. The sun is too powerful to be out in the middle of the day, unless there is an absolute necessity for it.

Since I have been in settled quarters, I rise at half past 5 in the morning, take a light breakfast at six, ride till ten, either coursing or otherwise. Then 10 to 11, engaged at a Second Breakfast, after which I am engaged on business till two, dress for dinner, dine at three, at six get on my horse & ride till 8, return to tea, and go to bed at ten. Thus it is I pass my time. There is no society here except among the officers. Inhabitants there are none with whom I could associate, so destitute are they of Education and Knowledge of the world.

I do not think I told you of my having visited Fundao with Carey, since the French had entered it during the absence of our Army at Badajoz. All the comfort that these poor people were in the enjoyment of but a few weeks before, they were now robbed of & in the utmost distress.

The face of the country was even different, all the cattle was driven away, & agriculture necessarily at a standstill. How miserable are the effects of war to the peaceable inhabitant, & how happy ought the People of England to feel for being spared this horrible calamity. Every article of life is intolerably dear, a chicken

> costs from six shillings to seven & sixpence. Bread enormously expensive, the consequence is that the people are nearly starved, which engenders fever, which is very prevalent in Portugal even in the most healthy parts of the Country.[1]

The relative quiet at Crato that month gave little indication of the build-up of armies in the surrounding area and what lay ahead. To the south of Salamanca, General Sir Rowland Hill led a daring raid that effectively destroyed the bridge at Almaraz across the river Tagus. The success of Hill's offensive prevented Marshal Soult in the south from easily reaching Marshal Marmont's army in central Spain.

One of the activities that kept the brigade occupied during downtime was hunting with dogs. At first, the officers used local dogs, but later, packs of foxhounds and harriers were sent over from England. Wellington himself had his own pack of foxhounds and would join in hunting twice a week. Carey wrote to his brother Denis in early spring:

> I am just returned from coursing, but without any sport. The day before yesterday we killed four hares. But the same luck is not to be expected every day, as the game is but scanty, and the ground being broken and covered with brushwood, furze, and stones, the dogs don't run well over it. I understand that we are likely to find much better sport in Spain, and certainly while we were in the neighbourhood of Zafra we had some capital runs, and saw abundance of hares. Altogether, I like the life I am leading in this country excessively, the constant change of scene is delightful, after having been cooped up so long in Cadiz, with nothing to do but garrison duty, which is, if possible, more tiresome abroad than at home.[2]

The month of June would see Wellington's army constantly on the move. Le Marchant received orders to join Wellington, who was assembling his infantry, cavalry and artillery for an assault on Salamanca. Leaving Crato, Le Marchant passed through Castelo

Branco and by 7 June had reached Caria, situated on the main road from Lisbon into Spain at the foot of the Estrela mountains. In Caria, the brigade left the Almeida road and turned right towards Cuidad Rodrigo.

That evening, they halted at Castanheira, a small hillside village. Two days later, they reached Lord Wellington's headquarters at Gallegos de Arganan, just across the border in Spain. The village, just a few houses, was now a hive of activity with over 40,000 allied troops camped in the vicinity.

It was here that all three regiments of Le Marchant's heavy brigade – the 3rd and 4th Dragoons and 5th Dragoon Guards – assembled on the banks of the Agueda river. By this stage, the men had become battle-hardened, tough and determined. Wellington took the opportunity to review Le Marchant's and Major-General Anson's brigades and the 11th Light Dragoons. A cavalry officer described the reviews: 'The regiments were in fine order, and strong. Sir Stapleton put them through some movements, contrary to the desire of Lord Wellington, who said he had no wish of the kind. After doing one or two things, the affair got confused, the Peer rode off in the midst of it, expressing what he thought, "What the devil is he about now?"'[3]

Around this time, Wellington received news of the defeat of a British cavalry brigade under Major-General John Slade at Maguilla, to the south of Badajoz. Slade's cavalry went up against the French General Lallemand, who had previously faced Le Marchant at Villagarcia. The British cavalry was successful at first, but then charged recklessly after the enemy, losing control and running into French cavalry reserves. The British were forced to retreat, pursued by the French for four miles until both sets of horses were completely exhausted. Wellington expressed his displeasure to Lieutenant-General Sir Roland Hill, commander of the campaign in southern Spain:

> I have never been more annoyed than by Slade's affair, and I entirely concur with you in the necessity of inquiring into it.

> It is occasioned entirely by the trick our officers of cavalry have acquired of galloping at everything, and their galloping back as fast as they gallop on the enemy. They never consider their situation, never think of manoeuvring before an enemy – so little that one would think they cannot manoeuvre, excepting on Wimbledon Common.[4]

On 13 June, the entire allied army crossed the river Agueda in three columns, each taking separate routes towards Salamanca. Le Marchant's brigade was in the column led by General Sir Thomas Picton, alongside the 3rd infantry division, Major-General Pack's Portuguese brigade and the 11th Light Dragoons. Picton had discovered an officer from the light dragoons asleep at his post while on watch. He was heard to comment, 'I always feel easy when General Le Marchant's men are between me and the enemy; they do their duty, and can be trusted; and I heartily wish the rest were like them.'[5]

Wellington had specifically asked for Picton to be sent out to the Peninsula, later describing him as 'a rough foulmouthed devil as ever lived, but he always behaved extremely well; no man could do better in different services I assigned to him'.[6]

The nature of the countryside had changed dramatically from the rugged charm of the Estrela mountains in Portugal to the expansive, rolling plains across the border in Spain. On 17 June, the allied army assembled just outside Salamanca. Wellington received information from the local inhabitants indicating that the French had left the city overnight, except for a garrison of around 800 men commanded by Lieutenant-Colonel Duchemin in three forts – San Vincente, San Cayetano and La Merced – in the southwest corner of the city. These forts overlooked the magnificent Roman bridge which, at the time, was the only crossing over the river Tormes in Salamanca. The bridge still exists today. The French had destroyed several buildings near the forts, including convents and colleges of the old university. They used the stone and wood from the buildings to reinforce the fortifications as well as leaving a clearer view, making it more difficult for the allied forces to approach.

The allies crossed the river Tormes both upstream and downstream, and Lord Wellington entered Salamanca that morning. The Anglo-Portuguese army received a warm welcome, with local residents trying to get close to Wellington as he rode through the city streets. Still, there were concerns among the population that the French were not too far away and might return. Those families sympathetic to the enemy had already left the city along with the retreating French army.

The splendid city of Salamanca made a lasting impression on the troops, especially the cathedral. Although the enemy had 'thrown a few shells into it'[7] it remained largely intact. The university, one of the oldest in Europe, was founded in 1218.

One of Le Marchant's junior officers described the city in glowing terms.

> The Cathedral, Square and some of the Colleges are the most Beautiful Buildings I ever saw, and not being exposed to severe Frosts or Smoky Chimneys, are as fresh and the Sculpture as entire as ever. I should conceive that Three of their Colleges were larger than Christ Church but the Quadrangles much smaller. Their Cathedral is truly magnificent both within and without, not so long as ours usually are, although richer in Sculpture. It had a very narrow escape of being demolished with the other Churches etc., but Marmont was graciously pleased to save it on condition of the Clergy paying a pretty severe contribution. The Cathedral was threatened as often as the French wanted Money.[8]

Le Marchant's brigade moved on to Cabrerizos, three miles away, to be joined by the rest of the army the following day. They took up a position on the heights of San Cristobal, with Le Marchant's brigade in the centre. On 20 June, Marmont advanced towards the allies with the intention of relieving the forts. A battle seemed imminent.

Lord Wellington held his position on the heights while Marmont's French army paraded below, with their regimental bands playing at full volume and drummers beating out a regular rhythm. The French artillery fired on the centre where Le Marchant was positioned, with little effect. Le Marchant's brigade lost thirteen horses killed, with several more wounded. There were no casualties amongst his men.

On the morning of 21 June, the allies readied themselves for action at the crack of dawn. However, Wellington was reluctant to engage in battle until the forts in Salamanca had been taken. The allied troops started the day in confident mood but grew restless as the hours passed without engaging the French. Some officers could not understand the delay. Carey Le Marchant expressed the sentiment of several when he recalled, 'If we had attacked the enemy, we must have annihilated him; we were so greatly his superior in numbers.'[9]

It was early summer, the sun rose high, blazing intensely during the day, while the nights still remained cool. Troops gathered up whatever wood they could find, the orange glow of small fires punctuated the dark around the camp. It was not uncommon for officers and troops alike to prefer sleeping out under the stars, rather than in uncomfortable billets in the company of fleas and rats. When resting outside, senior officers would get first pick of those trees that offered the best protection against the scorching Spanish sun. Le Marchant reflected on the conditions during the campaign: 'I have not halted a day in position since the first of last month, up at two every morning, sleeping constantly in the open air, with only a tree to shelter me from the heat and the dew. But this life does not disagree with me, and, thank God, I am so far in good health.'[10]

The siege of the French-held forts at Salamanca had made little progress. The allies had underestimated the strength of the walls, and the siege guns had soon run out of ammunition. An attempt to storm the forts using ladders on the night of 23 June had proved unsuccessful, with some reports claiming that the ladders were too short.

After receiving new supplies of ammunition, a ferocious bombardment began at around 3pm on 26 June, continuing throughout the night and into the next morning. The walls of the forts at San Cayetano and Le Merced were breached, and the two forts were taken by the allies. The red-hot shot from the cannons ignited the wooden roof of San Vincent, prompting the French garrison to surrender, fearful that the gunpowder magazine might explode. The French prisoners, six or seven hundred, were paraded through the streets of Salamanca, facing the anger of local inhabitants who would have taken revenge but for the protection provided by the allied soldiers.

The allies were now in complete control of Salamanca, and the jubilant inhabitants celebrated amidst the splendid illuminations of the *Plaza Mayor*. High mass took place, and the *Te Deum* was sung in the cathedral. Wellington hosted a dinner for senior officers and the noble families of the city, while the local council organised a ball. Neither event was as well attended as expected. Some locals opted to stay away out of fear that if the French were to retake the city, they might be viewed as collaborators with the enemy.

That night, upon learning of the forts' surrender, Marmont retreated in two columns to the northeast of Salamanca. One column headed in the direction of Toro, while the other withdrew towards Valladolid. Carey described the desolation left behind as the French army withdrew.

> He [Marmont] burnt and destroyed the houses and villages as he retired sparing nothing that he could injure, which has of course operated in our favour, and wherever we go the people receive us with enthusiasm, they curse the French, and show us the dilapidations they committed, and when a straggling Frenchman is unlucky enough to fall into their way, they never fail to cut his throat.[11]

Le Marchant, feeling the strain of the past few weeks, wrote to his daughter Katherine at the end of June from Fuentelapeña.

> I am too much fatigued by incessant marching to write you more than a few lines & I love you too much to pass you over in silence.
>
> For the last month the army has been constantly diverting its course to the North of Spain. The Spanish people of the North are very different from those whom I saw in the South. Nothing can exceed the picturesque appearance of these women & children. The women have their hair fastened behind in a kind of club with coloured tape, red is the favourite colour. Very large ear rings & necklaces of gold, a red cloth tippet that crosses before & fastens behind, edged with green or blue or yellow binding, a corset, the seams embroidered with black worsted & laced in front with coloured tape. A yellow cloth petit coat with a green or red border round the bottom. A brown or blue cloth apron with a border of cloth two inches wide round the sides of any colour they prefer. But at the bottom there are several rows of different coloured cloth one above the other. The shirt fastens round the neck with a silver button the same as men have theirs in England.
>
> The shoes are high heeled, laced in front & a large flap of leather that doubles over the laceing. When they wear a cloak it is of cloth. It is short & not much below the hips. It is worn over the head & a hat over it.
>
> When we are less occupied I shall make a collection of these most singular people. The men are not less striking in their clothes, but I have not time to write on this subject at present.[12]

The two armies now stood facing each other across the river Douro. Le Marchant established his headquarters at Nava del Rey with the advanced guard of Wellington's army. With both armies settled in their respective positions, Le Marchant caught up with correspondence with a letter to his eldest daughter, in which he looks forward to returning to visit his family. Dated 5 July, it was the last letter that Katherine was to receive from her father.

My dear Katherine
I have been so very much occupied ever since the army commenced its march for Spain that I have not been able to find time to write to many of my friends whom I have consequently neglected but to you I always continue to give a few lines.

The enemy being on the right bank of the Douro, leaves the Allied army a short repose & I profit of the opportunity of replying to your several letters.

I have told you very often that my regard for my children is in proportion to their endeavours to do my care of them justice, by their studying & attaining the accomplishments & education which it is fit they should possess.

I have not made up my mind whether I may not pass two or three of the winter months with my Family in England or Guernsey. It is most probable that I shall so that you have some months still left for exertion before we meet. I am far more anxious to see you accomplished than I have words to express. Let me see that you may bear in recollection the several points to which I have begged you to turn your attention. Your person, & carriage not to be overlooked, for the appearance, action, carriage & manner are all parts of an ensemble that belong & are indispensable from a well educated, well bred gentlewoman.

Beauty Education & Money are separately capable of obtaining an advantageous marriage. Money I am sorry to say is the most sought after, because the world is licentious. Accomplishments have an undoubted preference to Beauty, because the latter without accomplishments is insipid & makes no lasting impression on the sentiments of any but an idiot. As you have neither the Money nor the Beauty, your whole reliance is on an excellent education. I have said all this before, but I am not mindful of the time & trouble that I take to render you, my dear Katherine, everything that is perfect.

God bless you my dear Girl. I often think of you in my busiest moments looking forward to the pleasure of our meeting, believing me your most affectionate Father.[13]

Over time, an unofficial truce emerged between the two armies. It all began when allied soldiers were allowed to cross the river over to the French side to cut wood for building huts. In a surprising turn of events, hundreds of soldiers from both armies bathed together in the river, sometimes exchanging rations or sharing biscuits and rum. The cavalry brought their horses down the banks to drink from the river.

The camaraderie came to an end on the evening of 12 July, around the time that Marmont received reinforcements that would put his army on an equal footing with Wellington's. As they parted ways, soldiers from both sides bade each other farewell, with the French officers saying, 'We have met, and have been for some time friends. We are about to separate, and may meet as enemies. As friends we received each other warmly, as enemies we shall do the same.'[14]

The two armies now faced each other for nearly a fortnight on either side of the river Douro, each army keeping a cautious watch on the other. 'For the first Day or two we lived here very peaceably and had only a small Picquet out at Night, but as the French are expected to cross the River in order to serve it out to Lord Wellington, we are turned out bag and Baggage every Night at Ten, Breakfast on Beef and Onions at 4 in the Morning and afterwards go to Bed until evening.'[15]

It was now that Marmont went on the offensive. His army executed a number of manoeuvres designed to confuse Wellington as to where the French would cross the river Douro. His intention was to put pressure on Wellington by threatening to outflank him, potentially cutting off communications and supply lines. The allies responded to every French movement. Both commanders anxiously sought an opening, waiting for a mistake from the other side, like two grandmasters playing chess. Wellington started to think about withdrawing back into Portugal.

On the night of 16 July, Marmont crossed the Douro near the town of Toro, catching Wellington by surprise. Le Marchant's brigade, acting as the rearguard, engaged with the advancing

French cavalry on the wide-open plains north of Salamanca. Le Marchant, at the head of the 3rd Dragoons, rushed to the aid of the King's German Legion, who were struggling to fend off the French cavalry. On the morning of 18 July, skirmishes took place, keeping the French in check and resulting in the loss of three or four hundred men on both sides. Le Marchant left Nava del Rey for Fuentelapeña, then received orders to follow Wellington to Alaejos.

At sunrise on 20 July, both armies lined up against each other in order of battle. The French continued moving southwards along the meandering streams of the Guareña river. Throughout the day, both armies marched in parallel along their respective hills. A combined total of one hundred thousand troops strode in unison, often in view of each other and occasionally within musket range. Not a shot was fired. It was a brilliant and colourful spectacle, with little indication of the dreadful scenes that would soon unfold.

Wellington believed that the French army, although comparable in numbers to his own, held the advantage, certainly in terms of artillery. He anticipated that King Joseph's army, consisting of around 14,000 troops with a significant cavalry presence, would soon arrive to reinforce Marmont's forces.

On the 21st, the eve of the Battle of Salamanca, Wellington wrote to Henry Bathurst, Secretary of State for War and the Colonies, from Cabrerizos. 'I have therefore determined to cross the Tormes, if the Enemy should; to cover Salamanca as long as I can; and above all not to give up our communications with Ciudad Rodrigo; and not to fight an action unless under very advantageous circumstances, or it should become absolutely necessary.'[16]

19

THE DECISIVE BATTLE

On 21 July, both armies had reached the river Tormes to the west of Salamanca. The allied infantry occupied the high ground, with the cavalry on the broad plains below. Le Marchant rode along the grassland with his brigade, at times almost within touching distance of the enemy.

That afternoon, Le Marchant arrived at the village of Cabrerizos on the north bank of the river. It was here that he took a break from the rigours of the preceding weeks to complete a sketch of the countryside with the city of Salamanca in the background. His brigade crossed the river later that day and made camp in the vicinity.

In the dead of night, the soldiers were rudely awakened by a deafening crash, sending alarm through the ranks. Some feared they were under attack. Lieutenant William Grattan of the 3rd infantry division recorded the event:

> The evening of the 21st of July was calm, and appeared settled, but persons well versed in those symptoms on the horizon which were unobserved by others (who were unacquainted with their meaning, or so intensely occupied with the anticipations of the

events which the morrow was to produce that they did not remark them) pronounced that a hurricane was not distant.

Later in the night a storm arose, and the wind howled in long and bitter gusts. This was succeeded by peals of thunder and flashes of lightning, so loud and vivid, that the horses of the cavalry, which were ready saddled, took alarm, and forcing the pickets which held them, ran away affrighted in every direction. The thunder rolled in rattling peals, the lightning darted through the black and almost suffocating atmosphere, and presented to the view of the soldiers of the two armies the horses as they ran about from regiment to regiment, or allowed themselves to be led back to their bivouac by the troopers to whom they belonged. The vivid flashes of lightning, which seemed to rest upon the grass, for a few moments wholly illuminated the plain, and the succeeding flashes occurred with such rapidity, that a constant blaze filled the space occupied by both armies. It was long before the horses could be secured, and some in the confusion ran away amongst the enemy's line, and were lost. By midnight the storm began to abate, and towards morning it was evidently going farther. The lightning flashed at a distance through the horizon; the rain fell in torrents, and the soldiers of both armies were drenched to the skin before the hurricane had abated. Towards five o'clock the storm was partially over, and by six the dusky vapour which had before veiled the sun disappeared, and showed the two armies standing in the array they had been placed the evening before.[1]

In the midst of the chaos, Lieutenant-Colonel James Dalbiac of the 4th Dragoons in Le Marchant's brigade was lying beside his wife. Awoken by the startled horses running amok, he picked his wife up and got her to safety under a nearby gun carriage. Susanna Dalbiac was one of several wives who had joined their husbands. Most officers' wives who had travelled might have opted to stay in the relative comfort of Lisbon while their husbands were in the field. Not so Susanna Dalbiac. She had journeyed to the Peninsula in 1810 to nurse her husband after he had been taken ill. She accompanied him for the remainder of the campaign.

I am standing atop a ridge near the village of Calvarrasa de Arriba, to the south of Salamanca. It is here that the battle began. The landscape stretches out before me, very much as it would have done during the Peninsular War, with its expansive undulating plains of reddish-brown earth, punctuated by long, low ridges and rocky outcrops that would have concealed an entire army division from view.

The area is dominated by two prominent hills, standing less than half a mile apart, the Greater and the Lesser Arapiles. The Greater Arapile rises slightly higher and stretches almost twice the length of the smaller hill. In the distance, a few sparse trees gradually evolve into a dense wood, which disappears over the horizon.

Today, the battlefield is a protected area. No development is allowed on this historic site. The fields, once witness to the chaos of battle, are now used for agriculture. Cows graze serenely where thousands of soldiers once fought and fell. A tractor tills the land, and farmers even now continue to unearth musket shot as they plough the fields, revealing poignant remnants from the past.

Looking out over the scene on a warm, sunny October day, there is an eerie silence. The only discernible sound is the faint hum of distant traffic, in sharp contrast to the deafening cacophony of cannon fire, musket volleys, bugle calls, the thundering of horses' hooves and the cries of men in uniform that filled the air on 22 July 1812.

Le Marchant rose early that morning and was already inspecting the camp. He found that the 5th Dragoon Guards had lost thirty-one horses, with eighteen men injured, not due to the thunderstorm but as a consequence of the careering horses. The troops slowly resumed their duties, soaked through, as the bright sun rose with not a cloud to be seen. At seven o'clock, the trumpet sounded, and Le Marchant, at the head of his brigade, led his men into position in the line of the army.

The allied army under Wellington comprised 50,000 men, including seven divisions of British infantry and four brigades of cavalry. Leading those brigades were Le Marchant, Major-General Anson, Major-General Bock and Major-General von Alten, under the overall command of Lieutenant-General Sir Stapleton Cotton. The allies could also count on the support of three brigades of Portuguese cavalry and a division of Spanish infantry and cavalry. Marshal Marmont's army numbered around 47,000, made up of eight infantry divisions and two divisions of cavalry.

Marmont, like many others, regarded Wellington as a defensive commander unlikely to seek battle. Assuming that the allies would withdraw back to Portugal, Marmont devised a plan to cut off Wellington's escape route. And true to form, Wellington sent his baggage train off towards Ciudad Rodrigo as a precaution.

During the night, the French had advanced as far as Calvarassa de Arriba approaching the heights and the small chapel of Nuestra Señora de la Peña nearby. It was here that fighting broke out at around six o'clock on the morning of 22 July, as the French attacked the allied pickets on top of the ridge. Wellington retaliated by sending two battalions to drive the French back.

At the same time, a foot race had begun between the French and the allies for control of the Greater Arapile, a contest won by the French. From the hill's summit, Marmont had a clear view of the surrounding countryside from which he could direct his army on the plains below. It was on this hill that he positioned his artillery. In response, Wellington claimed the Lesser Arapile and the village of Los Arapiles. The stage was now set.

Wellington had instructed Lieutenant-Colonel Edward Pakenham, his brother-in-law, to bring the 3rd infantry division and the Portuguese cavalry down from north of the river Tormes at Salamanca, in the direction of the village of Aldea Tejada, to cover the road to Ciudad Rodrigo. They arrived at around two o'clock.

As the day unfolded, the likelihood of a battle grew increasingly unlikely. The French maintained a strong position, and Wellington, with his army deployed defensively, was reluctant to launch an attack unless he enjoyed a clear advantage. That afternoon, some of the British infantry had started preparing dinner, and at about two o'clock Le Marchant sent the 3rd Dragoons to the village of Las Torres to feed both men and horses. Just as they were about to start eating, they heard the sound of cannons. They were ordered to remount and return immediately to take up a position with the other regiments of Le Marchant's brigade, 'the consequence of which interruption was a privation of food for the men & horses from the commencement of the morning's march until the evening's conclusion of the Battle, excepting what the men might accidentally have had in their haversacks'.[2]

It was now that Marmont made a fateful mistake. From the summit of the Greater Arapile, he could see the dust clouds from the allied baggage train, already on its journey west, and from Pakenham's 3rd infantry division on its way to Aldea Tejada. Everything pointed to the allies in retreat. Marmont ordered the infantry divisions under General Jean Thomières and General Antoine de Maucune to quickly march west to outflank the British and block their escape route towards Portugal. Eager to outpace the allies, the French infantry quickened their step until gaps began to appear between the regiments.

Wellington was having lunch, still mounted on horseback, when an aide-de-camp arrived with the news that the French infantry continued to extend themselves and were strung out on the right of the allied army. This was the opportunity that Wellington had been waiting for. He cast aside his lunch and galloped over to Lieutenant-Colonel Pakenham and the 3rd infantry division, three miles away at Aldea Tejada.

> As Lord Wellington rode up to Pakenham, every eye was turned towards him. He looked paler than usual, but notwithstanding the sudden change he had just made in the disposition of his army, he was quite unruffled in his manner, and as calm as if the battle

> about to be fought was nothing more than an ordinary assemblage of the troops for a field-day. His words were few, and his orders brief. Tapping Pakenham on the shoulder, he said, 'Edward, move on with the third division, take the heights in your front, and drive everything before you.' 'I will, my Lord,' was the laconic reply of the gallant Sir Edward. Lord Wellington galloped on to the next division, gave, I suppose, orders to the same effect; and in less than half an hour the battle commenced.[3]

After issuing instructions to the commanders of the other infantry divisions, Wellington made his way over to join Stapleton Cotton and Le Marchant. The success of the advance of the 3rd infantry division would depend greatly on the support provided by Le Marchant's heavy brigade. Positioned between the infantry on the right and centre, Le Marchant was directed to remain in place until the opportunity arose. The orders from Wellington were straightforward: 'You must then charge at all hazards.'[4]

Le Marchant bided his time as Pakenham's division circled around from behind the low hills, still concealed from the enemy. The French artillery opened fire, the heavy brigade just within range. Le Marchant ordered his men to dismount and lie face down to avoid the cannon shot that whistled overhead. It was at this time that they saw a riderless horse emerge from the French line and dash across the battlefield. Not until the horse had arrived did they realise that it belonged to the 5th Dragoon Guards, and had bolted during the thunderstorm the previous night. Lieutenant Miles recognised the horse as his own, fetched it back into the line and rode it during the rest of the day.

The sudden appearance of the British 3rd infantry division from behind the hills took the French completely by surprise. General Thomières had expected the allies to be retreating back to Ciudad Rodrigo.

Pakenham's 3rd division reached the top of the hill and was met with a barrage of musket shot. Undeterred, they continued to press forward towards the enemy: 'His centre suffered, but still advanced. His left and right being less oppressed by the weight of the fire, continued to advance at a more rapid pace, and as his wings inclined forward and outstripped the centre, his right brigade assumed the form of a crescent.'[5]

The British returned gunfire and charged forward, bayonets at the ready, forcing the French to retreat back down the hill. The French quickly rallied and prepared to counterattack.

> While Le Marchant was preparing to take a part in the combat, Thomiere, with admirable presence of mind, remedied the terrible confusion of his division, and calling up a fresh brigade to his support, once more led his men into the fight, assumed the offensive, and Pakenham was now about to be assailed in turn. This was the most critical moment of the battle at this point.[6]

With the British infantry under threat, now was the time for Le Marchant to act. With Packenham in the distance on Le Marchant's right and the British 5th infantry division on his left, Le Marchant issued the order for his men to mount.

The heavy brigade advanced over a front of about 600 yards, heading for the gap between Thomières' troops and Maucune's division. Le Marchant led his brigade at a canter until they reached the crest of the hill previously occupied by Pakenham's infantry. Le Marchant had already dispatched Lieutenant-Colonel Dalbiac ahead and posted lookouts to alert them of any obstacles in their path. On both the left and right the battle was fierce, with the French bringing up reinforcements in support of their comrades.

Le Marchant arranged his troops into two lines, riding back and forth ahead of them. The 4th Dragoons and 5th Dragoon Guards took to the front, while the 3rd Dragoons remained in reserve. The French infantry ahead numbered five thousand men. Faced with such overwhelming numbers, Le Marchant's men initially hesitated: 'The French fired hotly, the rank began to waver. Colonel asked what was the matter, men said they could hardly make their horses face it.'[7] Le Marchant now gave the order to charge.

The British infantry, who were ahead of the heavy brigade, were at first startled by Le Marchant's sudden advance from behind. They quickly parted, creating a gap through which the cavalry could pass. The effect of Le Marchant's charge on the French was devastating and left a lasting impression on Lieutenant Grattan of the 3rd infantry division.

> The peals of musketry along the centre still continued without intermission; the smoke was so thick that nothing to our left was distinguishable; some men of the fifth division got intermingled with ours; the dry grass was set on fire by the numerous cartridge papers that strewed the field of battle; the air was scorching; and the smoke, rolling onward in huge volumes, nearly suffocated us. A loud cheering was heard in our rear; the brigade half turned round, supposing themselves about to be attacked by the French cavalry. Wallace called out to his men to mind the tellings-off for square. A few seconds passed, the trampling of horses was heard, the smoke cleared away, and the heavy brigade of Le Marchant was seen coming forward in line at a canter. 'Open right and left' was an order quickly obeyed. The line opened, the cavalry passed through the intervals, and, forming rapidly in our front, prepared for their work.
>
> The French column, which a moment before held so imposing an attitude, became startled at this unexpected sight. A victorious and highly excited infantry pressing close upon them, a splendid brigade of three regiments of cavalry ready to burst through their ill-arranged and beaten column, while no appearance of succour was at hand to protect them, was enough to appal the boldest intrepidity. The plain was filled with the vast multitude, retreat was impossible, and the troopers came still pouring in to join their comrades, already prepared for the attack. Hastily, yet with much regularity, all things considered, they attempted to get into square; but Le Marchant's brigade galloped forward before the evolution

> was half completed. The [French] column hesitated, wavered, tottered, and then stood still![8]

Clouds of dust and artillery smoke enveloped the land, carried by a strong breeze, the bright blue sky barely visible. Le Marchant led his men in at an angle towards two battalions of retreating French infantry. The infantry turned and fired at the charging cavalry, but the volley of musket shot had little impact. Before the French could reload, the heavy brigade was already upon them.

Le Marchant's three regiments now faced up to a second line of French infantry who were better prepared to receive the onrushing cavalry. The musket fire from the French was better timed, and some of Le Marchant's horsemen fell, but eventually the French succumbed to the onslaught of the heavy cavalry's swords.

The British 3rd infantry division, having initiated the attack, stood aside and observed the harrowing scene unfold ahead of them as Le Marchant's heavy brigade surged into action. The French infantry desperately sought refuge. Grattan continues:

> The conflict was severe, and the troopers fell thick and fast, but their long heavy swords cut through bone as well as flesh. The groans of the dying, the cries of the wounded, the roar of the cannon, and the piteous moans of the mangled horses, as they ran away affrighted from the terrible scene, or lying with shattered limbs, unable to move, in the midst of the burning grass, was enough to unman men not placed as we were. But upon us it had a different effect, and our cheers were heard far from the spot where this fearful scene was acting.
>
> Such as got away from the sabres of the horsemen sought safety amongst the ranks of our infantry and scrambling under the horses, ran to us for protection like men who, having escaped the first shock of a wreck, will cling to any broken spar, no matter how little to be depended upon. Hundreds of beings, frightfully disfigured, in whom the human face and form were almost

> obliterated, black with dust, worn down with fatigue, and covered with sabre-cuts and blood threw themselves amongst us for safety.[9]

After a brief pause while the brigade regrouped, Le Marchant continued forward towards a third, larger body of French infantry. The sparse wood of evergreen oaks became denser as the cavalry advanced. The speed and intensity of the cavalry charge caused Le Marchant's three regiments to lose formation, yet they still managed to maintain a steady line as they charged forward through the trees.

The French infantry, standing firm, withheld their fire, then unleashed a well-aimed volley when the dragoons were but a short distance away. Almost a quarter of the leading squadrons were brought down. Captain White on Le Marchant's staff, Lieutenant Selby of the 3rd Dragoons and Captain Osborne of the 5th Dragoon Guards were among those killed. Those still on horseback broke through the French lines, sword against bayonet. Eventually, the French gave way.

In the midst of the chaos, Lieutenant Norcliffe of the 4th Dragoons found himself detached from his regiment and joined a group of men from the 5th Dragoon Guards in the middle of the enemy's infantry. Soon after, his horse was shot through the ear, and at the same time, Norcliffe took a musket ball to the head. He fell unconscious.

The excitement amongst Le Marchant's brigade had now reached such an intense level that he had difficulty retaining control of his men as they chased down the fleeing French. He now sent his son Carey to find Sir Stapleton Cotton and request fresh cavalry support for his heavy brigade. Le Marchant continued forward and saw no more than half a squadron from the 4th Dragoons, led by Lieutenant Arthur Gregory, approaching a group of French stragglers who had formed into a square among the trees. Le Marchant took the lead and charged at full gallop from the front. The French waited until the British horsemen were nearly upon them and fired.

Le Marchant fell from his horse. A musket ball had entered through his groin and shattered his spine. The French infantry fled through the trees as soon as they had fired, leaving Le Marchant lying on the ground where they had stood moments before. The dragoons, along with men from General James Leith's 5th infantry division, rushed to his aid but found him unresponsive.

Lieutenant Gregory, wounded during the battle, later wrote:

> I forget what General Le Marchant exactly said, but the purport was satisfaction at seeing things going so well. He certainly never thought of retiring, but waved his sword for us to follow him, and shortly afterwards he was killed. I forgot to mention, that in one of the charges he was seen to cut down six of the enemy. I did not witness it, but it was told to me on the spot by a Dragoon, who was there at the time.[10]

Carey had by now returned to the area only to meet a sombre line of officers carrying a high-ranking officer, motionless. As he drew nearer, he saw that it was his father. Major Clowes described the scene in a letter to Le Marchant's son, Denis: 'I can only say that our final halt was ordered by Elly, of whom I had learned the melancholy loss we had sustained in your father, of whom your Brother at the same instant came to inquire of me, and I referred him to Elly being too much affected to communicate the sad news to him myself.'[11]

Sir Stapleton Cotton arrived on the scene and regrouped the dragoons. Exhausted, they returned to their lines, one by one, passing the advancing infantry engaged in mopping up and taking prisoners. Later that day, Stapleton Cotton was accidentally shot and badly wounded in the right arm by one of his own sentries who mistook him for the enemy.

Lieutenant-Colonel William Ponsonby of the 5th Dragoon Guards assumed command of Le Marchant's heavy brigade. He remained at the head of the brigade until the end of the Peninsular War. William Ponsonby was killed at Waterloo.

It had been no more than forty minutes since Le Marchant's charge had begun around five o'clock that afternoon. The charge had covered three miles from where the 3rd infantry division had first launched their attack. Lieutenant-Colonel Pakenham, who had witnessed the charge of the heavy brigade first-hand, wrote about Le Marchant's remarkable exploits.

> The Fellow died Sabre in hand, giving the Most Princely Example, leaving with his Companions an instance of the utility of combined Movement and of the confidence to be infused in all ranks by the energy of a leader. Nine children have to deplore his fate and poverty accompanies their Sorrow. I hope England will relieve the latter suffering.[12]

The allies had been less successful in the centre. The 4th infantry division suffered under a barrage from the French artillery and struggled to make headway against the opposing infantry. Major-General Pack's Portuguese cavalry were unable to dislodge the enemy from the Greater Arapile. As the sun set, the French regrouped, holding their positions in the centre and launching a counter-attack that slowed the British advance. Wellington called up the 6th infantry division. It was nearly dark, yet the sudden bursts of light from the cannon, the flashes of musketry and the flames from the tinder-dry grass illuminated the entire battlefield.

Despite fierce French resistance, the allies eventually regained the upper hand. It was all over by ten o'clock that night. The French retreated southeast from the battlefield, finding refuge in the forest. In a state of utter confusion, both cavalry and infantry crossed the bridge at Alba de Tormes on the east bank of the river, taking advantage of the cover provided by nightfall. It was at Alba that Marshal Marmont had an arm amputated as a result of an injury sustained early in the battle.

The allied victory was resounding, with various estimates placing the French losses between 12,000 to 17,000 men killed, wounded or taken prisoner. While the allies suffered around

5,000 casualties. Le Marchant was the highest-ranking British officer to sacrifice his life during the battle.

Le Marchant led what is considered to be one of the most successful British cavalry charges of the Peninsular War. This was a classic example of infantry, Pakenham's 3rd division, and cavalry, Le Marchant's heavy brigade, working in tandem. The timing of Le Marchant's attack was exemplary and demonstrated how a well organised and well led cavalry unit could have a significant impact in battle. Wellington is reported to have said of Le Marchant's charge, 'I never saw anything so beautiful in all my life.'[13]

The destruction of the French left flank by the 3rd infantry division and the heavy brigade was key to Wellington's success that day. Of the four cavalry brigades in Wellington's army, it was the heavy brigade of Le Marchant that suffered the greatest loss. Of the 136 troopers killed, wounded or missing, 105 came from Le Marchant's brigade.

That evening, there were wild celebrations in Salamanca. The streets reverberated with the jubilant sounds of singing and music. Wellington's victorious troops remained on the battlefield that night, with some reliving the action and sharing their experiences. Others, exhausted, succumbed to well-deserved sleep despite the chill that night, to wake before sunrise with the arrival of mules carrying rum. The inhabitants of Salamanca came with provisions, laden with fruit and water. The soldiers, once refreshed, took stock of the carnage from the previous day.

> The men of Wallace's brigade [part of the 3rd infantry division] naturally turned their attention to the hill they had won, and to the flat space behind it, where Le Marchant's horse had so gallantly seconded them: at both they found ample food for reflection – for a horrible massacre had taken place there! Hundreds of human beings lying dead, or what is worse, mutilated in a frightful manner – horses mangled by shot or shell, running here and there in disorder, or lying in a helpless state, still endeavouring to eat

> a mouthful of grass around the spot which it was evident they would never leave. These beautiful animals, unconscious of the cause of their agony, looked at us as we passed them, and their sufferings touched the heart of many a veteran, who never knew what it was to feel a tear moisten his cheek: but a field of battle, after a battle, is not easy of description; it is a fearful sight, even for those who are the victors. Men looking after their old friends and companions – women and children seeking for their husbands or fathers – looking for those whom destiny had decreed that they should never again behold, except as lifeless corpses, or as objects more to be shunned than sought after, is a frightful but too true a sketch of a battle-field. Those who but a short time before were in the prime of life and vigour, now lying dead – rode down – trampled into atoms, with not a vestige of face recognisable, is a melancholy feature in war, and a trying sight to witness, much less describe.[14]

Lieutenant Norcliffe, who had briefly fallen into French hands, had his head wound bandaged by a surgeon from the British 5th Foot regiment on the battlefield and stayed out in the cold that night. Susanna Dalbiac had set off on horseback with a dragoon to search for her husband after the battle had ended. She eventually received word that he had escaped unharmed. Early the next morning, she got to work helping the wounded when she came across Norcliffe, her cousin. Mrs Dalbiac arranged for him to be taken into Salamanca and once there tended to his wound. Lieutenant Norcliffe survived.

The French continued their retreat eastward the next day. Wellington soon realised that pursuing the French without adequate supplies would put his victory at risk. He allowed his men to rest before continuing at a slower pace into Valladolid on 30 July.

The victory at Salamanca had a profound impact on the Peninsular campaign. The threat against Portugal had been removed. The French army in the south under Marshal Soult abandoned the siege of Cadiz after two and a half years. The French withdrew from Madrid, allowing Wellington and the allied army to enter the city in August.

From Madrid, Wellington headed north to Burgos, where he attempted to wrest control of the town from the French. After a four-week siege that ended unsuccessfully, the allies withdrew back into Portugal where they spent the winter. In 1813, Wellington returned to Spain, passing through Salamanca once again. In June, he defeated the French at Vitoria and later captured San Sebastian in September. Crossing the border into France, the allies reached Toulouse in April 1814, where Wellington learned of Napoleon's abdication.

20

A MOST ABLE OFFICER

The body of Major-General Le Marchant was removed from the battlefield and laid in a stable nearby. The heavy brigade, along with the rest of the army, had moved on in pursuit of the retreating French, leaving only a handful to attend the burial. Major Onslow of the 5th Dragoon Guards, who was a medical officer caring for the wounded at Salamanca, remained, alongside Carey Le Marchant and a servant who had accompanied Le Marchant from England.

Major Onslow conducted a simple funeral service, Le Marchant's body wrapped in the same military cloak that he had worn during the battle. He was laid to rest among the trees near the spot where he had fallen.

The loss of Le Marchant was deeply felt by his superiors, friends and the men under his command. Lord Wellington wrote to Henry Bathurst, Secretary of State for War and the Colonies. In his letter, he described the demise of Le Marchant with the classic understatement of a British officer, as a 'most gallant and successful charge against a body of the enemy's infantry, which they overthrew and cut to pieces. In this charge Major Gen. Le Marchant was killed at the head of his brigade; and I have to regret the loss of a most able officer.'[1]

Prince Frederick, the Duke of York, is reported to have wept upon learning of Le Marchant's death. Captain William Bragge of the 3rd Dragoons, the junior officer who had once referred to Le Marchant as the 'schoolmaster' and a 'theoretical warrior', had over time come to appreciate the qualities of his commanding officer. Bragge wrote of Le Marchant's death, 'We lost our General in a square of Infantry and in him we have experienced a severe Loss.'[2]

Lieutenant-Colonel Robert Long wrote of the passing of his dear friend:

> Thus has fate put the seal to the misfortunes of his numerous and helpless Family by cutting off, in one short year, both their parents. Unable to secure the provision he wished for in and deserved from his country, he opened a new career in this, and Providence has very soon released him from all worldly cares and anxieties. Poor fellow, he was one of the few faithful and esteemed military friends left me, but as they continue to quit the stage my desire to remain upon it diminishes, and a short time, perhaps, will bring us all together again.
>
> What will become of his poor ten orphans [Le Marchant had nine children], I know not. They have only God and a few friends left for their protection. I hear my lamented friend and his brigade behaved nobly, and the Cavalry throughout have merited and received Lord Wellington's highest applause and admiration.[3]

Carey took charge of his father's affairs. He paid off the servants and orderlies who had served the Major-General during the campaign. He organised the sale of some of his father's possessions, sending the proceeds back to England to settle outstanding debts. It was not uncommon for a deceased officer's belongings to be put up for auction, except for those items of a sentimental value, which would remain with the family.

In September, Carey found himself in Lisbon, making preparations to return to England. He had left his regiment, sold his horse and mule, and was offered a passage back home by

General Sir Thomas Picton. Carey planned to spend a few months with his siblings.

His uncle, Colonel Thomas Carey, advised him to stay with the army on the Peninsula, echoing the same advice he had given to Carey's father a year earlier. Grateful for his uncle's support for the family, Carey found it hard to ignore his opinion. He decided to stay on the Peninsula, also aware that returning to England would hurt him financially.

That autumn, he sent a package of his late father's correspondence to his uncle:

> I have this morning been employed in reading & sorting over those letters of my poor Father, which I Send in the above mentioned package. I have destroyed several letters which were of no importance & which only added to the size of the parcel. The act of perusing the accompanying papers brought back all the melancholy ideas, the heaving of the loss we have sustained, with the worth and excellency of the character whom we mourn. These sorrowful images were again engraved upon my mind. Some of the papers are not upon business but only show the friendship & esteem which some of the best men entertained for my ever to be lamented parent, they will afford you a few hours of melancholy pleasure. It is always pleasing to know that a person so dear to us was esteemed & beloved by worthy & good men.
>
> I enclose the sash watch of my poor Father. They will remain as mementos of one who was dear to us & to whom his family owed everything, for indeed I believe that few such parents ever have existed.[4]

Several of the officers who knew Le Marchant paid heartfelt tributes to the Major-General. Major Clowes, who had served for seventeen years in the 3rd Dragoons, wrote of Le Marchant:

> I had ever been on the most friendly terms with him & the feeling manner in which he expressed himself in explanation to me so

> short a time before his death made an impression never to be forgotten. Many times during our march have I been delighted to hold his horse whilst he was with his pencil sketching various views & objects, & if his family become possessed as I hope they have, his collections must be most valuable to them.
>
> He was much active & zealous in his command & strict, but not unpleasantly so, in his discipline, exceedingly hospitable, not a day passing without some of the officers of the Brigade at his table.[5]

Clowes was soon to leave the service. In spite of his significant experience on the Peninsula, he was overlooked for promotion in favour of a far less experienced officer.

Lieutenant Norcliffe of the 4th Dragoons wrote to Le Marchant's son, Denis:

> He lived almost idolized. He died regretted by every individual on his Brigade. You may perhaps think I am flattering, not so I assure you. I never can forget your father's manner when he wanted any of us to go with an order. He would lay his hand on our shoulder & say 'Will you be kind enough my dear fellow to go & do this or that' & we felt we could have gone to the end of the world for him. We never knew his worth till he was gone, & then the void.[6]

It was not just Le Marchant's fellow officers who mourned his loss. About three or four years before his death, while at the Royal Military College, he had opened a bottle of vintage brandy dating back to 1707, brought from Guernsey. After enjoying two or three glasses, Le Marchant corked the bottle and secured it with his personal seal. He wished to preserve it as a family curiosity. On leaving High Wycombe, he had left the bottle in a box with Professor Isaac Dalby, the first master recruited by Le Marchant at the college. The box and bottle remained undisturbed. In the early summer of 1812, Le Marchant had written a lengthy letter to Dalby. Just as the professor was about to reply, he heard of the Major-General's demise. Dalby wrote to Le Marchant's son, offering to return the cherished bottle to the family. 'The Gen. in his letter (which I showed to Captain Wright) desired my acceptance of a mahogany table that stood in the Library, with an injunction to remember the donor when it supported a bottle; the request, however, was totally unnecessary, as I cannot but revere the memory of a man whom I honoured and esteemed when alive.'[7]

In the House of Lords, Henry Bathurst, Secretary of State for War and the Colonies, 'proceeded to pass high encomiums upon General Le Marchant, who, very unfortunately for the service, fell in the battle'.[8]

During a vote of thanks to the Duke of Wellington in the House of Commons on 3 December 1812, a resolution was passed to honour Le Marchant:

> That an humble Address be presented to his royal highness the Prince Regent, that he will be graciously pleased to give directions that a Monument be erected in the cathedral church of St. Paul, London, to the memory of major general John Gaspard Le Marchant, who fell gloriously on the 22nd of July last in the battle fought near Salamanca, when a decisive victory over the enemy was obtained by the allied army commanded by General the Marquis of Wellington; and to assure his Royal Highness that this House will make good the expence attending the same.[9]

After some delay, the monument was finally erected in St Paul's Cathedral in April 1817, at a cost of £1,500. The inscription on the monument reads: 'Erected at the public expence to the memory of Major General John Gaspard Le Marchant who gloriously fell at the Battle of Salamanca, July 22nd 1812.'

EPILOGUE

Le Marchant left behind four sons and five daughters. After his estate had been settled, it was revealed that he had substantially depleted his wealth over the years. He left just under £500 a year to support his nine children. The government made a generous provision for Le Marchant's family through the Royal Bounty Fund, originally set up for the relief of those in distress, at the discretion of the prime minister. His eldest son received an annual allowance of £300, while each daughter was granted £120. The three remaining sons received £100 each.

Following his father's death, Carey, the eldest surviving son, initially served on the Peninsula as an aide-de-camp to Lieutenant-Colonel Robert Long, a close friend of his late father. He then secured a permanent position in the 1st Regiment of Foot Guards as Captain and aide-de-camp to Lieutenant-General Sir William Stewart. Carey fought at the Battle of Vitoria and at the siege of San Sebastian during the summer of 1813.

As the Peninsular War was nearing its conclusion, Carey was wounded in the foot at the Battle of the Nive in the south of France, as he rallied a regiment that was on the brink of defeat. The prognosis for his recovery was positive. Carey received a letter from Sir William Stewart:

> I congratulate you, my dear Le Marchant on the prospect which we now have of your recovery with whole limbs from a dangerous wound. Our truly good friend Mr Nixon assures me, by a note which I have received from Crofton that he will make a good case of you yet, altho' you must expect your recovery to be tedious. This, comparatively with what might have been the case under so severe a foot wound as you have received, is what you might naturally expect, & be grateful that no worse consequences ensue. I will not have you, for a moment, entertain so unkind a sentiment towards yourself as well as towards me as you one day were so generous as to express, that of leaving my staff on account of your probably distant effectiveness for duty.[1]

Carey continued on to St Jean de Luz where he received care from Colonel George Scovell, Wellington's chief cypher officer, and Mrs Scovell, long-standing friends of his parents. Scovell would later be appointed as Lieutenant-Governor, then Governor of the Royal Military College at Sandhurst.

Sadly, Carey's condition deteriorated. In such instances, it was common practice for surgeons to amputate a soldier's injured limb to prevent the onset of gangrene, with rum the only anaesthetic. As Carey's health worsened, there was 'regret that the limb had not been amputated'.[2] He succumbed to his wound on 12 March 1814, at the age of twenty-three.

Denis Le Marchant was born on 3 July 1795 in Newcastle upon Tyne where his father was serving as a Major in the 16th Light Dragoons. Within a few months, the regiment had relocated to Weymouth. Denis, along with his mother, returned to Guernsey, staying with his maternal grandfather, while his father headed to London with his plans for the Royal Military College.

By the time the family had moved from Guernsey to High Wycombe, Denis was five years old. He did not speak any English, only the Guernsey French patois native to the island. He attended High Wycombe grammar school before moving on to Eton, where he had difficulty settling in. Denis expressed an interest in joining the navy. His father agreed that he could serve as a midshipman on HMS *Diomede*, part of a squadron commanded by Admiral Sir James Saumarez, a relative of the Le Marchant family. Denis's hopes were dashed when 'on further consideration Sir James and my father thought me too young for the Navy and I was sentenced to remain a couple of years longer at Eton.'[3]

Denis later went to work for a solicitor in London but did not take to the profession. He thought about joining the army to fight on the Peninsula, only to be dissuaded by his uncle Colonel Thomas Carey. Denis's older brother, Carey, advised him to continue with law, emphasising that Denis would have to take responsibility for their younger siblings should Carey die in action. Denis described how badly he was affected when he heard of Carey's death:

> I almost sunk under this blow. Often was I told that no family had perhaps ever suffered more heavy affliction. The fall from prosperity to extreme adversity had certainly been very abrupt. The deaths of Mother, Father and Brother in less than 3 years, poverty, obscurity, neglect. The present was most sad, the future most unpromising. The family scattered, and embarked thus early on the tempestuous ocean, with no hope but in God.[4]

Denis went to Trinity College, Cambridge, and looking back, he would fondly describe his time at university as the happiest period of his life. He reluctantly left university before completing his studies to return to Lincoln's Inn to pursue a career as a barrister.

In 1830, Denis was appointed as principal secretary to the Lord Chancellor and later became secretary to the Board of Trade. In 1846, he was elected as a Member of Parliament for Worcester, served as Chief Clerk to the House of Commons, and was granted the title of Baronet of Chobham Place in Surrey. He published a memoir of his father in 1841, wrote a biography of John Charles Spencer, 3rd Earl Spencer, and edited Horace Walpole's *Memoirs of the Reign of George III*.

The third son, named John Gaspard after his father, was born in 1803. Like his brother Denis, he attended High Wycombe grammar school and enrolled at the Royal Military College at Sandhurst. He joined the 10th Foot as an Ensign in 1820 and served in the colonies. He rose to the rank of Major in the 98th Regiment. In 1835, he joined the British auxiliary legion bound for Spain as Colonel and Adjutant-General. He was awarded the first and third crosses of St Fernande and the order of St Carlos.

Upon his return to England, John Gaspard was knighted for his distinguished service. He became Lieutenant-Colonel of the 99th Regiment and served as Governor of Newfoundland, followed by appointments as Lieutenant-Governor of Nova Scotia, then Governor of Malta. In later life, he became Commander-in-Chief of the Madras Army before retiring in 1868.

Katherine, the eldest daughter, was born in Guernsey. She had been in education under the tuition of Mrs de Minibus in Marlow when her father was killed. A few months later, she left Marlow and joined her uncle Peter Carey and his wife in Ireland. Katherine later married Reverend Thomas Lewis Fanshawe, whom she met through her brother Denis while he was at Eton. The wedding took place at St Martin's Church, Guernsey on 11 October 1821. The couple settled in Dagenham, where Thomas became the vicar. They had six children, one of whom Katherine named after her father.

Mary and Caroline were placed at a school in Hammersmith where they remained for several years. The fourth daughter, Helen, wife of Henry Shaw Lefevre, passed away prematurely in 1833, leaving three infant children. The youngest daughter, Anna Maria, married a Daniel Tupper in Guernsey in September 1823.

The youngest of the children, Thomas, born on 21 August 1811, never met his father, yet followed in his footsteps as a cavalry officer. He became a captain in the 7th Dragoon Guards and later served as an aide-de-camp to Charles Poulett Thomson, the British Governor General of Canada.

Carey's letter to Denis, written shortly after their father's passing, eloquently expresses the deep gratitude the family felt towards their uncle Colonel Thomas Carey and aunt Sophy Mourant. The letter acknowledges their unwavering care and support in looking after the orphaned children.

> How grateful ought we not to feel to our different relations for kindness they have shown on this ever melancholy occasion. Tom has always manifested the greatest desire for our own welfare, & I am certain would do anything for us. Look upon him as a Father, & take his advice as coming from a parent. For Sophy, how are we not indebted to her, for the motherly kindness she shows to the girls. What would become of them but for her goodness I know not, whilst we labour under such afflictions as the present we must thank Providence for bestowing on us such kind friends.[5]

Peter Carey, who had assisted Le Marchant with sword training in England and then on his own in Ireland, forged a successful career in the army. In 1806, he married Julia, the daughter of General Sir George Hewett. The marriage proved beneficial for Peter's career. Sir George became Commander-in-Chief of the forces in India, taking Peter onto his staff. When Sir George became Commander-in-Chief of Ireland, Peter served as his military secretary.

Major-General Le Marchant was actively involved in selecting the site for the college and made several visits to Sandhurst to check on the progress of the construction work. Sadly, he never lived to witness the Royal Military College move to its new, purpose-built premises.

Barely two months after his untimely death, it was announced that the Junior Department was about to be relocated from Marlow to Sandhurst. The distance between the Junior Department now at Sandhurst, and the Senior Department still at High Wycombe, was considered too great. So the Senior Department moved to temporary premises in West Street,

Farnham. The last exam at the Senior Department in High Wycombe occurred in early September 1812, with just one officer taking part. The first intake of thirty officers arrived at Farnham in 1813, and the Senior Department finally moved from Farnham to Sandhurst in 1820.

After Napoleon Bonaparte's defeat at Waterloo in 1815, military spending became less of a priority. The demand for qualified staff officers decreased, leading to a reduction in the number of students in the Senior Department, which fell to just fifteen, with only two instructors. It remained so until the Crimean War, when the need for specially trained staff officers became evident once more.

In 1855, the Select Committee of the House of Commons on Sandhurst highlighted the decline of the Senior Department and recommended that Parliament allocate funds to restore it to its former state. The report suggested giving priority to those educated at the Senior Department when appointing officers to staff positions within the army. The Senior Department was renamed to the Staff College, and competitive entry examinations were introduced.

In 1947, the Royal Military College at Sandhurst was merged with the military academy for the artillery at Woolwich, to become the Royal Military Academy, Sandhurst. One of the VIP dining rooms in the original college building at Sandhurst is still named after Le Marchant to this day, and features items from the Sandhurst Collection in honour of his legacy.

As we have noted, in his youth Le Marchant exhibited a somewhat volatile temperament, a trait that he learned to control as he grew older. He matured and mellowed with time. He was a man of detail, as seen in the effort and thoroughness he put into developing his plan for the Royal Military College. While he could be a strict disciplinarian, occasionally leading to conflicts with superiors and subordinates, especially as the Lieutenant-Governor of the Royal Military College, he also showed some liberal tendencies. In his original vision for the college, he had proposed a 'Legion' dedicated to educating the sons of soldiers, a concept deemed too progressive by the military establishment at the time. And he ensured that the orphans of officers, even if they were the most likely to be expelled, were afforded a fair opportunity.

Le Marchant appears to have been something of a perfectionist, setting high standards for himself, his associates and even his family. This sometimes led to frustration when those standards were not met. When it came to his children, his second son, Denis, considered that his father 'had been a severe tho' never intentionally an unjust parent, but his affection for his children was deep, and he had no object so much at heart as their welfare'.[6]

In spite of the absence of significant wealth and family connections, Le Marchant achieved a highly distinguished career in the army. His promotions later in his career were earned through merit rather than purchase. His rise through the ranks was a testament to an innovative mind and hard work. His skill as an artist, which first brought him to the attention of senior politicians and the royal family itself, also contributed to his success. His skill as a cavalry officer was recognised by many. General Clinton wrote, 'Had he outlived the war, he would have achieved actions with the British cavalry that would have astonished not his country only, but all Europe.'[7]

Le Marchant personally witnessed the shortcomings of the British army during the Flanders campaign. Back then, officers were usually selected for promotion based on social status and wealth, rather than ability. This meant that both regimental and staff officers, regardless of their courage or enthusiasm, often lacked the necessary military competence required in wartime. The Senior Department of the Royal Military College was established to address this issue, aiming to equip officers with the skills required to effectively lead regiments, and qualify them for positions in the Quartermaster-General's and the Adjutant-General's Departments.

Motivated by the shortcomings of the British forces during the French Revolutionary Wars, Le Marchant initially focused his efforts on improving swordsmanship in the army and designing a new cavalry sword. But his greatest achievement was the creation of the Royal Military College, which eventually evolved into the esteemed Royal Military Academy at Sandhurst.

Several individuals played crucial roles in both establishing the college and contributing significantly to its subsequent success. General Jarry, drawing on his experience in training officers in the Prussian army, made a substantial contribution in the early days of the college. He was highly respected by Le Marchant. Prince Frederick, the Duke of York, who found more success as a reformer when Commander-in-Chief of the British Army than as a commander during the Flanders campaign, actively supported Le Marchant's vision for the college and secured its approval at the highest level.

Without Le Marchant's unwavering drive and determination, it is doubtful whether the establishment of the Royal Military College would have taken place, certainly not at that time. He overcame numerous obstacles and opposition to realise his vision of providing high-quality training for infantry and cavalry officers at a national level. He succeeded where previous attempts had failed.

His success can be measured not only by the establishment of the college but also by the contribution made by its graduates to subsequent campaigns. Many early graduates from the Senior Department played crucial roles during the Peninsular War and the Battle of Waterloo.

The fact that many of these officers stayed in touch with Le Marchant after leaving the college is testament to the respect and admiration in which he was held.

And so we come to the end of the life and times of a man, like many who came before and followed after, who was cut down in his prime. We can only speculate about what John Gaspard Le Marchant might have achieved had he survived the Battle of Salamanca on that fateful day, 22 July, 1812.

APPENDIX A

Statement of the service of J. G. Le Marchant
Colonel and Lieutenant Governor R. M. College
1st January 1810

To His Excellency Sir David Dundas K B, Commander-in-Chief

Sir.
I do myself the honor to enclose a statement of my services in compliance with his Excellency the Commander-in-Chief's instructions & which I was prevented doing sooner, owing to the difficulty of getting at the several parts relating thereto.

Where employed, specifying the period of each service, the names of any siege, battle or considerable action, where personally present, Regimental leave or absence. Modern foreign language acquired.

Ensign: 2nd Battalion 1st Regiment of Foot February 18th 1783
I served with the Regiment in Ireland twelve months, afterwards in Gibraltar during four years.

Cornet: 6th Dragoons May 30th 1787
The Governor of Gibraltar not receiving an official notification of my removal into the Dragoons, I continued to do duty with the Royals several months after my appointment

Lieutenant: 2nd Dragoon Guards November 18th 1789
I obtained His Majesty's leave to go to the continent, but was absent only six months owing to a preparation for war with Russia

Captain: 2nd Dragoon Guards December 21st 1791 / Major Brigade May 15th 1793
I embarked with the Regiment for Flanders on the 23rd of May 1793 and was present at the several battles and principal actions fought by the Allied army under the orders of His Royal Highness the Duke of York during the years 1793 and 94

Major: 16th Light Dragoons March 1st 1794
At the close of the campaign of Flanders after the allied army had crossed the Meuse, I received orders to take up command of that part of the Regiment that was in England in which I continued until the British army returned from the continent.

In 1796 I presented to his Royal Highness the Duke of York a system for the instruction of the Cavalry in the exercise of the sword, until which time the Cavalry was not instructed in the proper use of the weapon. I afterwards completed the instruction of the Cavalry within the space of nine months.

A treatise that I had written on the exercise of the sabre was printed by authority of the Adjutant-General which continues to be observed as regulations. Several editions of this work have been sold at prime cost for the benefit of the service from which I derived no emolument.

Lieutenant Colonel: Humpesch's or Prince of Wales Hussars April 6th 1797
I proposed a plan to His Royal Highness the Commander-in-Chief for constructing & mounting in a different manner the swords of the Cavalry which was adopted and continues to be observed as regulation.

Lieutenant Colonel: 29th Light Dragoons May 29th 1797
As an acknowledgement of the utility of this suggestion, I received a letter of thanks from the Master General of the Ordnance accompanied with a present of the sword

Lieutenant Colonel: 7th Light Dragoons June 1st 1797
I delivered to His Royal Highness Commander-in-Chief a work entitled an elucidation of Cavalry movements. It was afterwards printed by authority of the Adjutant-General & went through several versions which were sold at prime cost for the benefit of the service, but without any emolument to myself.

At the same period was likewise printed by authority of Adjutant-General. "Instructions for the Formation & Discipline of the Provisional Cavalry" which also was sold at a reduced price.

Lieutenant Colonel: 2nd Dragoon Guards October 25th 1799
In January 1799 I had the honor of presenting to His Royal Highness the Commander-in-Chief a plan proposing to found a Military college for the Education of persons intended for the land service, also comprising a course of instruction applicable to officers intended to serve on the General Staff. My suggestions having approved of by his Majesty & subsequently in parliament, the Senior Department of the Royal Military College opened on the 4th of May 1799 & the Junior Dept on the 1st of June 1801.

Lieutenant Governor: Royal Military College June 25th 1801
I have continued at the Military College since my appointment to the Lieutenant Government, with the exception of a couple of months when I joined the Queens Dragoon Guards then under orders for foreign service.

In December 1802 I submitted to His Royal Highness the Commander-in-Chief the outline of a plan for the organization of the General Staff of the army comprehending the formation of a permanent field staff to be attached to the 2 Master Generals Department also of an office for the deposit of Military plans and charts.

Lieutenant Colonel: 15th Light Dragoons half pay 10th July 1803
I was afterwards placed on full pay as an unattached Lieutenant Colonel of cavalry from the date of my appointment to the 15th Light Dragoons

Colonel: October 30th 1805
I cannot charge my recollection with the leave of absence that I may have had. I never was on the recruiting service, nor otherwise on half pay than as above stated

I am acquainted with the French language.

Signed J. G. Le Marchant

(The Sandhurst Collection, Le Marchant papers, Letterbook 6)

APPENDIX B

Outline of a Plan for a Regular course of Military Education 1799

It is proposed to found a Royal Military College, to be conducted under the direction of officers of approved ability and experience, over which establishment the Commander In Chief shall preside as Chancellor.

The immediate object of this Institution will be, to instruct the body of the service in the degree of science requisite to subordinate stations, and to afford the means of a regular education to those, who aspiring to rank and responsibility apply early to the study of their profession.

To effect these purposes, the instruction must be arranged & conducted under separate courses of study, forming three distinct departments of the college, each appropriated to the views under which individuals may enter into the service as officers. At the same time extending the plan to instruction to the education of soldiers' sons who thereby may eventually become intelligent Non Commissioned Officers peculiarly useful to the Corps of the army in which they may afterwards serve.

Of the Three Departments, the Third is intended to instruct youth in the several branches of Military science after their having finished their classical studies.

The Second is to receive the cadets of the Army, & soldiers' sons who are to be formed to the practical duties of the service.

The First is to give to the Staff of the Army the Intelligence necessary to assist Generals commanding armies in the execution of their orders, and of the very extensive & various details which relate to the operations of war.

Third Department

For the Instruction of Youth

This department would constitute the Junior course, and be calculated for the instruction of those who are from early life intended for the Military profession, and who by becoming students in this department, may be well grounded in Science, previous to their attaining that age which at present entitles them to hold commissions.

The points of instruction to which their attention will be directed, consist in the study of Mathematics in its several branches, of Field Fortification, with the General principles of Gunnery and Artillery service. They are to be instructed in Drawing of Plans, Military movements & Perspective. Likewise in a knowledge of Tactics, Military Geography & History, together with the German & French languages.

Frequent lectures will be given the Students on the subjects of Moral and Natural Philosophy. Riding, Fencing the Sabre & swimming are also to be included among their acquirements.

As it is proposed to receive cadets of the East India Company's service in this Department, it is intended to have Professors in the Hindoo & Persian Languages, as immediately requisite to the service of India. Also Masters in the Geography of India, who are to instruct the Cadets in the local knowledge of the settlement for which they are severally intended.

Quarterly examinations will be held for the several degrees of progress, when those students who are found qualified, will be considered as eligible for the army.

The students are to be admitted from the age of Fourteen to Sixteen, and with the approbation of the Chief Governor. They are to be boarded, and educated in the several branches of science; the particulars of which will be here after detailed in the Regulations of the Department, and this at a fixed allowance of seventy pounds annually for each student, free of all other charges whatsoever.

The number of Pupils admitted to this department will be limited to Two Hundred, of which, Fifty are to be on the foundation, being officers & the sons of officers who have died in His Majesty's Service.

Fifty Cadets of the East India Company's service.

One Hundred Students, the sons of Gentlemen intended for His Majesty's service of the line, making altogether Two Hundred.

These are to be formed into Four Companies of Fifty each, with proper officers appointed to them, as it will be a principal object with this Department to conduct the education according to the strictest principle of the Military subordination, in order to instil early impressions of Military duty in the minds of those whom it may be supposed will eventually form the staff of the Army, & arrive at the highest rank & responsibility in the service.

Although the acquirements treated are directed to military views, yet they enter into a finished education equally, whether men are designed for military or civil stations. The regulations of the Department should therefore not operate to the exclusion of those whose rank and circumstances entitle them to aspire to elevated stations.

The officers entrusted with the conduct of this and the other Departments of the College, together with the several Professors, Masters & Attendants are specified in the details of the Institution under the head of Finance.

Second Department

For the Cadets of the Army and Soldiers Sons

This first branch of the Second Department is calculated to inform the body of the Army, by instructing those who enter the service without having been qualified for the Profession by previous military instruction.

With this view, every person, before a commission is granted him, must be required to enter as a Cadet, in order that he may attain a competent knowledge of the service; and by passing an examination in that probationary state, prove himself equal to the duties of a Subaltern officer.

The Cadets will do duty with a Legion, consisting of four companies, composed of Two Hundred Soldier's sons recruited without bounty, who are to be educated on the establishment in the practical duties of that service to which their natural genius may lead them.

The course of instruction attached to this Department (as far as cadets are concerned) will be elementary in point of science, whilst its practice will be directed to every situation comprised in regimental arrangement, whether of Cavalry or Infantry.

The Cadets of both services will be taught plain Geometry and Trigonometry, to make sketches of an outpost or country when sent on patrol, to draw the different manoeuvres treated of in his Majesty's regulations, writing therefrom the words of command appropriated to every rank that directs the execution of each movement, & as far as time and circumstances might admit, such means to confirm them in a knowledge of the theory, as will insure their becoming correct and intelligent officers in practice.

Such cadets as were intended for the Cavalry, will be instructed in Horsemanship and the use of the sword. They will be attached to that division of the Legion which is mounted & formed to the Cavalry service, thereby become acquainted with the treatment of Horses & the interior economy of a Regiment in quarters, as well as with its movements in the Field.

Their drills will be conducted indiscriminately together with the Legion, in order to unite practice with theory, which is indispensably necessary to a perfect knowledge of a military system. Upon the same principle, the Cadets destined for the Infantry will be attached to companies, & receive instructions in the several branches of duty which relate to that particular service.

In order to obtain admission to the College as Cadet, every person must first be approved of by the Commanding Officer of a Regiment as successor to a vacant commission (and if by purchase) the purchase money is to be lodged with the Regimental Agent before the Commissioned Officer applies to the Chief Governor for an order of admission.

The Cadets will remain six months at the College, during which time they will have to pass two examinations for their qualification, which having taken, they will be entitled to hold commissions in the several corps for which they are intended.

Notice of their being qualified to become Officers will be officially transmitted by the board to the Chief Governor, who will cause their commissions to be made out antedated to the period at which they entered the College.

During the time they are at the College, their whole pay goes to the funds of the Department. They pay for their clothing, washing & diet, which is rated at £36 for the six months they are under instruction.

Legion

The establishment of the Legion will be a very necessary branch of this Department of the College, and an institution not less munificent than beneficial to the service. It will be formed according to the rules & regulations established for the army. They will be taught reading, writing, and arithmetic, and at such seasons as the weather may be unfavourable to Military Exercises, they will be employed in working at several branches of trade they may be considered most appropriated to the wants of the service.

By being educated in the habits of laborious industry & the constant practice of military exercise, it will ensure to the Army a regular succession of persons qualified to become Non Commissioned Officers, whilst they contribute essentially to improve the Cadets, by affording them the means of exemplifying what they have at first acquired in theory.

Three years residence at the College will enable the Legion to become soldiers and of a proper age for service. In consequence, a draft of one third will be made annually into Regiments of the line.

The Legion is to be recruited from Soldier's sons not under the age of thirteen & not exceeding sixteen years old. These are to be recommended by Commanding Officers of Regiments to the resident Governor, after which & having passed the Board, they will be attested and admitted on the foundation of the College.

Seventy boys only are to be admitted into the Legion in the first year, a like number in the second year, and sixty in the third year. At the commencement of the fourth year, sixty-five are to be discharged from the College & returned to the several regiments from which they were sent. This draft will be made every year & the Legion recruited to its usual establishment.

The Legion will be divided into four companies, to whom Officers and Non Commissioned Officers are to be appointed from the line.

The horses required to mount one company of the legion, to be recruited from foresters, at twelve guineas each, measuring from thirteen to fourteen hands, and tails not docked.

Twenty horses are to be received the first year, & the number to be completed in the second year to fifty eight.

No distinction is to be made in the Pay between the mounted and dismounted companies, but the general pay to be fourteen pence per day.

This allowance will be found fully adequate to the expense of clothing and subsistence.

The whole of this Department will be conducted under the immediate direction of Officers of the line as a Military Establishment founded on the system of Discipline established by His Majesty's regulations, having in view the future uniformity of practice throughout every rank & situation in the British Army.

First Department

To qualify Officers intended to serve in the General Staff

This Department is only intended for Officers of experience in the duties of Regimental service, who possess a competent knowledge of the several branches of science pursued in the Junior department of the College.

The immediate purpose of this establishment is to lead progressively from minutiae to a knowledge of military operations, upon those principles which direct the great scale of war, & thereby to expand the genius, that responsibility may not precede information. For tho' no reluctance is felt in acknowledging inexperience while in subordinate stations, yet having once arrived at rank, enquiry after information too naturally ceases, from a dread of ridicule, or the galling imputation of incapacity.

The instruction appropriated to this First Department of the College will be calculated to qualify officers to become Aid De Camps, & fill other staff appointments in the General Staff of the army with the ability due to their high importance. It will explain the nature of the country, & form the eye to that perfect knowledge of ground that is necessary to a judicious choice of position, & to the conduct of offensive & defensive war.

It will point out the modes of attack & defence, appropriated to local situation, with the several duties inseparable from an advanced corps cooperating with the movements of an army.

It will minutely detail the sections that compose an army, & specify the proportion that troops of each branch of service should bear to the other with the proper distribution of them (in camp) according to the nature of the country and the local circumstances of ground.

It will enumerate the different Departments of an army, comprised under the heads of Military & Civil Staff, enter into the particular duties of each, their relative powers, & their connection with the general conduct of an army, as well in what relates to the interior system as to its service in the field. The principle upon which movements are conducted & the general motives that determine the choice of position for an army, both in the field & cantonments.

It will treat of the great principle which should regulate command, & the policy requisite to high authority, in order to maintain discipline, to inspire energy in the troops, & insure a perfect cooperation in every branch of the service.

It will point out generally the resources of an army in the various means of procuring supplies of forage & provisions, the power of influencing the good disposition and support of the natural inhabitants of the country that may be the Theatre of War, thro' whose means intelligence of the enemy can be obtained, with the several other aids so indispensable to the operations of active service.

Finally, it will show the proper administration of finance in regulating the expenditure, and checking the accounts of the several departments.

Officers who have not attained an age sufficiently ripe for reflection & who have nor some experience of the service will not be considered eligible to enter the course of study.

Apartments are to be provided in the College where each officer will be allowed forage for two horses, and accommodation for one servant.

Every necessary means of messing will be provided, but subject to the rules of the Department.

Application to the Chief Governor for admission, is to be made through the Commanding Officers of corps.

No person will be adequate to conduct this department under the rank of a Field Officer, as the instruction required to give it can only result from great ability & much experience.

As Officers educated for the Duties of the General Staff are those who probably (in their turn) will arrive at command and great responsibility, it is of the utmost importance that their instruction shall not be confined to Military Theories alone, but be made as universal as the mind shall be capable of embracing. For it is evident, that the operations of war in the conduct of Armies are interwoven with general knowledge, which combines with the Military and Political History of Europe, the habit of judging correctly of men and measures, by placing in a true point of view the influence of national prejudice, acting under the pressure of local circumstances.

It is therefore proposed (as soon as proper funds can be provided for the purpose) that five Officers of the most distinguished talents shall be sent annually from the First Department to visit the several Courts of Europe, to become acquainted with the interior discipline and conduct of Foreign Armies, to view with a military eye, country rendered memorable by having been the theatre of brilliant achievements in war, and by directing their enquiries to points of useful knowledge they will acquire that intelligence which hereafter will best qualify them for Military Command.

These Officers are to remain two years abroad, and will be allowed from the funds of the College a sum sufficient to defray their travelling expenses.

They are to correspond with the Governor (resident at the College) to whom they will communicate their observations on Political and Military occurrences.

They are to keep a Military Journal according to the form delivered to them. These journals are to be deposited in the Library of the College on their return to England.

The Supreme Committee is to examine at the close of the Winter term those Officers of the First Department who are candidates for going to the Continent, and the Committee is to determine in favour of such as are of the most improved and acknowledged talents.

The route of these Officers will be regulated by order of the Supreme Committee.

The detailed rules & reflections for the College, the immediate course of instruction proposed to be followed together with the examinations to be made in every branch of science, as appropriated to the several departments are omitted, it being the immediate object to submit for consideration the Outlines of a Plan, which may afterwards be examined in detail.

(The Sandhurst Collection, Le Marchant Papers, Packet 7, Item 1)

NOTES

Prologue

1. Le Marchant, *Memoirs of The Late Major-General Le Marchant*, p.13
2. Lunt, *Scarlet Lancer*, p.38
3. The *Sun* newspaper, 2 September 1812

Chapter One – Of all the Dunces

1. Le Marchant, *Memoirs Of The Late Major-General Le Marchant*, p.6
2. Parliamentary Archives, LEM/1/2/20, Letter from Miss Katherine Le Marchant to Denis Le Marchant
3. Bragge, *Peninsular Portrait 1811-1814*, p. 33-34
4. Bruce, *The Purchase System in the British Army*, p. 2

Chapter Two – A Disastrous Campaign

1. Watkins, John, *A Biographical Memoir of His Late Royal Highness Frederick, Duke of York*, p. 206
2. Fortescue, *A History of the British Army, Volume IV*, p. 80-81
3. Thoumine, *Scientific Soldier*, p. 14

4. Le Marchant, *Memoirs of The Late Major-General Le Marchant*, p. 14
5. Ibid., p. 16-17
6. Ibid., p. 17-18
7. Ibid., p. 20
8. Thoumine, *Scientific Soldier*, p. 22
9. Le Marchant, *Memoirs of The Late Major-General Le Marchant*, p. 23
10. Ibid., p. 23
11. Ibid., p. 26
12. Burne, *New light on the Flanders Campaign*, p. 121
13. Le Marchant, *Memoirs of The Late Major-General Le Marchant*, p. 29-30
14. Ibid., p. 32
15. Ibid., p. 34
16. Thoumine, *Scientific Soldier*, p. 34
17. Ibid., p.35
18. Le Marchant, *Memoirs of The Late Major-General Le Marchant*, p. 38-39
19. Ibid., p.41
20. Fortescue, *A History of the British Army, Volume IV*, p. 320-321
21. Fullom, *The Life of General Sir Howard Douglas*, p. 85
22. Thomas, *The Story of Sandhurst*, p. 20
23. Fortescue, *A History of the British Army, Volume IV*, p. 296-297
24. Longford, *Wellington*, p.29

Chapter Three – Live by the Sword

1. Tomkinson, *The Diary of a Cavalry Officer*, p. 135
2. Le Marchant, *Memoirs of The Late Major-General Le Marchant*, p. 45
3. The Sandhurst Collection, Le Marchant papers, Packet 5, Item 5
4. Le Marchant, *The Rules and Regulations for the Sword Exercise of the Cavalry*, p.3

5. National Archives, WO 3/17, Circular to Commanding Officers
6. Le Marchant, *Memoirs of The Late Major-General Le Marchant*, p. 53
7. The Sandhurst Collection, Le Marchant papers, Packet 14, Item 1
8. Ibid., Packet 5, Item 5
9. Le Marchant, *Memoirs of The Late Major-General Le Marchant*, p. 48-49
10. Anglesey, Marquess of, *One-Leg: The Life and Letters of Henry William Paget*, p. 54
11. Ibid., p. 54
12. Thoumine, *Scientific Soldier*, p. 57

Chapter Four – The French General

1. Combermere, *Memoirs and Correspondence of Field-Marshal Viscount Combermere*, p. 29
2. Bunbury, *Narratives of some passages in the Great War with France, from 1799 to 1810*, p. VII
3. Auckland, William and Robert, *The Journal and Correspondence of William, Lord Auckland, Volume III,* p. 70
4. National Archives, WO/3/19, Adjutant General's Circular of 12 December 1798

Chapter Five – The Outline of a Plan

1. Le Marchant, *Memoirs of The Late Major-General Le Marchant*, p. 64-65
2. Ibid., p. 65-66
3. The Sandhurst Collection, Le Marchant papers, Packet 7, Item 1
4. Le Marchant, *Memoirs of The Late Major-General Le Marchant*, p. 80-82
5. The Sandhurst Collection, Le Marchant papers, Packet 14, Item 4
6. Thoumine, *Scientific Soldier*, p. 70

7. Jarry, *Treatise on the Marches and Movements of Armies*, p. 22-23
8. Cole, *Memoirs of British Generals*, p. 246
9. Ibid., p. 246
10. Parliamentary Archives, LEM/1/20/2, p. 7
11. Le Marchant, *Memoirs of The Late Major-General Le Marchant*, p. 88
12. Ibid., p. 89
13. Ibid., p. 89

Chapter Six – The Seal of Approval

1. Le Marchant, *Memoirs of The Late Major-General Le Marchant*, p. 93
2. Auckland, William and Robert, *The Journal and Correspondence of William, Lord Aukland, Volume IV*, p. 102-103
3. National Archives, WO 1-943, p. 53
4. Ibid., p.41-42
5. The Sandhurst Collection, Le Marchant papers, Packet 11, item 14
6. National Archives WO1-943, p. 69

Chapter Seven – The Royal Military College

1. National Archives WO1-943, p. 85
2. Le Marchant, *Memoirs of The Late Major-General Le Marchant*, p. 102
3. The Sandhurst Collection, Le Marchant papers, Packet 12, Item 4
4. Whitehall Evening Post, 9 June 1801
5. Farington, *The Farington Diary, Volume 8*, p. 68
6. The Sandhurst Collection, WO99/5, Supreme Board minutes, 1801-1802, p. 60
7. British Library, 188b22, *His Majesty's Warrant Containing the Rules Order and Regulations for the Junior Department of the Royal Military College*, p.9-11

8. Mockler-Ferryman, A.F., *Annals of Sandhurst*, p. 10
9. Farington, *The Farington Diary, Volume 3*, p. 7
10. The Sandhurst Collection, WO99/5, Supreme Board minutes, 1801-1803, p. 254-255
11. Cole, *Memoirs of British Generals*, p. 253
12. Le Marchant, *Memoirs of The Late Major-General Le Marchant*, p. 114
13. The Sandhurst Collection, Letterbook 3, p. 152-153
14. Farington, *The Farington Diary, Volume 1*, p. 344
15. Ibid., *Volume 2*, p.68
16. Ibid.
17. The Marlow Historian, Volume 1, p. 21
18. Le Marchant, *Memoirs of The Late Major-General Le Marchant*, p. 139
19. Ibid., p. 140
20. Parliamentary Archives, LEM/1/2/20, Letter from Miss Katherine Le Marchant to Denis Le Marchant
21. The Sandhurst Collection, Le Marchant Papers, Letterbook 3, p. 97
22. Ibid., Packet 1a, Item 5

Chapter Eight – Mutiny and Rebellion

1. Le Marchant, *Memoirs of The Late Major-General Le Marchant*, p. 119
2. Ibid., p. 110
3. The Sandhurst Collection, Le Marchant papers, Letterbook 3, p. 1
4. Ibid., p. 23
5. National Archives, WO3-37
6. The Times, 21 September 1804
7. Le Marchant, *Memoirs of The Late Major-General Le Marchant*, p. 145-146
8. The Sandhurst Collection, Le Marchant papers, Letterbook 2, p. 208

9. Ibid., p. 271
10. The Sandhurst Collection, Le Marchant papers, Letterbook 3, p.104-106
11. Ibid., Packet 5, Item 15
12. Ibid., Letterbook 3, p. 148
13. Ibid., p. 149
14. Ibid., p. 155
15. Ibid., p. 193
16. The Sandhurst Collection, Le Marchant papers, Letterbook 4, Appendix
17. Ibid., Letterbook 3, p. 223-224
18. Ibid., p. 225
19. Ibid., p. 232-233
20. The Sandhurst Collection, Le Marchant papers, Letterbook 4, Appendix
21. Ibid., Letterbook 3, p. 269-270
22. Ibid., Letterbook 4, Appendix
23. Ibid., Letterbook 3, p. 247
24. Ibid., p. 271-272
25. Ibid., Packet 10a, Item 2

Chapter Nine – Reconciliation

1. The Sandhurst Collection, Le Marchant papers, Packet 13, Item 15
2. Ibid., Letterbook 3, p. 288
3. Ibid., p. 272
4. Ibid., p. 152
5. Morning Chronicle, 20 March 1807
6. The Sandhurst Collection, Le Marchant papers, Letterbook 3, p. 284
7. Jarry, *Treatise on the Marches and Movements of Armies*, p. 4
8. The Sandhurst Collection, Le Marchant papers, Letterbook 3, p. 298
9. Ibid., Packet 10a, Item 1

10. Thoumine, *Scientific Soldier*, p. 31-32
11. The Sandhurst Collection, Le Marchant papers, Letterbook 5, p. 127-128
12. Ibid., p. 132

Chapter Ten – A Seminary of Vice

1. McCallum, *Observations On H.R.H The Duke of Kent's Shameful Persecution*, p. i
2. Ibid., p. 17
3. Ibid., p. 24-25
4. Ibid., p. 25
5. Ibid., p. 32
6. Ibid., p. 26
7. Ibid., p. 34-35
8. The Sandhurst Collection, Le Marchant papers, Packet 13, Item 14
9. Ibid.
10. The Sandhurst Collection, Le Marchant papers, Letterbook 3, p. 91
11. Ibid., Packet 5, Item 3
12. *Morning Chronicle*, 2 February 1809
13. Ibid.
14. Ibid.
15. Peithmann, *A Refutation of Pierre Franc McCallum's Remarks on the Royal Military College*
16. The Sandhurst Collection, Le Marchant papers, Letterbook 3, p. 95-96
17. Ibid., Letterbook 6, 30 July 1809
18. Ibid., 15 June 1810

Chapter Eleven – Sandhurst

1. The Sandhurst Collection, Le Marchant papers, Packet 13, Item 12
2. Ibid., Packet 14, Item 4
3. National Archives, WO 1-943, p. 65

4. The Sandhurst Collection, Le Marchant papers, Letterbook 3, p. 99
5. Ibid., p. 104
6. The Sandhurst Collection, WO99/5, Supreme Board minutes, 1806-1803, p. 406
7. Ibid., 1808-1812, p. 75

Chapter Twelve – On Active Service

1. The Sandhurst Collection, Le Marchant papers, Letterbook 6, 9 June 1811
2. Ibid., 17 June 1811
3. Ibid., 3 July 1811
4. Ibid., 6 July 1811
5. McGuffie, *Peninsular Cavalry General*, p. 124
6. The Sandhurst Collection, Le Marchant papers, Letterbook 6, 20 July 1811
7. Le Marchant, *Memoirs of The Late Major-General Le Marchant*, p. 157

Chapter Thirteen – The Peninsular War

1. The Sandhurst Collection, Le Marchant papers, Packet 1, Item 2
2. Ibid., Packet 8a, Item 2
3. Ibid., Packet 10, Item 6
4. Ibid., Packet 10, Item 5
5. Ibid., Packet 10, Item 8
6. Ibid., Packet 8a, Item 1
7. Ibid., Packet 10, item 9
8. Ibid., Packet 14, Item 5
9. Gurwood, *The Dispatches of Field Marshal the Duke of Wellington, Volume Seven*, p. 374
10. Ibid., *Volume Seven*, p. 412
11. Ibid., *Volume Eight*, p. 231

Chapter Fourteen – An Incomparable Loss

1. Fisher, *A Sketch of the City of Lisbon*, p. 3
2. Bragge, *Peninsular Portrait 1811-1814*, p. 6
3. Fisher, *A Sketch of the City of Lisbon*, p. 9
4. National Army Museum, 1968-07-213, *Memoirs of a Dragoon*, p. 2
5. Ibid.
6. Bragge, *Peninsular Portrait 1811-1814*, p. 8
7. McGuffie, *Peninsular Cavalry General*, p. 128
8. The Sandhurst Collection, Le Marchant papers, Packet 14, Item 13

Chapter Fifteen – Journey Through Portugal

1. National Army Museum, 1968-07-213, *Memoirs of a Dragoon*, p. 2
2. Bragge, *Peninsular Portrait 1811-1814*, p. 11
3. Ibid., p. 18
4. Valence House Archive, BD16/3/12, Letter book of General Le Marchant, p. 86-88
5. Parliamentary Archives, LEM/1/20/2, p. 6
6. Valence House Archive, BD16/3/12, Letter book of General Le Marchant, p. 91
7. The Sandhurst Collection, Le Marchant papers, Packet 3a, Item 7
8. Ibid., Packet 3a, Item 6
9. Ibid., Packet 3a, Item 5
10. Ibid., Packet 14, Item 13
11. Tomkinson, *The Diary of a Cavalry Officer*, p. 136
12. Valence House Archive, BD16/3/12, Letter book of General Le Marchant, p. 5-15
13. Ibid., p. 3
14. Le Marchant, *Memoirs of The Late Major-General Le Marchant*, p. 173
15. Ibid., p. 174
16. Ibid., p. 175
17. Ibid.

Chapter Sixteen – Siege of Ciudad Rodrigo

1. Le Marchant, *Memoirs of The Late Major-General Le Marchant*, p. 177-178
2. Bragge, *Peninsular Portrait 1811-1814*, p. 28-29
3. Greenwood, *Through Spain with Wellington*, p. 88
4. Tomkinson, *The Diary of a Cavalry Officer*, p. 125
5. Valence House Archive, BD16/3/12, Letter book of General Le Marchant, p. 25-27
6. Ibid., p. 80
7. Gurwood, *The Dispatches of Field Marshal the Duke of Wellington, Volume Eight* p. 316
8. Bragge, *Peninsular Portrait 1811-1814*, p. 36
9. Le Marchant, *Memoirs of The Late Major-General Le Marchant*, p. 234-235
10. Bragge, *Peninsular Portrait 1811-1814*, p. 38-39
11. The Sandhurst Collection, Le Marchant papers, Packet 21a, Item 2
12. Valence House Archive, BD16/3/12, Letter book of General Le Marchant, p. 34
13. Bragge, *Peninsular Portrait 1811-1814*, p.. 41-42
14. Ibid., p. 48
15. Tomkinson, *The Diary of a Cavalry Officer*, p. 145-146

Chapter Seventeen – Success at Villagarcia

1. Le Marchant, *Memoirs of The Late Major-General Le Marchant*, p. 213
2. Tomkinson, *The Diary of a Cavalry Officer*, p. 150
3. Ibid., p. 151
4. Ibid., p. 153
5. Combermere, *Memoirs and Correspondence of Field-Marshal Viscount Combermere*, p. 250
6. The Sandhurst Collection, Le Marchant papers, Packet 28a, Item 2
7. Gurwood, *The Dispatches of Field Marshal the Duke of Wellington, Volume Nine*, p. 63

8. The Sandhurst Collection, Le Marchant papers, Packet 28a, Item 1
9. Ibid., Packet 28a, Item 2
10. Ibid.
11. The Sandhurst Collection, Le Marchant papers, Packet 26a & 27a
12. Holmes, Richard, *Wellington: The Iron Duke*, p. 144
13. Brett-James, *Life in Wellington's Army*, p. 200-201
14. Bragge, *Peninsular Portrait 1811-1814*, p. 45
15. Le Marchant, *Memoirs of The Late Major-General Le Marchant*, p. 226
16. Valence House Archive, BD16/3/12, Letter book of General Le Marchant, p. 82-83
17. Le Marchant, *Memoirs of The Late Major-General Le Marchant*, p. 230-231

Chapter Eighteen – Destination Salamanca

1. Valence House Archive, BD16/3/12, Letter book of General Le Marchant, p. 45-50
2. Le Marchant, *Memoirs of The Late Major-General Le Marchant*, p. 238
3. Tomkinson, *The Diary of a Cavalry Officer*, p. 159
4. Gurwood, *The Dispatches of Field Marshal the Duke of Wellington, Volume Nine*, p. 238
5. Cole, *Memoirs of British Generals*, p. 275
6. Henry, Philip, *Notes of Conservations with the Duke of Wellington*, p. 96
7. Boutflower, Charles, *The Journal of An Army Surgeon During The Peninsular War*, p. 141
8. Bragge, *Peninsular Portrait 1811-1814*, p. 75
9. Le Marchant, *Memoirs of The Late Major-General Le Marchant*, p. 253
10. Ibid., p. 275
11. Ibid., p. 255
12. Valence House Archive, BD16/3/12, Letter book of General Le Marchant, p. 58

13. Ibid., p. 65
14. Grattan, *Adventures with the Connaught Rangers*, p. 41
15. Bragge, *Peninsular Portrait 1811-1814*, p. 61
16. National Archives, WO1-255, p.86

Chapter Nineteen – The Decisive Battle

1. Grattan, *Adventures with the Connaught Rangers*, p. 50
2. The Sandhurst Collection, Le Marchant papers, Packet 29a, Item 4
3. Grattan, *Adventures with the Connaught Rangers*, p. 54
4. Le Marchant, *Memoirs of The Late Major-General Le Marchant*, p. 289
5. Grattan, *Adventures with the Connaught Rangers*, p. 57
6. Ibid., p. 60
7. The Sandhurst Collection, Le Marchant papers, Packet 17a
8. Grattan, *Adventures with the Connaught Rangers*, p. 60
9. Ibid., p. 62
10. The Sandhurst Collection, Le Marchant papers, Packet 17a, Item 3
11. Ibid., Packet 29a, Item 4
12. Pakenham, *Packenham Letters 1800-1815*, p. 173
13. Heathcote, T.H., *Wellington's Peninsular War Generals*, p. 36
14. Grattan, *Adventures with the Connaught Rangers*, p. 73

Chapter Twenty – A Most Able Officer

1. Gurwood, *The Dispatches of Field Marshal the Duke of Wellington, Volume Nine*, p. 303
2. Bragge, *Peninsular Portrait 1811-1814*, p. 64
3. McGuffie, *Peninsular Cavalry General*, p. 211
4. The Sandhurst Collection, Le Marchant papers, Packet 3a, Item 5
5. Ibid., Packet 29a, Item 1
6. Ibid., Packet 29a, Item 5
7. Ibid., Packet 1, Item 1
8. https://hansard.parliament.uk/Lords/1812-12-03
9. https://hansard.parliament.uk/commons/1812-12-03

Epilogue

1. The Sandhurst Collection, Le Marchant papers, Packet 23a
2. Parliamentary Archives, LEM/1/20/2, p. 12
3. Ibid., p. 3
4. Ibid., p. 13
5. The Sandhurst Collection, Le Marchant papers, Packet 3a, Item 8
6. Parliamentary Archives, LEM/1/20/2, p. 10
7. Ibid., LEM/1/3/2

BIBLIOGRAPHY

Manuscript Sources

British Library, London

188b18 – His Majesty's Warrant, appointing a Supreme Board of Commissioners, for the Affairs of the Royal Military College, 24 June 1801

188b18 – His Majesty's Warrant, containing Statutes for the Government and Conduct of the First Department of the Royal Military College, 9 December 1801

188b22 – His Majesty's Warrant, containing the Rules, Orders, and Regulations for the Junior Department of the Royal Military College, 4 March 1802

British Newspaper Archive

Morning Chronicle, 20 March 1807

Morning Chronicle, 2 February 1809

The Sun, 2 September 1812

The Times, 21 September 1804

Whitehall Evening Post, 9 June 1801

National Archives, London

WO 1/255 – British Army in Spain, Portugal and France (1808-1820)

WO 1/943 – Papers on the foundation of a Royal Military college

WO 3/17 – General letters 1797 Jan.-1798 Feb.
WO 3/19 – General letters 1798 Oct.-1799 July.
WO 3/37 – General letters 1804 Jan.-1804 Sept.
TS 11/806 – Treasury Solicitor and HM Procurator General, Papers

National Army Museum, London
1968-07-213 – Typescript: Memoirs of a Dragoon, 1811-1838

Parliamentary Archives, London
LEM/1/2/20 – Letter from Miss C Le Marchant
LEM/1/3/2 – Letter from W W Clinton
LEM/1/20/2 – Part of a diary of Sir Denis Le Marchant

Priaulx Library, Guernsey
PLS LL940.27 LEM – Peninsula Letters: Le Marchant 1811-1812
PLS LAG929.2 DES – De Saumarez, Le Marchant and Dobrée families
PLS LOC355.547 LEM – Rules and regulations for the sword exercise of the cavalry

The Sandhurst Collection, Sandhurst
NRA 184 – Le Marchant papers
WO99/5 – Supreme Board minutes

Valence House Collections, Dagenham
BD16/3/12 – Transcriptions of the letters of General John Gaspard Le Marchant, 1811-1812
BD16/3/19 – Transcription of the journal of Carey Le Marchant, circa. 1810-1813

Printed Sources

Anglesey, Marquess of, *One-Leg: The Life and Letters of Henry William Paget* (London: Jonathan Cape, 1961)

Auckland, William and Robert, *The Journal and Correspondence of William, Lord Auckland Vol. III & Vol. IV* (London: Richard Bentley, 1862)

Berry, William, *The History of the Island of Guernsey* (London: Longman et al, 1815)

Boutflower, Charles, *The Journal of An Army Surgeon During The Peninsular War* (Staplehurst: Spellmount Ltd, 1997)

Bragge, William, Edited by S.A.C. Cassels, *Peninsular Portrait 1811-1814: The Letters of Captain William Bragge* (London: Oxford University Press, 1963)

Brett-James, Antony, *Life in Wellington's Army* (London: George Allen & Unwin Ltd, 1972)

Bruce, Anthony, *The Purchase System in the British Army 1660-1871* (London: Royal Historical Society, 1980)

Bunbury, Sir Henry, *Narratives of some passages in the Great War with France, from 1799 to 1810* (London: Richard Bentley, 1854)

Cole, John William, *Memoirs of British Generals Distinguished During the Peninsular War Vol. II* (London: Richard Bentley, 1856)

Combermere, Mary, *Memoirs and Correspondence of Field-Marshal Viscount Combermere* (London: Hurst and Blackett, 1866)

Dalby, Isaac, *A Course of Mathematics Designed for the Use of the Officers and Cadets of the Royal Military College* (London: Glendinning, 1807)

Duncan, Jonathon, *The History of Guernsey; With Occasional Notices of Jersey, Alderney, and Sark, and Biographical Sketches* (London: Longmans, 1841)

Farington, Joseph, Edited by James Greig, *The Farington Diary* (London: Hutchinson & Co, 1922)

Fletcher, Ian, *Galloping at Everything: The British Cavalry in the Peninsular War and at Waterloo 1808-15* (Staplehurst: Spellmount Limited, 1999)

Fisher, R.B., *A Sketch of the City of Lisbon and its Environs* (London: J Ridgway, 1811)

Fortescue, J.W., *A History of the British Army Volume IV*, (London: MacMillan and Co, 1906)

Fullom, S.W., *The Life of General Sir Howard Douglas* (London: John Murray, 1863)

Glover, Richard, *Peninsular Preparation: The Reform of the British Army 1795-1809* (Cambridge: Cambridge University Press, 1963)

Grattan, Lieutenant William, *Adventures with the Connaught Rangers: From 1808 To 1814, Volume II* (London: Henry Colburn, 1847)

Greenwood, Adrian, *Through Spain with Wellington: The Letters of Lieutenant Peter Le Mesurier of the Fighting Ninth* (Stroud: Amberley Publishing, 2016)

Gurwood, Lieutenant Colonel, *The Dispatches of Field Marshal the Duke of Wellington During His Various Campaigns*, Volumes Seven, Eight and Nine (London: John Murray, 1838)

Heathcote, T.H., *Wellington's Peninsular War Generals and Their Battles* (Barnsley: Pen & Sword, 2010)

Henry, Philip, *Notes of Conservations with the Duke of Wellington* (London: John Murray, 1889)

Hibbert, Christopher, *George III: A Personal History* (London: Penguin, 1998)

Holmes, Richard, *Wellington: The Iron Duke* (London: Harper Collins, 2003)

Holmes, Richard, *Redcoat: The British Soldier in the Age of Horse and Musket* (London: Harper Collins, 2002)

Jarry, François, Translated by Richard Rochfort, *Treatise on the Marches and Movements of Armies* (London: James Ridgeway, 1807)

Johnston, Peter, *A Short History of Guernsey* (Guernsey: Peter Johnston, 1987)

Le Marchant, Denis, *Memoirs of The Late Major-General Le Marchant* (London: Samuel Bentley, 1841)

Le Marchant, John Gaspard, *The Rules and Regulations for the Sword Exercise of the Cavalry* (London: T. Egerton, 1796)

Long, Robert Ballard, Edited by T.H. McGuffie, *Peninsular Cavalry General (1811-13)* (London: George Harrap, 1951)

Longford, Elizabeth, *Wellington* (London: Weidenfeld and Nicholson, 1992)

Lunt, James, *Scarlet Lancer* (London: Rupert Hart-Davis, 1964)

McCallum, Pierre Franc, *Observations on H.R.H The Duke of Kent's Shameful Persecution* (London: McCallum, 1808)

Mockler-Ferryman, A.F., *Annals of Sandhurst: A Chronicle of The Royal Military College* (London: William Heinemann, 1900)

McGuffie, T.H. (Edited), *Peninsular Cavalry General, 1811-13: The Correspondence of Lieutenant-General Robert Ballard Long* (London: Harrap & Co, 1951)

Pakenham, Edward Michael, *Packenham Letters 1800-1815* (London: John and Edward Bumpus Ltd, 1914)

Peithmann, Lewis, *A Refutation of Pierre Franc McCallum's Remarks on the Royal Military College* (London: Wyatt, 1809)

Thomas, Hugh, *The Story of Sandhurst* (London: Hutchinson & Co, 1961)

Thoumine, R.H., *Scientific Soldier: A Life of General Le Marchant 1766-1812* (London: Oxford University Press, 1968)

Tomkinson, William, Edited by James Tomkinson, *The Diary of a Cavalry Officer in the Peninsular War and the Waterloo Campaign 1809-1815* (London: Swan Sonnenschein & Co, 1895)

Watkins, John, *A Biographical Memoir of His Late Royal Highness Frederick, Duke of York and Albany* (London: H. Fisher, 1827)

Journals and Websites

Beckett, Ian, *The Royal Military College at Marlow and High Wycombe* (Marlow Historian, Volume 5)

Burne, Alfred, *New Light on The Flanders Campaign Of 1793: Contemporary Letters Of Captain J. G. Le Marchant* (Journal of the Society for Army Historical Research, Vol. 30, No. 123, Autumn 1952)

Marquis, Hugues, *Le Général François Jarry au service de l'Angleterre* (Annales historiques de la Révolution française, 2009)

Peaty, John, *Architect of Victory: The Reforms of The Duke Of York* (Journal of the Society for Army Historical Research Vol. 84, No. 340, Winter 2006)

Wethered, Anthony, *The Gentlemen Cadets of Marlow* (Marlow Historian, Volume 1)

The Family of Major-General John Gaspard Le Marchant, Priaulx Library, Guernsey https://www.priaulxlibrary.co.uk/articles/article/family-major-general-john-gaspard-le-marchant

Sword Exercise of the Cavalry, Priaulx Library, Guernsey https://www.priaulxlibrary.co.uk/articles/article/sword-exercise-cavalry

Vote of Thanks to The Marquis of Wellington – Victory Of Salamanca https://hansard.parliament.uk/commons/1812-12-03; https://hansard.parliament.uk/Lords/1812-12-03

PICTURE CREDITS

John Gaspard Le Marchant, artist Philip Jean, courtesy of the Priaulx Library, Guernsey
Mary Le Marchant (wife), artist Philip Jean, courtesy of the Priaulx Library, Guernsey
John Le Marchant (father), courtesy of the Priaulx Library, Guernsey
Illustrations from Le Marchant's *Rules and Regulations for the Sword Exercise of the Cavalry*, Le Marchant papers, courtesy of the Sandhurst Collection
1796 pattern light cavalry sword, © Royal Armouries
1796 pattern heavy cavalry sword, © Royal Armouries
St Peter Port and Castle Cornet, Guernsey, artist J G Le Marchant, © Sir Piers Le Marchant, Bt
Bordeaux Harbour, Guernsey, artist J G Le Marchant, © Sir Piers Le Marchant, Bt
La Coupée, Sark, artist J G Le Marchant, © Sir Piers Le Marchant, Bt
General Jarry, artist J D Harding, Le Marchant papers, courtesy of the Sandhurst Collection
Issac Dalby, artist James Thomson, courtesy of the Welcome Collection under Creative Commons CC0 1.0
High Wycombe, home of the Senior Department, artist J G Le Marchant, © Sir Piers Le Marchant, Bt
Military review at the Junior Department, Marlow, courtesy of the Marlow Society
Plaque at the site of the Senior Department, High Wycombe, © Paul Le Messurier
Plaque at the site of the Junior Department, Marlow, © Paul Le Messurier
Belem Tower, Lisbon, artist J G Le Marchant, © Sir Piers Le Marchant, Bt
Sintra, Portugal, artist J G Le Marchant, © Sir Piers Le Marchant, Bt
Lord Wellington's Quarters at Santarem, artist J G Le Marchant, © Sir Piers Le Marchant, Bt
Salamanca from Cabrerizos, artist J G Le Marchant, © Sir Piers Le Marchant, Bt
View of the battlefield at Salamanca, © Paul Le Messurier
Mural illustrating Le Marchant's cavalry charge, Los Arapiles, Spain, © Paul Le Messurier

INDEX